AF149401

American Corporate Identity '98

'98

The 13th annual showing
of the best new work
in the USA

editor—**DAVID E. CARTER**

BOOK DESIGNER—Suzanna M.W. Brown

American Corporate Identity 1998
First published 1997 by Hearst Books International
1350 Avenue of the Americas
New York, NY 10019

ISBN: 0-688-15686-X

Distributed in the U.S. and Canada
Watson-Guptill Publications
1515 Broadway
New York, NY 10035
Tel: 800-451-1741
         908-363-4511 in NJ, AK, HI
Fax: 908-363-0338

Distributed throughout the rest of the world by
Hearst Books International
1350 Avenue of the Americas
New York, NY 10019
Tel: 212-261-6770
Fax: 212-261-6795

Printed in Hong Kong by Everbest Printing Company through
Four Colour Imports, Louisville, Kentucky.

Table
of Contents

Complete
Identity
Programs

Client   MasterCard International
Design Firm   Interbrand Schechter
Designers   Gerald Berliner, Andrew Bogucki

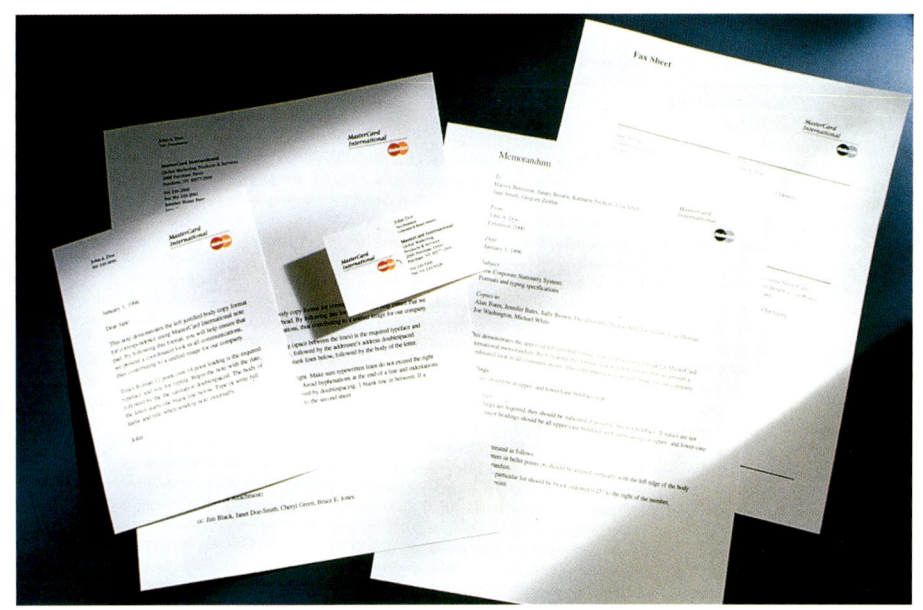

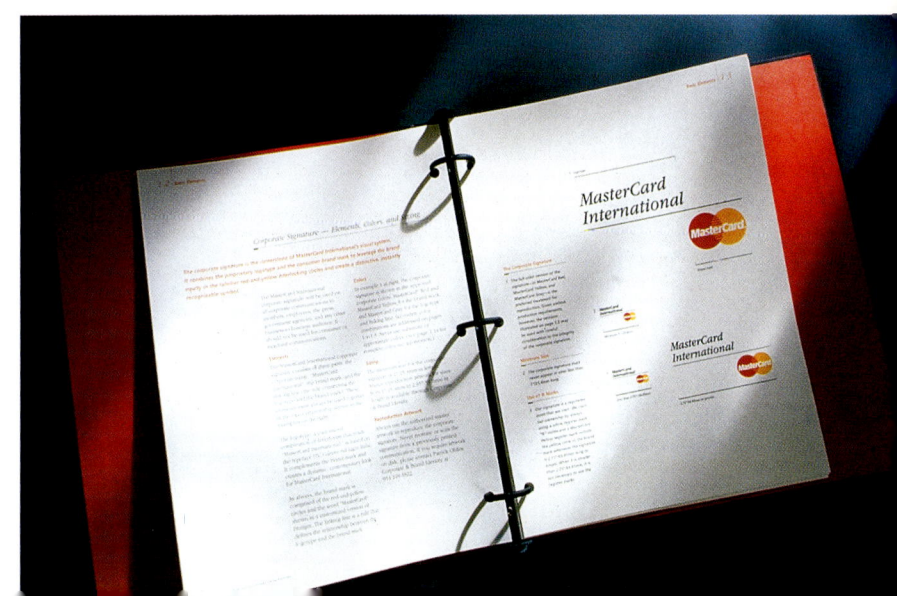

United States Post Office

Client   UNITED STATES POSTAL SERVICE
Design Firm   KING CASEY INC
Designers   EUGENE J. CASEY, JOHN CHRZANOWSKI,
              STEVE BRENT, JEFF REDSTON, JOHN RYAN

Client   ANALYTIX PITTSBURGH
Design Firm   BALLY DESIGN, INC.
Designer   FRANK GARRITY

analytix

Client   ALLEGIANCE HEALTHCARE CORPORATION
Design Firm   LIPSON • ALPORT • GLASS & ASSOCIATES
Designers   KEITH SHUPE, KATHERINE HOLDEREID, BRIAN CARROW, JEFF RICH

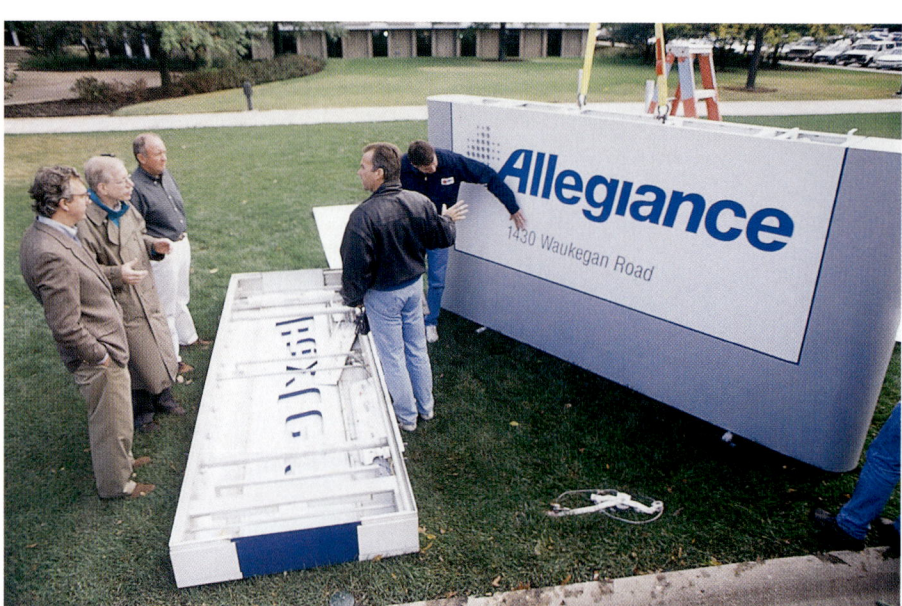

AquaPenn
spring water company

Client	AQUAPENN SPRING WATER COMPANY
Design Firm	SOMMESE DESIGN
Designers	KRISTIN SOMMESE, LANNY SOMMESE

BENEVIA

Client
Design Firm
Designers

MONSANTO CORPORATION
TDC/THE DESIGN COMPANY SAN FRANCISCO
CRAIG FRAZIER, SANDRA KOENIG

BENEVIA

Client BEST WESTERN INTERNATIONAL
Design Firm LISTER BUTLER
Designer JOHN LISTER

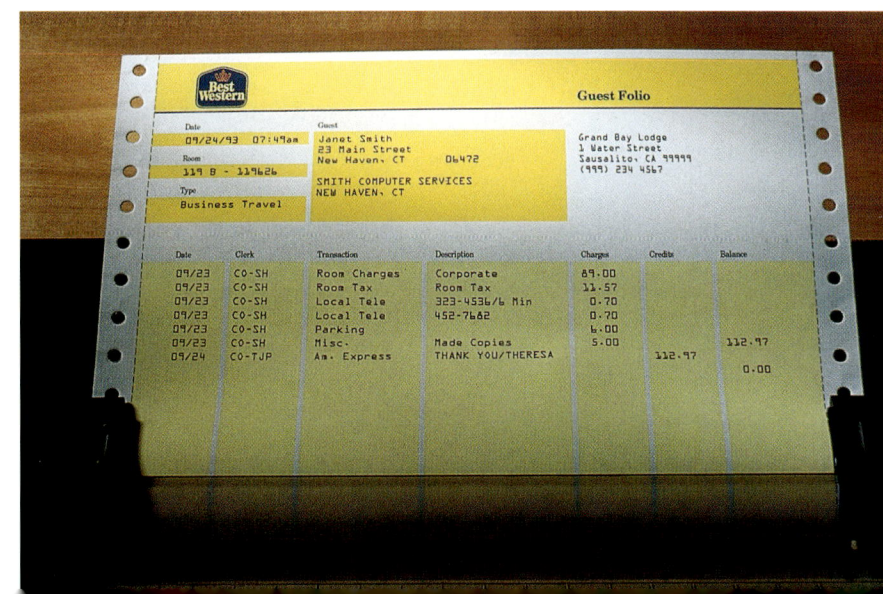

B R O̲ W N

Client	BROWN PRINTING
Design Firm	LARSEN DESIGN + INTERACTIVE
Designers	RICHELLE HUFF, MIKE HAUG, SASCHA BOECKER,
	PETER DE SIBOUR, TODD NESSER

Client   CHASE MANHATTAN BANK
Design Firm   DESOLA GROUP, INC.
Designers   STAFF

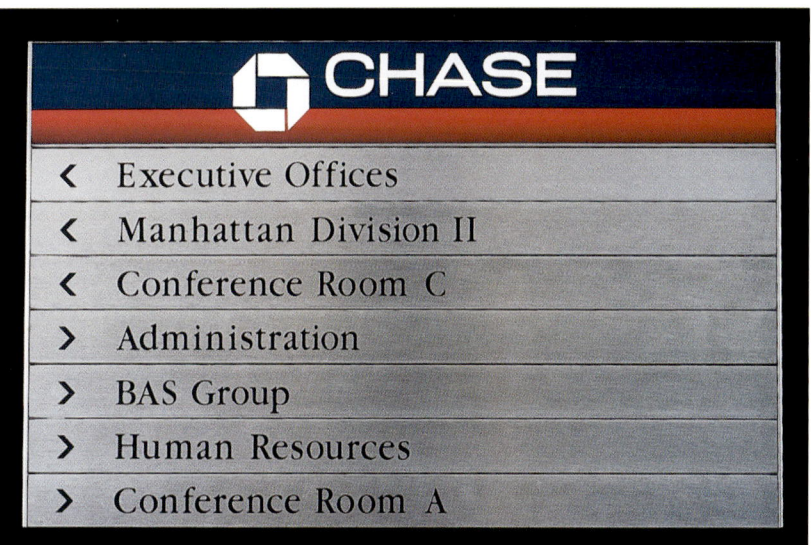

Client   CHICK-FIL-A
Design Firm   COPELAND HIRTHLER DESIGN + COMMUNICATIONS
Creative Directors BRAD COPELAND, GEORGE HIRTHLER
Designers   DAVID BUTLER, MARK LIGAMERI
Environmental Designers ERIC BROWN, JEFF HAACK
Copywriters   GEORGE HIRTHLER, JASON HIRTHLER
Producers   LAURA PERLEE, DONNA HARRIS, TOR GUNDERSON
Account Executives WARD COPELAND, JEAN MCCLURE

Client   Bordeaux Printers
Design Firm   Mires Design
Creative Director José A. Serrano
Designers   José A. Serrano, Miguel Perez
Illustrator   Tracy Sabin

24

Client   CHILDREN'S HEALTH CARE
Design Firm   LARSEN DESIGN + INTERACTIVE
Designers   NANCY WHITTLESEY,
              ELIZABETH LONGHURST,
              KRISTINE THAYER

Client   CMP MEDIA INC.
Design Firm INTERBRAND SCHECHTER
Designers   GERALD BERLINER, JANINE BRUTTIN

San Juan 2004

Client   COMMISSION FOR THE 2004 OLYMPIAD
Design Firm   GRAF, INC.
Designer   LYDIMARIE APONTE

PALOMINO PARK

Client THE FELD COMPANY
—WELLSFORD RESIDENTIAL PROPERTY TRUST
Design Firm NOBLE•ERICKSON INC
Designers JACQUELYN NOBLE, STEVEN ERICKSON, DAVID LANSDOH

FLUOROWARE

Client   FLUOROWARE
Design Firm   LARSEN DESIGN + INTERACTIVE
Designers   RICHELLE HUFF, GAYLE JORGENS, TODD MANNES

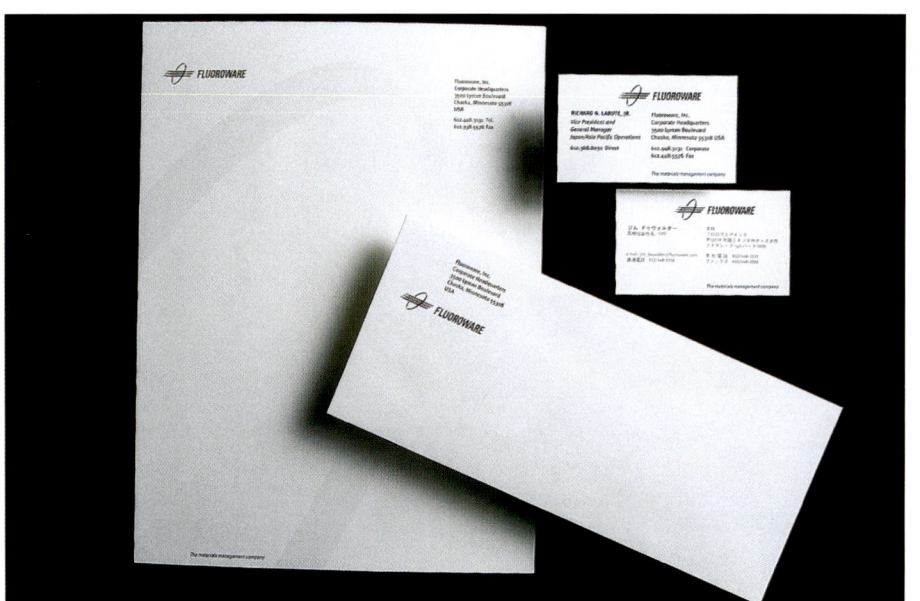

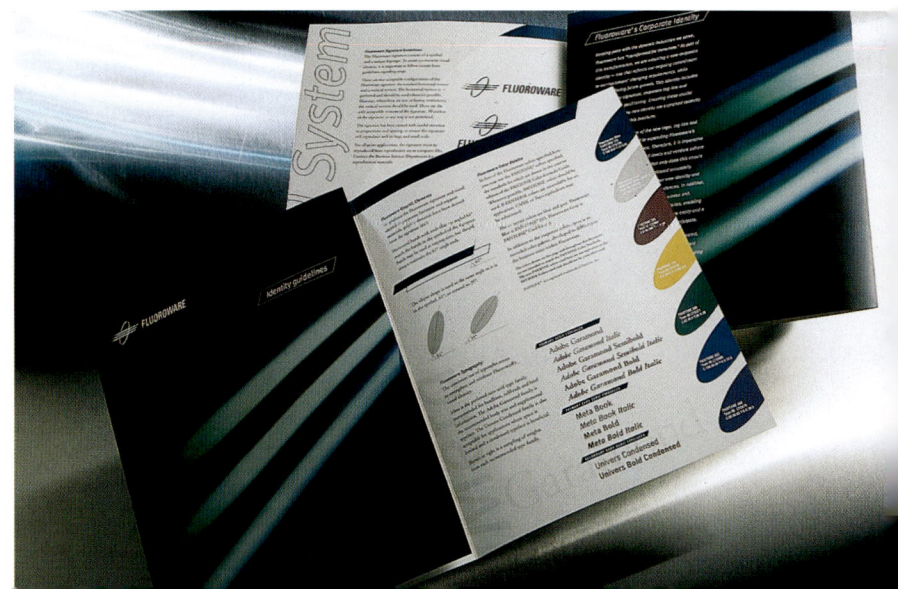

Client   H.C. BERGER BREWING COMPANY
Design Firm   COONTS DESIGN GROUP
Designers   DAVID BACK, GREG RATTENBORG

Client   CoreStates Bank
        —Networth Café
Design Firm   DSI • LA
Designers
       Rod Parker,
       Bryan Murphy,
       Chris Steiner,
       Lonnie Carnaggio

Client   HEWLETT-PACKARD
Design Firm   ANVIL
Designers   LAURA BAUER, STACEY FISCHER, JANICE WONG, HENNI AENGNENDT

Client   **IBM**
Design Firm   **SUPON DESIGN GROUP.**
Designers   **SUPON PHORNIRUNLIT, ANDY DOLAN,**
               ANDREW BERMAN, DEBBI SAVITT

Client   IBM Aptiva POP
Design Firm   Desgrippes Gobé & Associates
Creative Director   Joanna Feldheim
Art Director   Francine Germano
Designer   Andre Metzger

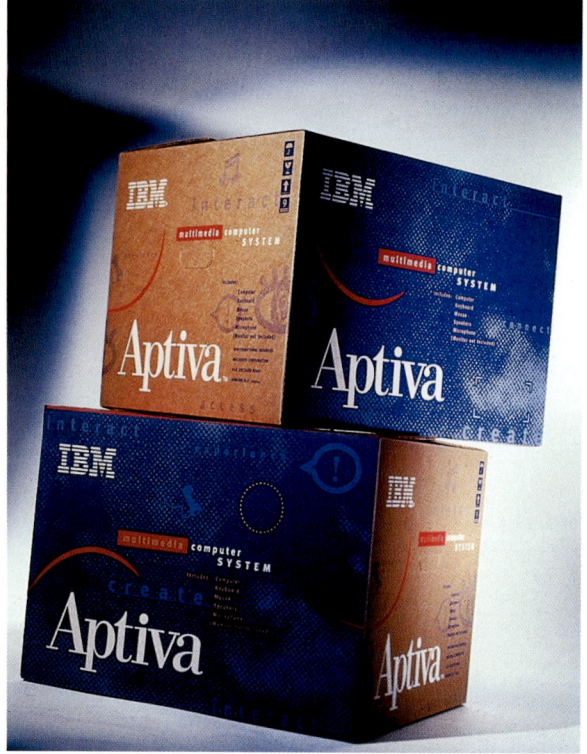

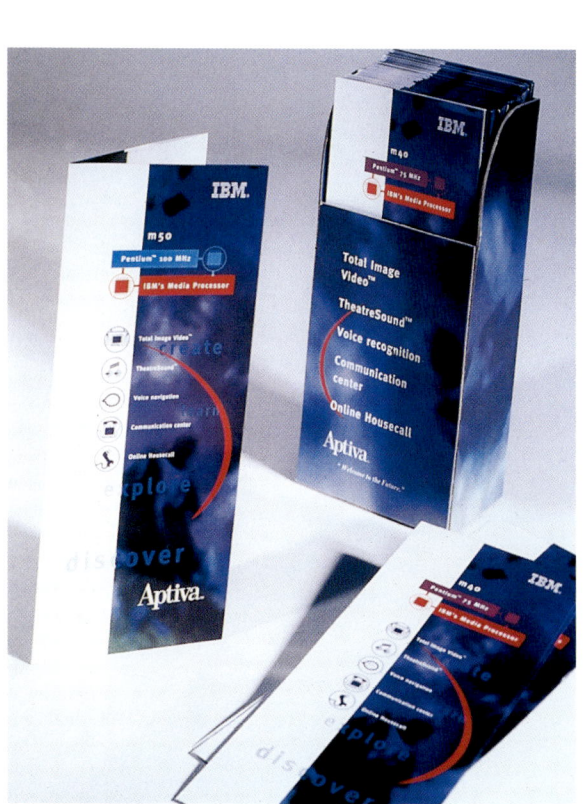

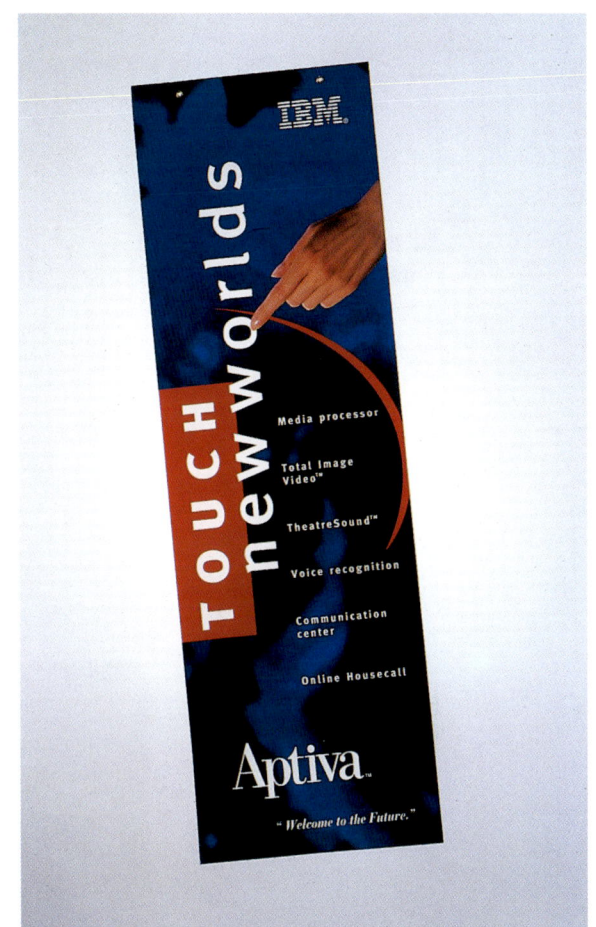

Client   IMATION
Design Firm   INTERBRAND SCHECHTER
Designers   GERALD BERLINER,
              GARY STILOVICH

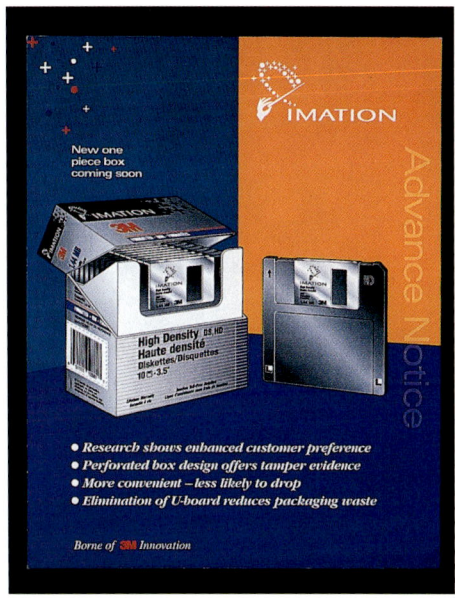

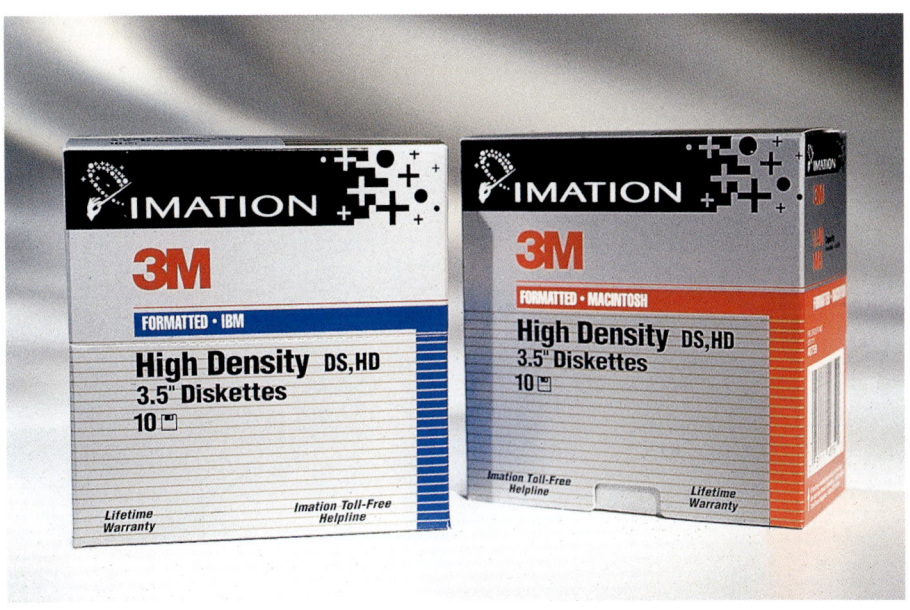

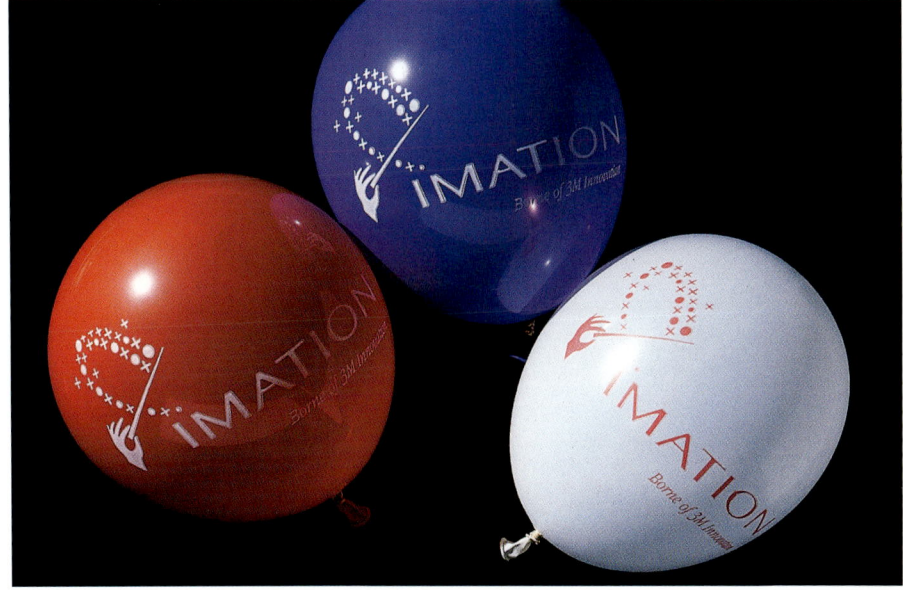

Client   MAJOR LEAGUE BASEBALL PROPERTIES
Design Firm   HERIP DESIGN ASSOCIATES, INC.
Designers   JOHN R. MENTER, WALTER M. HERIP

Client MCI
Design Firm INTERBRAND SCHECHTER
Designers GERALD BERLINER, ANDREW BOGUCKI

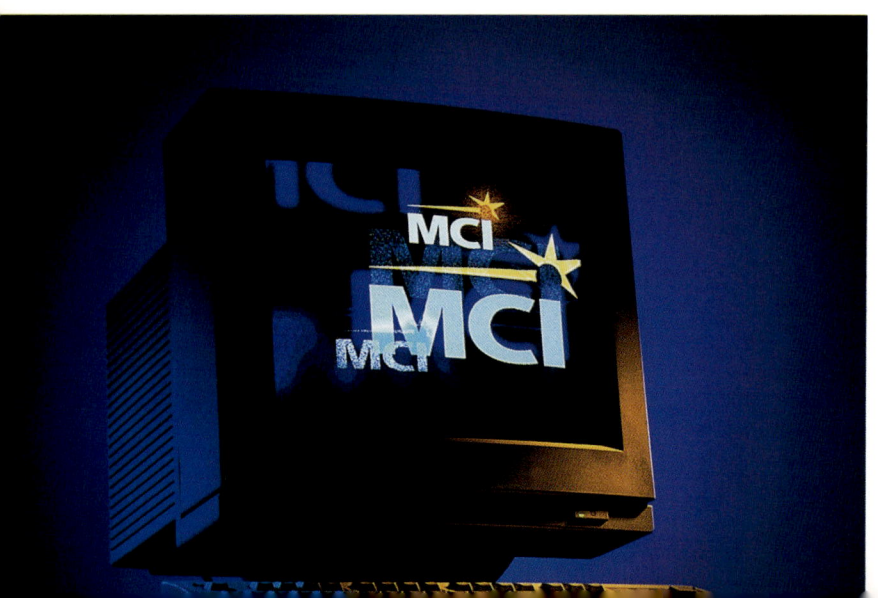

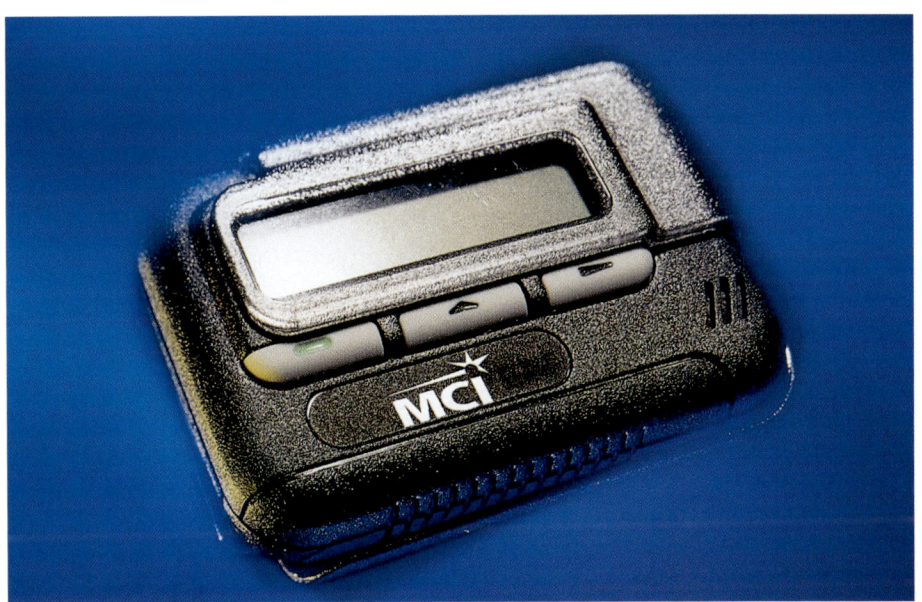

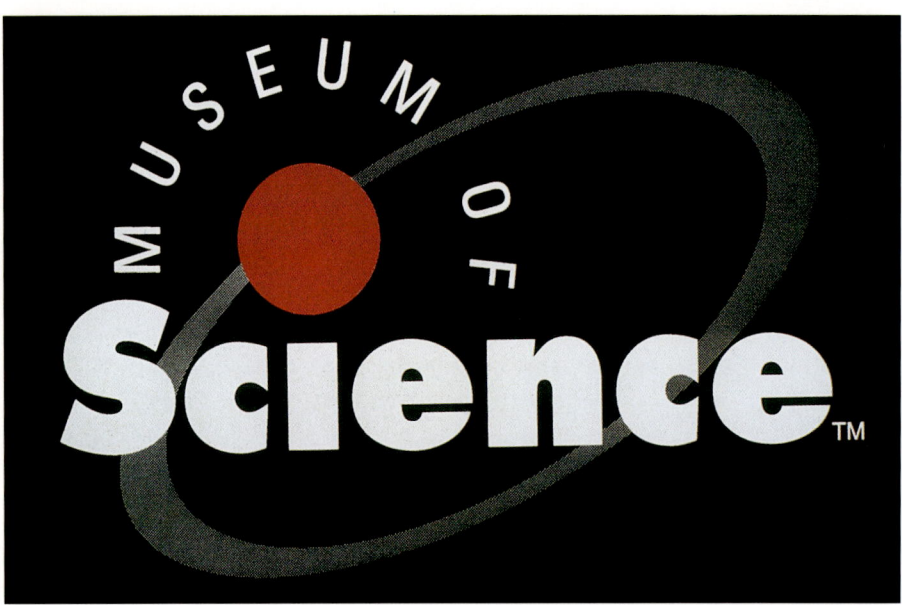

Client   MUSEUM OF SCIENCE
Design Firm BrandEquity International
Design Director JOE SELAME, IDSA
Project Team JOE SELAME, STEVEN SMITH, GREG KOLLIGIAN

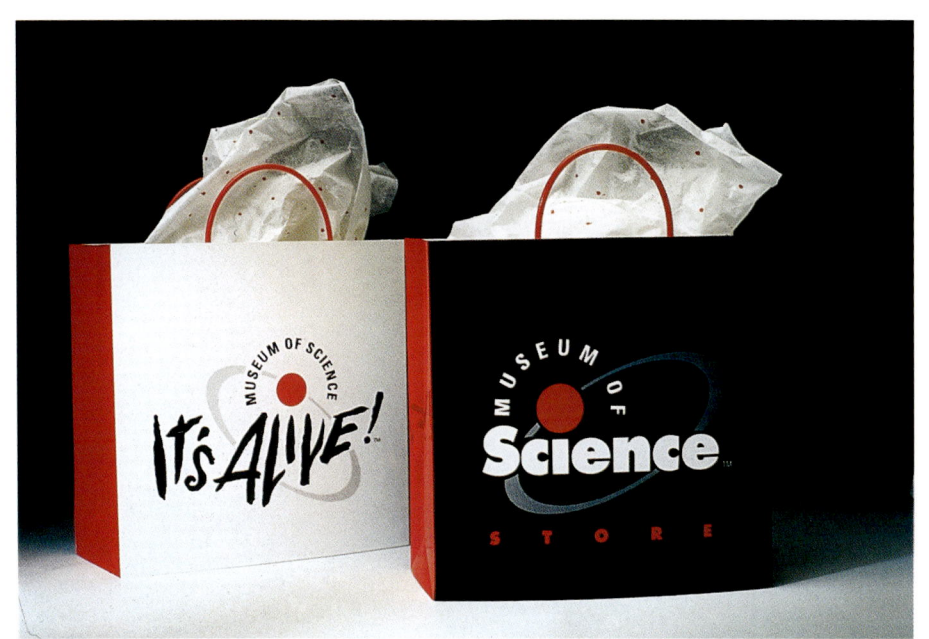

N C T D

Client   North County Transit District
Design Firm Crouch & Naegeli/Design Group West
Designer   Jim Naegeli

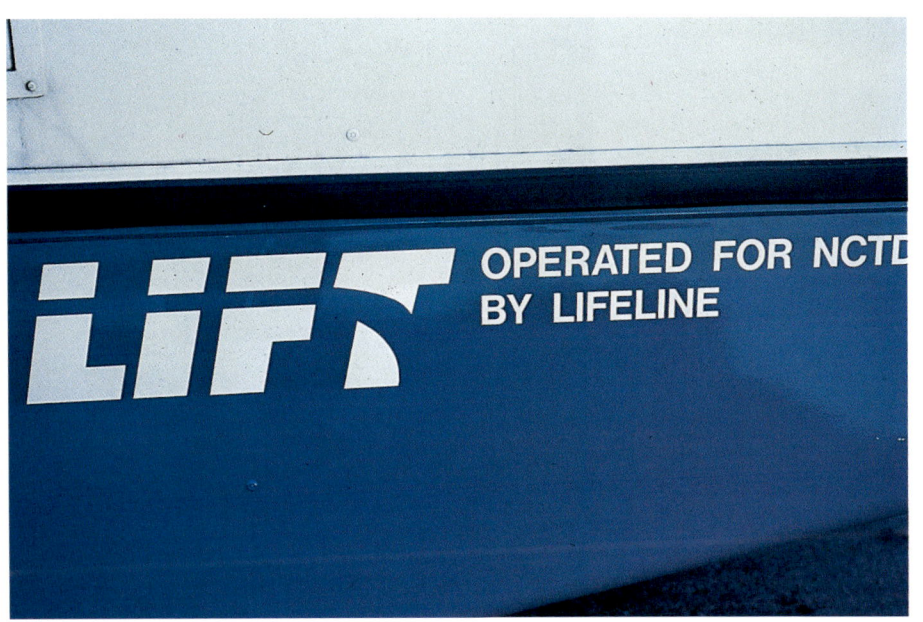

pcsHealthSystems℠

Client   PCS HEALTH SYSTEMS INC.
Design Firm   THE DELOR GROUP, INC.
Designers   CHRIS ENANDER, KEVIN WYATT

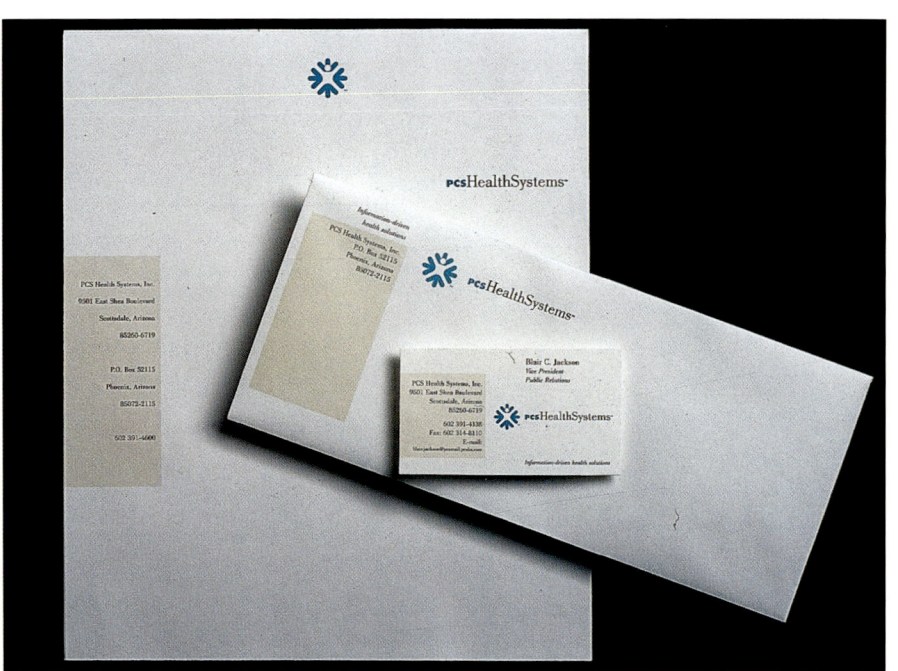

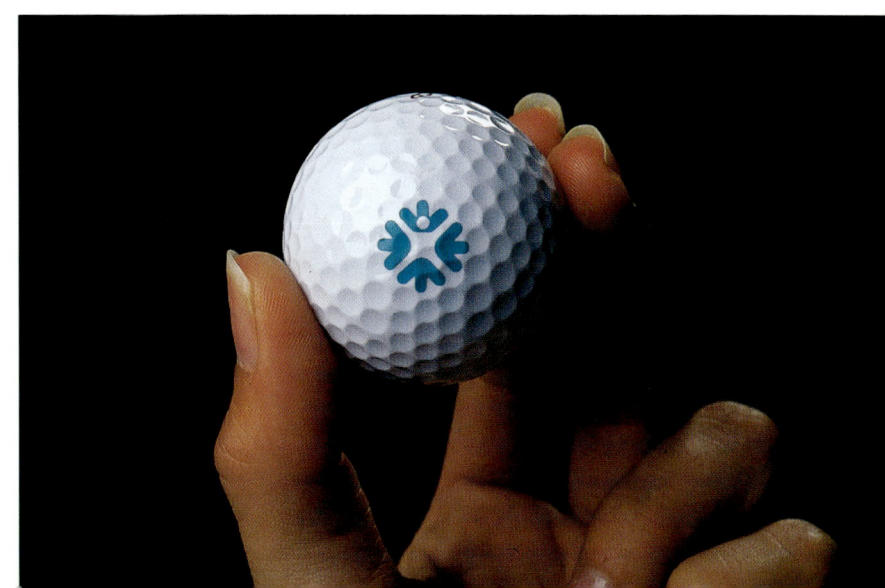

Client   NEXTLINK CORPORATION
Design Firm   HORNALL ANDERSON DESIGN WORKS, INC.
Designers   JACK ANDERSON, DAVID BATES,
                MARY HERMES, JOHN ANICKER,
                MARY CHIN HUTCHISON

RELIASTAR

Client   ReliaStar Corporation
Design Firm   Larsen Design + Interactive
Designers   Nancy Whittlesey, Marc Kundmann,
                 Richelle Huff, Peter de Sibour,
                 Karin Heidemann

Client   SPRINT
Design Firm   LISTER BUTLER
Designer   JOHN LISTER

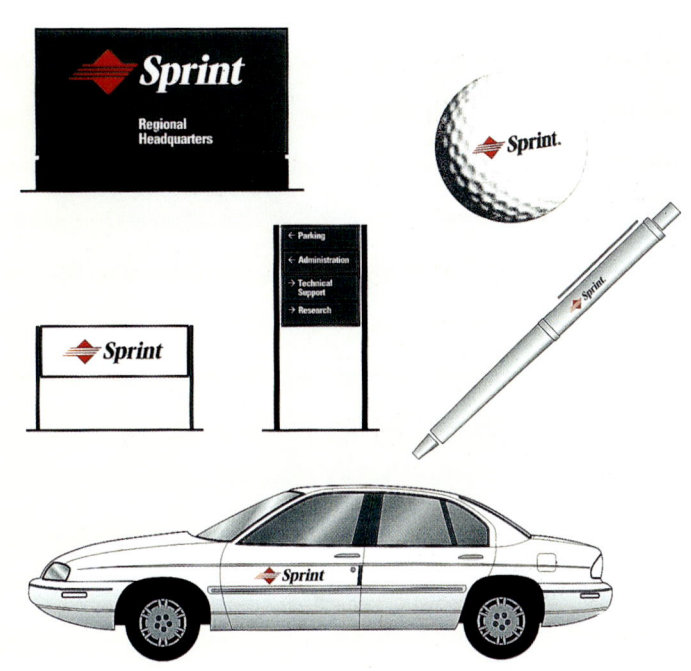

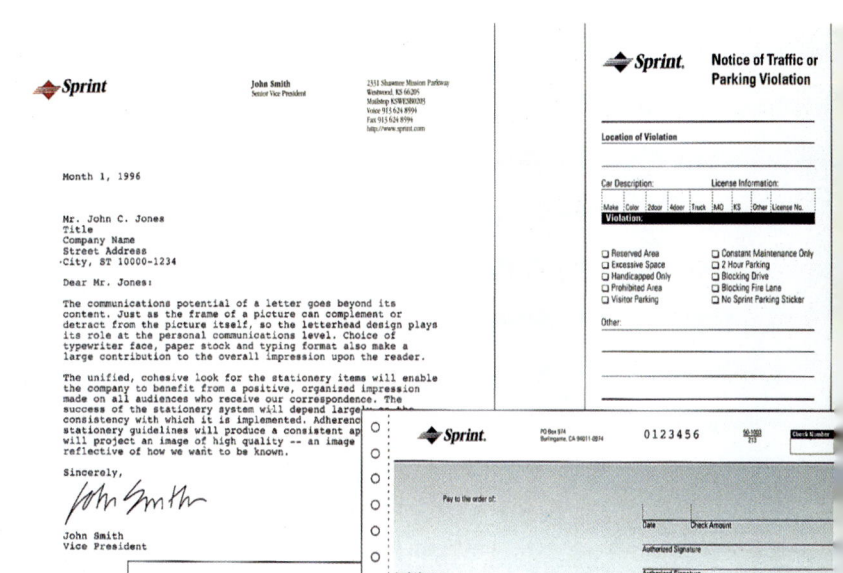

Client   **67 WINE & SPIRITS** (RETAIL LIQUOR STORE)
Design Firm   **SUSAN MESHBERG GRAPHIC DESIGN**
Designer   **SUSAN MESHBERG**

Client   UNITED STATES POSTAL SERVICE
                —POSTMARK AMERICA
Design Firm   KING CASEY INC
Designers   JOHN CHRZANOWSKI, JEFF REDSTON

Client   Venture Design Group
                Steve Morris, Design Director
Design Firm   Phoenix Creative
Designers   Eric Thoelke, Kathy Wilkinson

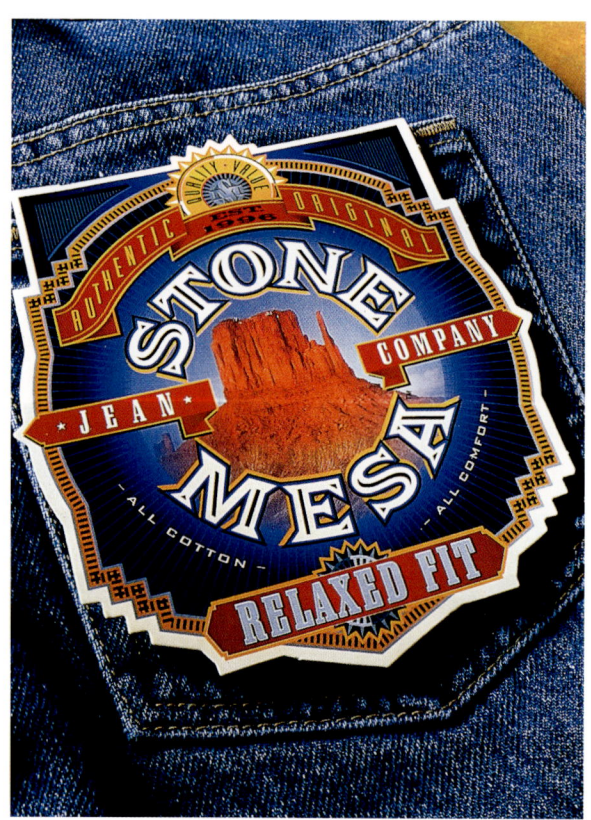

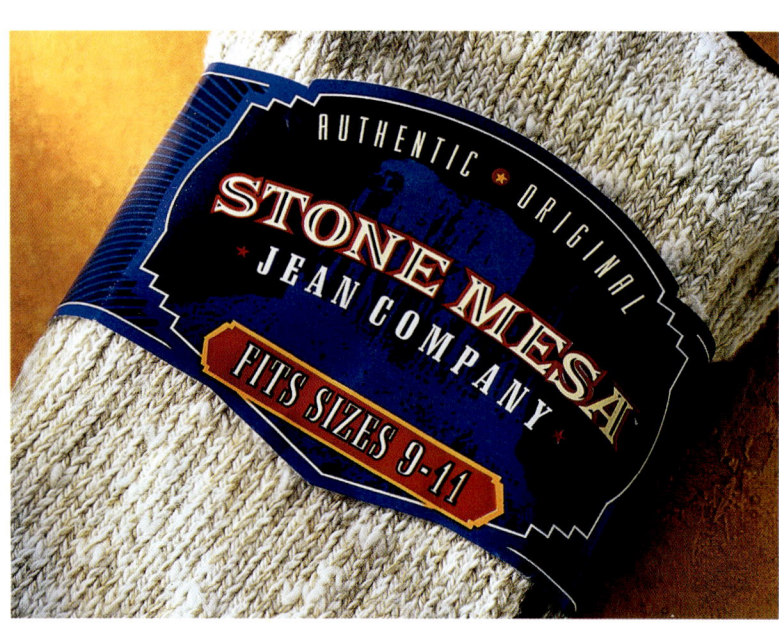

WANA ZOO

Client   WANA ZOO
Design Firm   SUPON DESIGN GROUP.
Designers   SUPON PHORNIRUNLIT, SHARISSE STEBER,
                    BRENT ALMOND, TOM KLINEDINST

Client   World Wrapps
Design Firm   Design One
Designers   Alisa Rudolff, Dave Hurlbert,
              Gayle Marsh, Chris Peterson,
              Jacqueline Ghosin, Jim Fash,
              Franz Platte

Package
Designs

Client   THE SURFARIS
Design Firm BERRYHILL PRODUCTIONS
Designer GENE BERRYHILL

Client   VISUAL ASYLUM (NUTCASE PROMO)
Design Firm VISUAL ASYLUM
Designers AMY LEVINE, MAELIN LEVINE

Client   BROWN & HALEY ALMOND ROCA
     (HOLIDAY HOUSE BOX & MUG)
Design Firm DAVID LEMLEY DESIGN
Designer DAVID LEMLEY

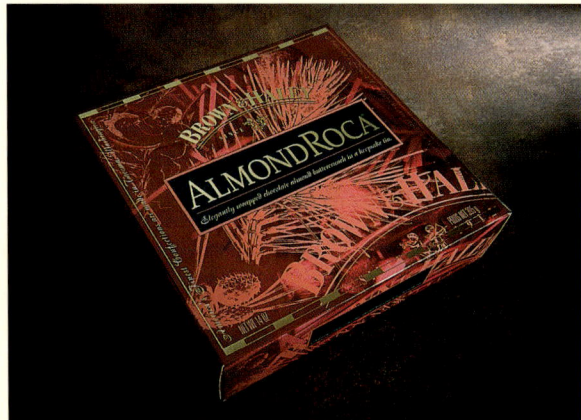

Client   BROWN & HALEY ALMOND ROCA (HOLIDAY PACKAGING)
Design Firm DAVID LEMLEY DESIGN
Designer DAVID LEMLEY

Client   BROWN & HALEY ALMOND ROCA (CHRISTMAS BOX)
Design Firm DAVID LEMLEY DESIGN
Designer DAVID LEMLEY

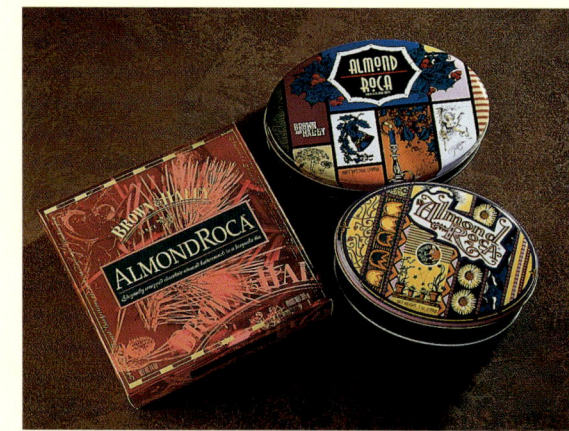

Client ANDERSON PRINTING
Design Firm EVENSON DESIGN GROUP
Designer AMY HERSHMAN

Client DELTA AIRLINES
Design Firm COPELAND HIRTHLER DESIGN + COMMUNICATIONS
Creative Directors BRAD COPELAND, GEORGE HIRTHLER
Art Directors BRAD COPELAND, DAVID BUTLER
Designers DAVID BUTLER, MARK LIGAMERI
Copywriter JASON HIRTHLER
Producers LAURA PERLEE, DONNA HARRIS
Account Executives WARD COPELAND, SHENNA PRICE

Client KNOLL, INC. (SELF-PROMO)
Design Firm KNOLL, INC.
Designer EILEEN BOXER

Client ZUNDA DESIGN GROUP (SELF-PROMO)
Design Firm ZUNDA DESIGN GROUP
Designers CHARLES ZUNDA, TODD NICKEL

Client KILMER & KILMER, INC. (SELF-PROMO)
Design Firm KILMER & KILMER, INC. DESIGN & ADVERTISING
Designers RANDALL MARSHALL, BRENDA KILMER, RICHARD KILMER

Client THOMA & THOMA
(SELF-PROMO)
Design Firm THOMA & THOMA CREATIVE
Designer TERRI PARKER-WEST

Client   MATTHEW'S MUSTARDS
Design Firm PAT CARNEY STUDIO, INC.
Designer   LIZ MONTGOMERY

Client   BEAVERTON FOODS—OLD SPICE GOLD MUSTARDS
Design Firm FAINE/OLLER PRODUCTIONS, INC.
Designer   CATHERINE OLLER

Client   BOSTON BRANDS
Design Firm HILLIS MACKEY & COMPANY
Designer   JOHN HILLIS

Client   HEINZ USA
Design Firm GERSTMAN+MEYERS INC
Design Director SABRA WAXMAN

Client   STONEWALL KITCHEN
Design Firm LESLIE EVANS DESIGN ASSOCIATES
Designers   LESLIE EVANS, CHERI BRYANT

Client   SOE TRADING &
               MANAGEMENT CO.
Design Firm BOLDPRINT
Designer   MICHAEL FOX

Client   SMUCKER'S
Design Firm   LANDOR ASSOCIATES
Creative Director NICOLAS APARICIO
Designer   JENNIFER BOSTIC

Client   ROBISON RANCH SPECIALTY FOODS
                —ROBISON RANCH PICKLED PRODUCTS
Design Firm   FAINE/OLLER PRODUCTIONS, INC.
Designers   CATHERINE OLLER, BARBARA FAINE

Client   OCEAN SPRAY CRANBERRIES INC.
Design Firm   LIBBY MACDONALD + SHEAR
Designer   RICHARD SHEAR

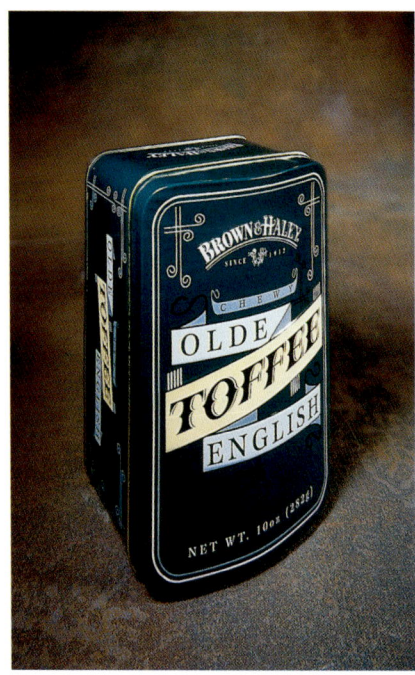

Client   AMISH FAMILY RECIPES
Design Firm   DEAN DESIGN/MARKETING GROUP, INC.
Designers   PEGGI ZWALLY, RUSS COX, LORI HESS

Client   BROWN & HALEY OLDE ENGLISH TOFFEE
Design Firm   DAVID LEMLEY DESIGN
Designer   DAVID LEMLEY

Client   OCEAN BEAUTY SEAFOOD
Design Firm   MARK OLIVER, INC.
Designers   MARK OLIVER,
              PATTY DEVLIN-DRISKEL

Client   AIDELLS
Design Firm   AXION DESIGN, INC.
Designers   LISA BRUSSELL, NANCY WAGSTAFF

Client   ICICLE SEAFOODS, INC.—SHIP AHOY SNOW CRAB
Design Firm   FAINE/OLLER PRODUCTIONS, INC.
Designer   CATHERINE OLLER

Client   JIMMY DEAN
Design Firm   AXION DESIGN, INC.
Designers   ERIC READ, TIM FERDUN

Client   ALASKAN HARVEST SEAFOODS (CANNED SEAFOOD)
Design Firm   FAINE/OLLER PRODUCTIONS, INC.
Designers   CATHERINE OLLER, JERRY NELSON, BARBARA FAINE

Client   SNOW BALL FOODS
Design Firm   KOLLBERG/JOHNSON ASSOCIATES
Designer   PENNY JOHNSON

Client   BORDEN, INC.—REALEMON LEMON JUICE
Design Firm HERMSEN DESIGN ASSOCIATES, INC.
Designers   CYNTHIA CHYLIK, JERRY DYER,
               JACK HERMSEN, BRUCE MAHAN,
               CHRISTINE PASIENSKI

Client   CARGILL SEA SALT
Design Firm PEDERSEN GESK
Designers   ROGER REMALEY, RONY ZIBARA,
               KRIS MORGAN, MARK ORTON

Client   CPC INTERNATIONAL
Design Firm WALLACE CHURCH ASSOCIATES, INC.
Designers   STAN CHURCH, SIMON LINCE, JOHN BRUNO

Client   WOLFGANG PUCK FOOD CO.—WOLFGANG PUCK BROWNIES
Design Firm ANTISTA FAIRCLOUGH DESIGN
Designers   TOM ANTISTA, THOMAS FAIRCLOUGH

Client   CAFE 222
Design Firm VISUAL ASYLUM
Designers   JOEL SOTELO, MAELIN LEVINE

Client   WILLIAMS-SONOMA
Design Firm SBG PARTNERS
Designers   MARK BERGMAN, VICKI CERO

Client   NATURIA, INC.
Design Firm   ROGER CHRISTIAN & CO.
Designer   JASON BROWN

Client   NEWMAN'S OWN INC.—CAESAR DRESSING
Design Firm   ZUNDA DESIGN GROUP
Designer   CHARLES ZUNDA

Client   GRAND PALACE FOODS INTERNATIONAL
Design Firm   SUPON DESIGN GROUP.
Designers   MIMI EANES, SUPON PHORNIRUNLIT

Client   PECOS VALLEY SPICE COMPANY
Design Firm   KILMER & KILMER, INC. DESIGN & ADVERTISING
Designers   RICHARD KILMER, BRENDA KILMER, RANDALL MARSHALL

Client   PAULA'S
Design Firm   KIMBERLY BAER DESIGN ASSOC.
Designer   BARBARA COOPER

Client   THE CHASE COLLECTION
Design Firm   ARISTA ADVERTISING, INC.
Designers   FANNY CHAKEDIS, PATTIE GERDING, JOE FERRARO

Client   DREYER'S
Design Firm   LANDOR ASSOCIATES
Creative Director NICOLAS APARICIO
Designer   JON WEDEN

Client   GOOD HUMOR—BREYERS
Design Firm   SMITH DESIGN ASSOCIATES
Designer   EILEEN BEREZNI

Client   BLUE BELL CREAMERIES
Design Firm   METZDORF, INC.
Designer   LYLE METZDORF

Client   SCHWAN'S SALES ENTERPRISES, INC.
                (ICE CREAM AND FROZEN YOGURT)
Design Firm   RAPP COLLINS COMMUNICATIONS
Designer   YVES ROUX

Client   H.P. HOOD, INC.
Design Firm   THE COLEMAN GROUP
Designers   ED MORRILL, STEPHANIE SIMPSON, CIRO GIORDANO

Client   BLUE BELL CREAMERIES
Design Firm   METZDORF, INC.
Designer   LYLE METZDORF

Client   UPSTATE FARMS
               —MILK FOR LIFE
Design Firm   FORWARD DESIGN, INC.
Designers   JONATHAN FORWARD,
               DAPHNE STOFER,
               JON EMERY

Client   ALL SEASON'S KITCHEN, L.L.C.
Design Firm   GRIFFIN GRAPHICS
Designer   DAVID GRIFFIN
Illustrators   MIKE BARRETT, DAVID GRIFFIN

Client   GOOD HUMOR BREYERS—CREAMSICLE
Design Firm   SMITH DESIGN ASSOCIATES
Designers   JAMES C. SMITH, CAROL KONKOWSKI

Client   BLUE BELL CREAMERIES
Design Firm   METZDORF, INC.
Designer   ROBERT VAN LENTEN

Client   DUO DELIGHTS (GOURMET CANDY COMPANY)
Design Firm   LAMBERT DESIGN
Designer   JOY CATHEY PRICE

Client   BROWN & HALEY EXTRA STRENGTH PEPPERMINT
Design Firm   DAVID LEMLEY DESIGN
Designer   DAVID LEMLEY

Client   CAPA FOODS
Design Firm MCNULTY & CO.
Designers   RON CRAIN, DAN MCNULTY

Client   HUNGRY SULTAN MEDITERRANEAN GOURMET
Design Firm   LANDOR ASSOCIATES
Creative Director NICOLAS APARICIO
Designer   CARL MAZER

Client   KASHI COMPANY—GOOD FRIENDS
Design Firm   MARK OLIVER, INC.
Designers   MARK OLIVER, PATTY DEVLIN-DRISKEL

Client   KASHI COMPANY
                —PILLOWS
Design Firm   MARK OLIVER, INC.
Designers   MARK OLIVER,
                PATTY DEVLIN-DRISKEL

Client   GERBER
Design Firm   LANDOR ASSOCIATES
Designers   NICOLAS APARICIO, JENNIFER BOSTIC, MARGIE DRECHSEL

Client   KASHI COMPANY—BABY
Design Firm   MARK OLIVER, INC.
Designers   MARK OLIVER, PATTY DEVLIN-DRISKEL

Client   HUNGRY SULTAN MEDITERRANEAN GOURMET
Design Firm LANDOR ASSOCIATES
Designers   NICOLAS APARICIO, CARL MAZER

Client   ADVANCED NUTRITIONALS
Design Firm POLIVKA LOGAN DESIGN, INC.
Designer   CHRIS ADAMS

Client   COCA-COLA
             INTERNATIONAL
             —TAI PEAR DRINK
Design Firm ANTISTA FAIRCLOUGH
             DESIGN
Designers   TOM ANTISTA,
             THOMAS FAIRCLOUGH

Client   CHIPPEWA
             SPRINGS, LTD.
Design Firm HILLIS
             MACKEY &
             COMPANY
Designer   TJODY DeVAAL

Client   ALTA BEVERAGE
             COMPANY
Design Firm HORNALL ANDERSON
             DESIGN WORKS, INC.
Designers   JACK ANDERSON,
             LARRY ANDERSON,
             JULIE KEENAN

Client   PUBLIC LABEL BRANDS
Design Firm FAYE KLEIN DESIGN
Designer   FAYE KLEIN

Client   R.W. GARCIA
Design Firm PROFILE DESIGN
Designers   RUSSELL BAKER, ANTHONY LUK, LENA TONSETH

Client   NORTHAMPTON PEANUT COMPANY
Design Firm BERNI DESIGN
Designers   BERNI STAFF

Client   DIAMOND TOASTED WALNUTS
Design Firm SBG PARTNERS
Designers   MARK BERGMAN, JESSIE MCANULTY

Client   GARDETTO'S
Design Firm DESIGN NORTH, INC.
Designers   GWEN GRANZOW, JANE MARCUSSEN

Client   QUAKER OATS COMPANY-QUAKER BAGGED CEREAL
Design Firm DESIGN NORTH, INC.
VP Creative Director GWEN GRANZOW
Designer   PAT COWAN

Client   GENERAL MILLS, INC.
Design Firm HILLIS MACKEY & COMPANY
Designer   RANDY SZARZYNSKI

Client   SARA LEE—BAGEL CHIPS
Design Firm AXION DESIGN, INC.
Designer   KENN LEWIS

Client   TOM'S FOODS, INC.
            —PUFFED CHEEZERS
Design Firm HERMSEN DESIGN
            ASSOCIATES, INC.
Designers   JACK HERMSEN,
            JERRY DYER

Client   THE BACHMAN
            COMPANY
Design Firm DIXON & PARCELS
            ASSOCIATES, INC.
Designers   DIXON & PARCELS
            ASSOCIATES, INC.

Client   AUSTIN
            FOODS, INC.
            (FAT FREE
            PRETZELS)
Design Firm HERMSEN
            DESIGN
            ASSOCIATES,
            INC.
Designers   JACK
            HERMSEN,
            JERRY DYER

Client   FRITO-LAY, INC.
Design Firm APPLE DESIGNSOURCE INC
Creative Director BARRY SEELIG
Designers   NANCY BROGDEN, JOHN RUTIG

Client   KRAFT GENERAL FOODS,
            POST DIVISION—WAFFLE CRISP
Design Firm MONNENS-ADDIS DESIGN
Designers   CALDWELL TOLL, ROBIN MACLEAN,
            JUSTIN CARROLL, DEBBIE SMITH,
            JOANNE HOM

Client   TRADER JOE'S
Design Firm   VINCE RINI DESIGN
Designer   VINCE RINI

Client   SARA LEE GARLIC BREAD
Design Firm   AXION DESIGN, INC.
Designer   KENN LEWIS

Client   KATZ FOOD CORP.
Design Firm   FILOSI JONES
Designer   SANDRA PIRIE-ST. AMOUR

Client   CPC INTERNATIONAL
Design Firm   FISHER DESIGN, INC.
Designers   PETER M. SEXTON, RICHARD W. DEARDORFF

Client   BORDEN, INC.—TORTELLINI PASTA
Design Firm   HERMSEN DESIGN ASSOCIATES, INC.
Designers   CYNTHIA CHYLIK, JACK HERMSEN

Client   SCHWAN'S SALES ENTERPRISES
Design Firm   PEDERSEN GESK
Designers   KRIS MORGAN, RONY ZIBARA,
               MARK ORTON

Client   WILDFLOWER BREAD COMPANY
Design Firm   ESTUDIO RAY
Designers   JOE RAY, CHRISTINE RAY, LESLIE LINK

Client   STOCK POT COMPANY
Design Firm   PROFILE DESIGN
Designers   THOMAS MCNULTY, BRIAN JACOBSON, BRUCE BOWLES

Client   NEW ITALY FOODS
Design Firm   GREG WELSH DESIGN
Designer   GREG WELSH

Client   HANNAFORD BROS. CO.
Design Firm   GERSTMAN+MEYERS INC
Creative Director JUAN CONCEPCION
Design Director SUSAN PAYNE

Client   CRUM CREEK MILLS
Design Firm   MINKUS & ASSOCIATES
Designers   ROBERT MINKUS, LISA BRUEGGEMANN

Client   GENUARDI'S FAMILY MARKETS
Design Firm   DESIGN FORUM
Designer   DAVE NIXON

Client   BARI & GAIL CHOCOLATIER
Design Firm   FILOSI JONES
Designer   SANDRA PIRIE-ST. AMOUR

Client   GHIRARDELLI CHOCOLATE COMPANY
Design Firm   CURTIS DESIGN
Designer   JOAN BITTNER

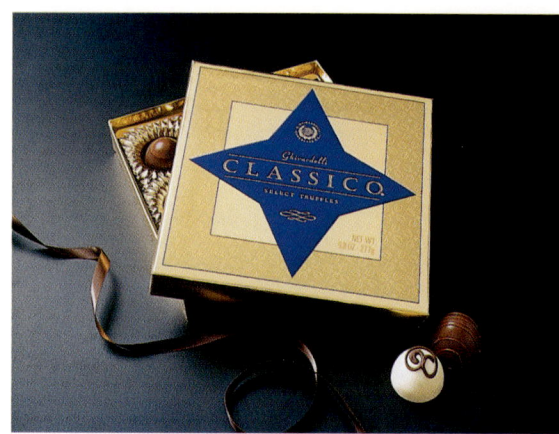

Client   FRAN'S CHOCOLATES, LTD.
Design Firm   WALSH AND ASSOCIATES
Designer   MIRIAM LISCO

Client   JOSEPH SCHMIDT CONFECTIONS
Design Firm   MÜHLHÄUSER & YOUNG
Designer   BARBARA MÜHLHÄUSER

Client   LEAF, INCORPORATED
Design Firm   CASSATA & ASSOCIATES, LTD.
Designer   JAMES WOLFE

Client   SEATTLE CHOCOLATES
Design Firm   HORNALL ANDERSON DESIGN WORKS, INC.
Designers   JACK ANDERSON, JANA NISHI

Client ELEGANT SWEETS—HANNAH'S DELIGHTS
Design Firm TIP TOP CREATIVE
Designers DEBBIE CAMPBELL, DAVID DAY

Client ELEGANT SWEETS—IL BISCOTTO
Design Firm TIP TOP CREATIVE
Designers DEBBIE CAMPBELL, DAVID DAY

Client NABISCO—STELLA D'ORO
Design Firm HABER DESIGN GROUP
Designers LEE HABER, EILEEN STRAUSS

Client VAN DE KAMP'S, INC.—PET-RITZ COBBLERS
Design Firm MOONINK COMMUNICATIONS
Designer MOONINK COMMUNICATIONS

Client HERSHEY CHOCOLATE U.S.A.
Design Firm ZUNDA DESIGN GROUP
Designers CHARLES ZUNDA, TODD NICKEL

Client PRESIDENT BAKING COMPANY, INC.
Design Firm FISHER DESIGN, INC.
Designers RICHARD W. DEARDORFF, BILL DUEBBER

Client   FRAN'S CHOCOLATES, LTD.
Design Firm   WALSH AND ASSOCIATES
Designer   MIRIAM LISCO

Client   STARBUCKS COFFEE COMPANY—FRAPPUCCINO
Design Firm   HORNALL ANDERSON DESIGN WORKS, INC.
Designers   JACK ANDERSON, JULIE LOCK, JANA NISHI, JULIE KEENAN,
          JULIA LAPINE, MARY CHIN HUTCHISON

Client   MAJESTIC CHOICES
Design Firm   TAB GRAPHICS DESIGN, INC.

Client   KRAFT FOODS
Design Firm   HUGHES DESIGN
Designers   SIRI KORSGREN, MICHAEL ENDY, SCOTT FISHER

Client   COFFEE PLANTATION
Design Firm   ESTUDIO RAY
Designers   JOE RAY, CHRISTINE RAY, LESLIE LINK

Client   KRAFT FOODS
Design Firm   HUGHES DESIGN
Designers   SIRI KORSGREN, MICHAEL ENDY, SCOTT FISHER

Client   ROYAL CROWN COLA CO.
                —MO JAVA COFFEE SODA
Design Firm   ANTISTA FAIRCLOUGH DESIGN
Designers   TOM ANTISTA,
                THOMAS FAIRCLOUGH

Client   BASKIN ROBBINS FLAVORS INC.—FAVORITE BLEND
Design Firm   THE DUPUIS GROUP
Designers   NOBUKO KOMINE, STEVEN DUPUIS

Client   KRAFT
Design Firm   HANS FLINK DESIGN INC.
Designers   STEPHEN HOOPER, HANS FLINK,
                HARRY BERTSCHMANN

Client   COFFEE PLANTATION
Design Firm   ESTUDIO RAY
Designers   JOE RAY,
                CHRISTINE RAY,
                LESLIE LINK

Client   BONJOUR BAGEL CAFE
Design Firm   MCNULTY & CO.
Designers   JENNIFER MCNULTY, DAN MCNULTY

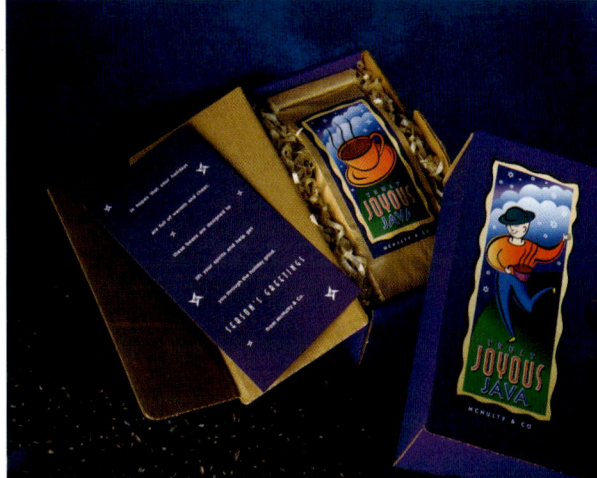

Client   INNOVATION SPECIALISTS
                MARKETING GROUP
Design Firm   SABAJ WILLIAMS & ASSOCIATES
Designer   JIM WILLIAMS

Client THE COCA-COLA COMPANY
Design Firm HILLIS MACKEY & COMPANY
Designer TERRI GRAY

Client COCA-COLA
Design Firm SBG PARTNERS
Designers MARK BERGMAN, PHILIP TING

Client THE COCA-COLA COMPANY
Design Firm MURRELL DESIGN GROUP
Designer STAN ZIENKA

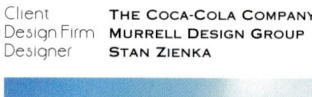

Client PEPSI-COLA
Design Firm ADDIS GROUP
Designer JAMES ELI

Client TALKING RAIN
Design Firm HORNALL ANDERSON DESIGN WORKS, INC.
Designers JACK ANDERSON, JANA NISHI, JULIA LAPINE

Client DR PEPPER COMPANY
Design Firm BERNI DESIGN
Designer PETER ANTIPAS

Client   MOTT'S U.S.A.
Design Firm   HABER DESIGN
     GROUP, INC.
Designers   LEE HABER,
     EILEEN STRAUSS

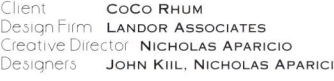

Client   THE COCA-COLA
     COMPANY
     (OLYMPIC
     PACKAGING)
Design Firm   DESGRIPPES
     GOBÉ &
     ASSOCIATES
Creative Director   JOANNA
     FELDHEIM
Art Director   LORI YI
Designer   THOMAS
     DAVIDSON

Client   AUSTIN NICHOLS
Design Firm   KOLLBERG/
     JOHNSON
     ASSOCIATES
Designers   KOLLBERG/
     JOHNSON
     ASSOCIATES

Client   HEUBLIN INC.
Design Firm   HUGHES DESIGN
Designer   SIRI KORSGREN

Client   HIRAM WALKER & SONS, INC.
Design Firm   THE VAN NOY GROUP
Designers   JIM VAN NOY, JOE HUIZAR

Client   FIRESTONE VINEYARD—CURTIS
Design Firm MARK OLIVER, INC.
Designers MARK OLIVER, PATTY DEVLIN-DRISKEL

Design Firm CALDEWEY DESIGN
Designer   JEFFREY CALDEWEY

Client   ESTRELLA CELLARS
Design Firm CALDEWEY DESIGN
Designer   JEFFREY CALDEWEY

Client   EDGEWOOD VINEYARDS
            —PIQUE-NIQUE
Design Firm CALDEWEY DESIGN
Designer   JEFFREY CALDEWEY

Client   WILLIAM ARBIOS WINERY
Design Firm CALDEWEY DESIGN
Designer   JEFFREY CALDEWEY

Client   FETZER VINEYARDS—BONTERRA
Design Firm CALDEWEY DESIGN
Designers JEFFREY CALDEWEY, DAN MACLAIN, JIM MURPHY

Client   BOISSET USA—JOLIESSE
Design Firm   CALDEWEY DESIGN
Designer   JEFFREY CALDEWEY

Client   SEAGRAM CLASSICS WINE CO.
Design Firm   MONNENS-ADDIS DESIGN
Designers   JOANNE HOM, ROBIN MACLEAN,
                CRAIG MARSHALL

Client   BORDEAUX
                PRINTERS
Design Firm   MIRES DESIGN
Creative/Art Director
                JOSÉ A. SERRANO
Designers   JOSÉ A. SERRANO,
                MIGUEL PEREZ
Illustrator   TRACY SABIN

Design Firm   SBG PARTNERS

Client   CHINA BASIN BALLPARK CO. LLC
                —AFFILIATED WITH SAN FRANCISCO GIANTS
Design Firm   THE GNU GROUP
Designers   NANCY DANIELS, JENI OLSEN, TODD TRUE

Client   BROWN & WILLIAMSON TOBACCO CORP.
Design Firm   FISHER DESIGN, INC.
Designer   BILL DUEBBER

Client ANHEUSER BUSCH, INC.
(BUD ICE OLYMPIC SPECIALTY PACKAGING)
Design Firm ANTISTA FAIRCLOUGH DESIGN
Designers THOMAS FAIRCLOUGH, TOM ANTISTA,
JAMEY WAGNER

Client ANHEUSER BUSCH, INC.
(BUDWEISER INDY CAR SPECIALTY PACKAGING)
Design Firm ANTISTA FAIRCLOUGH DESIGN
Designers THOMAS FAIRCLOUGH, TOM ANTISTA, JAMEY WAGNER

Client THE LUTSIK GROUP—AVALOS & BOURSE
Design Firm PROFILE DESIGN
Designers KENICHI NISHIWAKI, BRIAN JACOBSON

Client ANHEUSER BUSCH, INC.—WINTER BREW
Design Firm ANTISTA FAIRCLOUGH DESIGN
Designers THOMAS FAIRCLOUGH, TOM ANTISTA, JAMEY WAGNER

Client BOSTON BEER CO.—DOUBLE BOCK
Design Firm MUTS & JOY & DESIGN
Designer AKIRA OTANI

Client BOSTON BEER CO.—LONGSHOT
Design Firm MUTS & JOY & DESIGN
Designers GISELE SANGIOVANNI, AKIRA OTANI, JOY GREENE

Client   ANHEUSER BUSCH, INC.
              —ROSCOE RED
Design Firm   ANTISTA FAIRCLOUGH DESIGN
Designers   THOMAS FAIRCLOUGH,
              TOM ANTISTA, JAMEY WAGNER

Client   ANHEUSER BUSCH, INC.—BUD ICE and BUD ICE LIGHT
Design Firm   ANTISTA FAIRCLOUGH DESIGN
Designers   THOMAS FAIRCLOUGH, TOM ANTISTA

Client   BLACK MOUNTAIN BREWING COMPANY
              —CAVE CREEK GOLD
Design Firm   TIEKEN DESIGN
              & CREATIVE
              SERVICES
Designer   FRED E. TIEKEN

Client   ANHEUSER BUSCH,
              INC.—RIO CRISTAL
Design Firm   ANTISTA FAIRCLOUGH
              DESIGN
Designers   THOMAS FAIRCLOUGH,
              TOM ANTISTA,
              JAMEY WAGNER

Client   JOSEPH E. SEAGRAM & SONS
Design Firm   KOLLBERG/JOHNSON ASSOCIATES
Designer   PENNY JOHNSON

Client   BLACK MOUNTAIN BREWING COMPANY—CHILI LIGHT BEER
Design Firm   TIEKEN DESIGN & CREATIVE SERVICES
Designers   FRED E. TIEKEN, RIK BOBERG

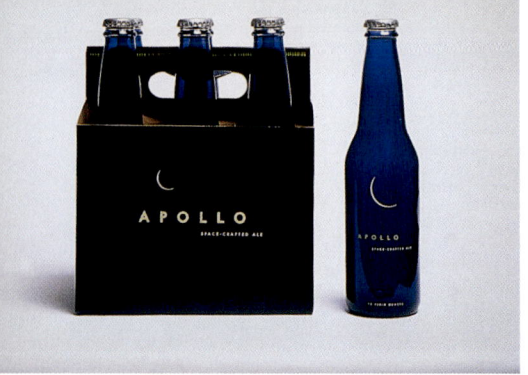

Client   BOISSET USA—APOLLO ALE & LAGER
Design Firm   CAHAN & ASSOCIATES
Designer   KEVIN ROBERSON

Client   MAYER BROS.
Design Firm   MCELVENEY & PALOZZI
Designers   MATT NOWICKI, JONATH[108
AN M. WESTFALL,
            STEVE PALOZZI, DENNIS DESILVA

Client   BOSTON BEER CO.—HARDCORE
Design Firm   MUTS & JOY & DESIGN
Designers   AKIRA OTANI, GISELE SANGIOVANNI, JOY GREENE

Client   PETE'S BREWING COMPANY
Design Firm   LANDOR ASSOCIATES
Designers   NICOLAS APARICIO, JENNIFER BOSTIC

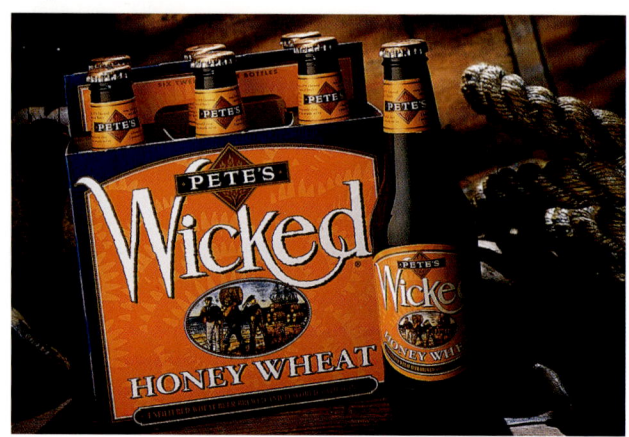

Client   PETE'S WICKED ALE
Design Firm   LANDOR ASSOCIATES
Creative Director NICOLAS APARICIO
Designer   JOHN KIIL

Client   BOSTON BEER CO.—CREAM STOUT
Design Firm   MUTS & JOY & DESIGN
Designers   GISELE SANGIOVANNI, AKIRA·OTANI

Client   MILLER BREWING COMPANY
Design Firm   TONG/MCKNEW ASSOCIATES
Designer   DEXTER J.C. LEE

Client   BOSTON BEER CO.—GOLDEN PILSNER
Design Firm   MUTS & JOY & DESIGN
Designer   AKIRA OTANI

Client   BOSTON BEER CO.—WINTER LAGER
Design Firm   MUTS & JOY & DESIGN
Designer   AKIRA OTANI

Client   GENESEE BREWING COMPANY
Design Firm   MCELVENEY & PALOZZI
Designers   MATT NOWICKI, STEPHEN PALOZZI

Client   CHAMPION BEVERAGES, INC.
Design Firm   GREEN RIVER & ASSOC.
Creative Director/Designer ELIZABETH SANTIAGO
Illustrator   PAUL DILLON

Client   JOSEPH VICTORI WINES, INC.
Design Firm   LIBBY MACDONALD & SHEAR
Designer   RICHARD SHEAR

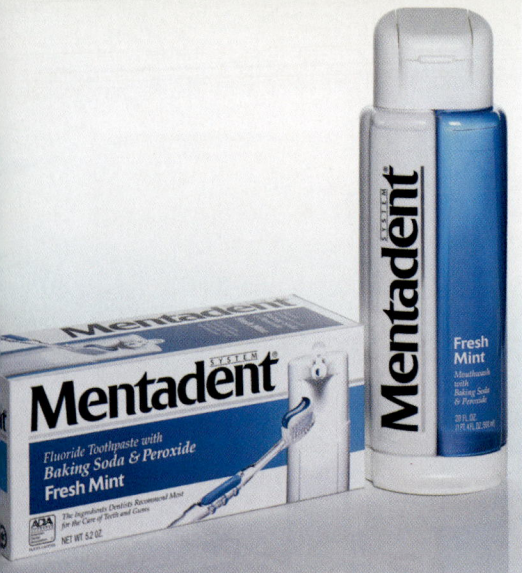

Client   ULTRAFEM, INC.
Design Firm   WALLACE CHURCH ASSOCIATES, INC.
Designers   STAN CHURCH, WENDY CHURCH, DEREK SAMUEL

Client   CHESEBROUGH-PONDS USA
Design Firm   HANS FLINK DESIGN INC.
Designers   HANS FLINK, CHANG MEI LIN

Client   HANES HER WAY
Design Firm   MONNENS-ADDIS DESIGN
Designers   JOANNE HOM, SHIRLEY NG-BENITEZ

Client   ANN TAYLOR INC.—ANN TAYLOR DESTINATION
Design Firm   DESGRIPPES GOBÉ & ASSOCIATES
Design Director   FRANCE ULLENBERG
Designer   KATHRIN JANKE

Client   SEASONAL SPECIALTIES ELECTRICS
Design Firm   SEASONAL SPECIALTIES LLC
Creative Director JENNIFER SHEELER
Designer   LISA MILAN

Client   PHARMACIA UPJOHN—PROGAINE
Design Firm   GERSTMAN+MEYERS INC
Design Director   LARRY RIDDELL

Client   DEP JAPAN STYLING GELS
Design Firm   DAVID SLAVIN DESIGN
Designers   DAVID SLAVIN, ALFRED TENAZAS

Client   AGREE CANADA STYLING PRODUCTS
Design Firm   DAVID SLAVIN DESIGN
Designers   DAVID SLAVIN, ALFRED TENAZAS

Client   HARNETT'S
Design Firm   STUDIO IZBICKAS
Designer   EDMUND V. IZBICKAS

Client   NATURES FAMILY
                INT'L BOTANICAL
                SHAMPOOS
Design Firm   DAVID SLAVIN
                DESIGN
Designers   DAVID SLAVIN,
                ALFRED TENAZAS

Client   GOLDEN NEO-LIFE DIAMITE INTERNATIONAL
Design Firm   LOUISA SUGAR DESIGN
Designer   LOUISA SUGAR

Client   SEASONAL
                    SPECIALTIES ELECTRICS
Design Firm   SEASONAL
                    SPECIALTIES LLC.
Creative Director   JENNIFER SHEELER
Art Director   BARBARA ROTH

Client   FRAGONARD SOLEIL
Design Firm DESGRIPPES GOBÉ & ASSOCIATES
Creative Director JOEL DESGRIPPES
Art Director SOPHIE FARHI
Designer   VERONIQUE MOROTTI

Client   ELOGEN, INC.
Design Firm LOVE PACKAGING GROUP
Designer   BRIAN MILLER

Client   AVON PRODUCTS, INC.—COLOR COSMETICS
Design Firm IN-HOUSE
Designer   E. MARK SMITH

Client   NEO DERMA LABORATORIES
Design Firm SHIMOKOCHI/REEVES
Designers   MAMORU SHIMOKOCHI, ANNE REEVES

Client   SEARS—TIME OUT
Design Firm   DESGRIPPES GOBÉ & ASSOCIATES
Creative Director KENNETH HIRST
Design Director SUSAN BERSON

Client   AVON
Design Firm IN-HOUSE
Designer   KIMBERLY MCCOY-FIDALEO

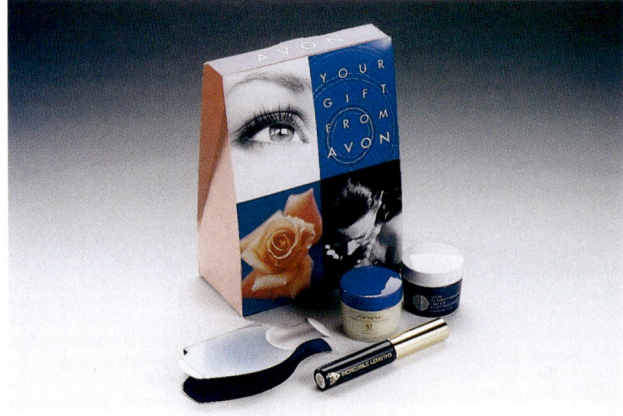

Client   CARTIER SO PRETTY
Design Firm DESGRIPPES GOBÉ &
            ASSOCIATES
Creative Director JOEL DESGRIPPES
Designers   ELIE HASBANI,
            FRANCK WEIDEL

Client   NOEVIR INTERNATIONAL CORPORATION
Design Firm GERSTMAN+MEYERS INC
Design Director SUSAN PAYNE

Client   PRIVATE PORTFOLIO
Design Firm BAGBY AND COMPANY
Designer   JANE GITTINGS

Client   DEL LABORATORIES, INC.
Design Firm ELEANOR WONG DESIGNS
Designer   ELEANOR WONG

Client   PRIVATE PORTFOLIO
Design Firm BAGBY AND COMPANY
Designer   JANE GITTINGS

Client   ANN TAYLOR CORP.—DESTINATION
Design Firm DESGRIPPES GOBÉ & ASSOCIATES
Creative Directors PETER LEVINE, KENNETH HIRST
Designers   FRANCES ULLENBERG, KIM TYSKA, CHRISTOPHER FREAS

Client   LASER PUBLISHING GROUP
Design Firm   KENG'S DESIGN
Designer   ROBERT KENG

Client   GAA CORPORATION
Design Firm   SMITH DESIGN ASSOCIATES
Designer   DWIGHT ADAMS

Client   ATTACHMATE CORPORATION
Design Firm   HORNALL ANDERSON DESIGN WORKS, INC.
Designers   JOHN HORNALL, LARRY ANDERSON, JANA NISHI

Client   ABKCO MUSIC + RECORDS
Design Firm   RUSSELL DESIGN ASSOCIATES
Designer   CODY RASMUSSEN

Client   HUNTER DOUGLAS WINDOW FASHIONS
Design Firm   POLLMAN MARKETING ARTS, INC.
Designer   JENNIFER POLLMAN

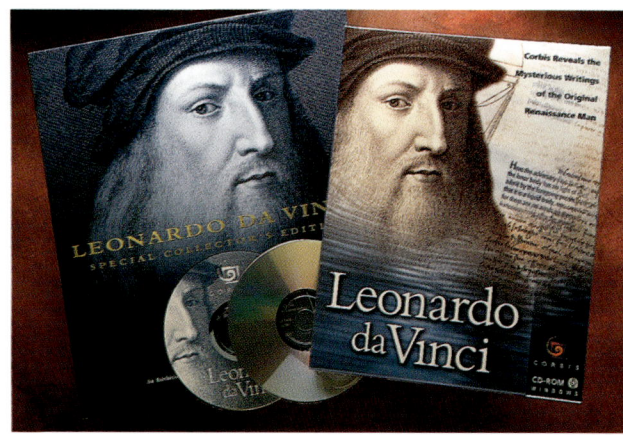

Client   CORBIS CORPORATION
Design Firm   HORNALL ANDERSON DESIGN WORKS, INC.
Designers   JACK ANDERSON, JOHN ANICKER, MARGARET LONG

Client   VH1
Design Firm   PARHAM SANTANA, INC.
Art Directors   RICK TESORO, JOHN PARHAM
VH1 Art Director DEAN LUBENSKY
Designer   PAULA KELLY
Photographer   PETER MEDELIK
VH1 Project Manager   MARY RUSSELL
VH1 Director   WAYNE WILKINS

Client   SUN MICRO SYSTEMS
Design Firm   SBG PARTNERS
Designers   MARK BERGMAN,
                JESSIE McANULTY

Client   SCOTT FORESMAN/ADDISON-WESLEY
Design Firm   LEE/McCOY CREATIVE CENTER
Designer   CINDY LEE

Client   SUPPORTFOLIO SERIES—SILICON GRAPHICS
Design Firm   SILICON GRAPHICS CREATIVE
Art Director   ELINOAR ALMAGOR
Designers   NICOLA GINZLER, AYLIN UNYAL

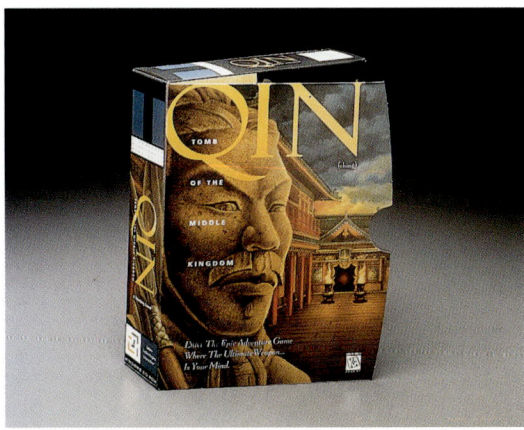

Client   TIME WARNER ELECTRONIC PUBLISHING
Design Firm   PLATINUM DESIGN
Designer   KATHLEEN PHELPS

Client   NEIL CLARK WARREN & ASSOCIATES
Design Firm   DENNIS S. JUETT & ASSOCIATES INC
Designers   DENNIS S. JUETT, DENNIS SCOTT JUETT

Client   XINET SOFTWARE
Design Firm   GEE + CHUNG DESIGN
Designers   EARL GEE,
   FANI CHUNG,
   ROBERT PASTRANA

Client   ALTEC LANSING TECHNOLOGIES INC.
   —TRUE SOUND
Design Firm   RONALD EMMERLING DESIGN INC.
Designers   JERRY FIELDS, RONALD EMMERLING

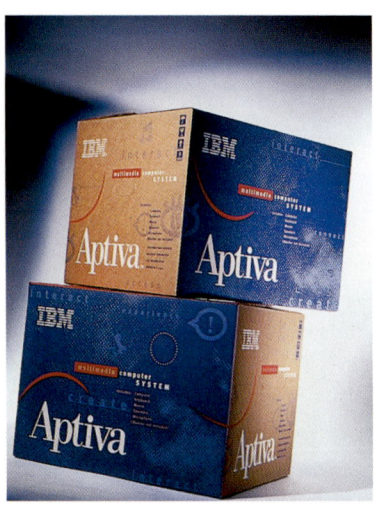

Client   SIERRA ON LINE
   —LAND DESIGNER
Design Firm   NBBJ GRAPHIC DESIGN
Designers   LEO RAYMUNDO,
   KERRY BURG

Client   IBM APTIVA
Design Firm   DESGRIPPES GOBÉ & ASSOCIATES
Creative Director   JOAANA FELDHEIM
Art Director   FRANCINE GERMANO
Designer   ANDRE METZGER

Client   WALL DATA—ARPEGGIO
Design Firm   TIM GIRVIN DESIGN, INC.
Designers   STEPHEN PANNONE,
   MARC GREEN,
   ROB MAGERIA

Client   WRITEPLACE SOFTWARE
Design Firm   LINCOLN DESIGN
Designers   TOM LINCOLN, PAUL HAGOOD

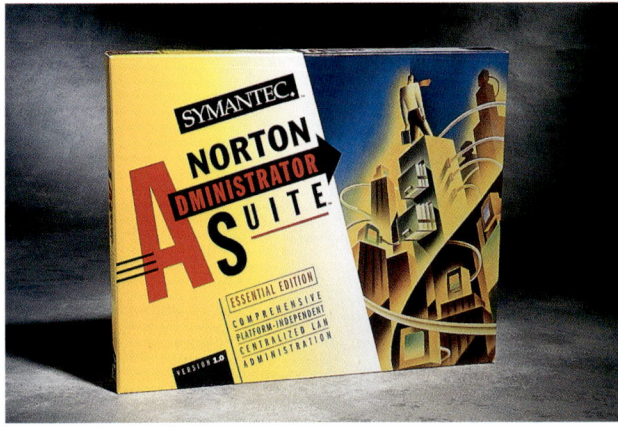

Client SYMANTEC NORTON ADMINISTRATOR SUITE
Design Firm GEE + CHUNG
Designers EARL GEE, FANI CHUNG, NIKOLAI PUNIN

Client TELEVIDEO MULTIMEDIA
Design Firm 3 MARKETEERS ADVERTISING
Designers IN-HOUSE DESIGN TEAM

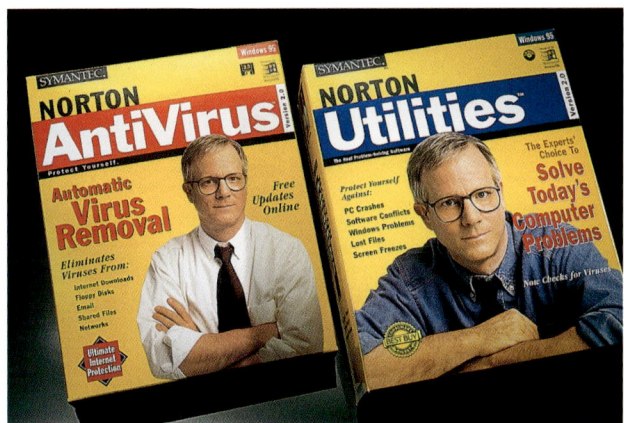

Client SYMANTEC
Design Firm TDC/THE DESIGN COMPANY SAN FRANCISCO
Designers SANDRA KOENIG, SHANNON BUTLER

Client P.F. MAGIC
Design Firm TDC/THE DESIGN COMPANY SAN FRANCISCO
Designer DAWN JANNEY

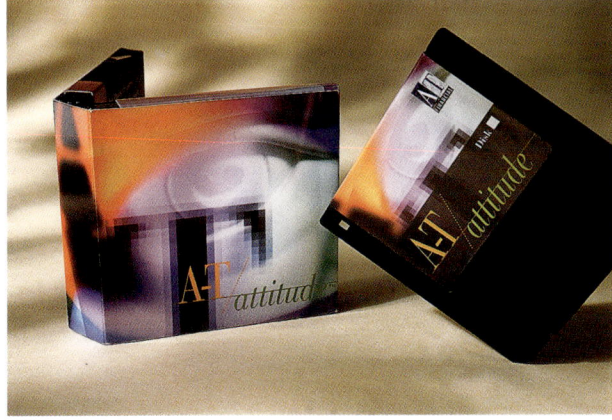

Client A-T FINANCIAL
Design Firm CULLINANE DESIGN INC.
Designer LUCINDA WEI

Client POWERSIM—POWERSIM 2.5
Design Firm CORYELL DOUGLAS DESIGN
Designer DWAYNE CORYELL

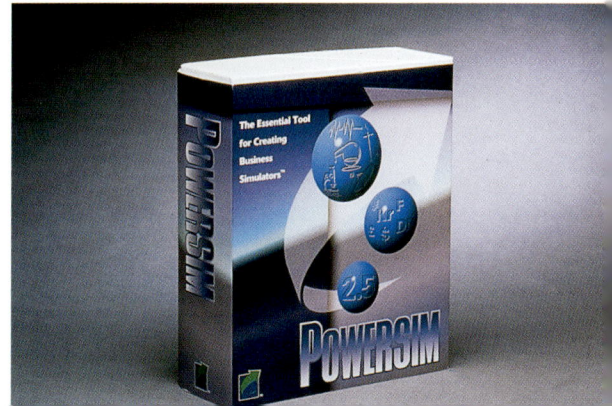

Client NETSTART, INC.—TEAM BUILDER
Design Firm ELLIOTT VAN DEUTSCH
Designers RACHEL DEUTSCH, ERIKA MAXWELL,
ROB RHINEHART, LOU CARAGAN,
HUGETTE ROE

Client SIERRA ON LINE—SIERRA HOME
Design Firm NBBJ GRAPHIC DESIGN
Designers LEO RAYMUNDO, KERRY BURG

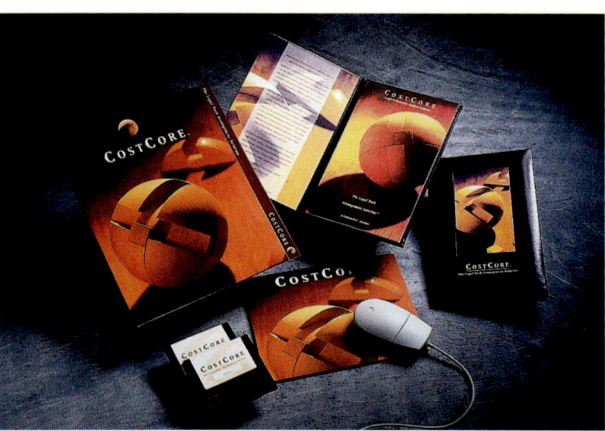

Client CHRYSALIS SOFTWARE
Design Firm LAURA COE DESIGN ASSOC.
Art Director LAUREN BRUHN
Designer DARRYL GLASS

Client IBM CORPORATION
Design Firm C3 INCORPORATED
Art Director BILLIE HARBER
Senior Designer SCOTT WILLIAMS

Client TRACKER BC—BENJAMIN FRENDEL
Design Firm DOINK INC.
Designer CHARLIE CALDERIN

Client NOVA DEVELOPMENT
Design Firm OGDEMLI/FELDMAN DESIGN, INC.
Designer SHAN OGDEMLI

Client   SUPPORTFOLIO
                —SILICON GRAPHICS
Design Firm SILICON GRAPHICS CREATIVE
Art Director ELINOAR ALMAGOR
Designers ELINOAR ALMAGOR,
                AYLIN UYSAL

Client   XEROX CORP.—5390 DEMONSTRATION ORIGINALS
Design Firm MCELVENEY & PALOZZI
Designers TOM CONE, WILLIAM MCELVENEY

Client   SILICON GRAPHICS INC.
Design Firm SILICON GRAPHICS CREATIVE
Art Director ELINOAR ALMAGOR
Designers FRANCI LU, STEWART MCSHERRY

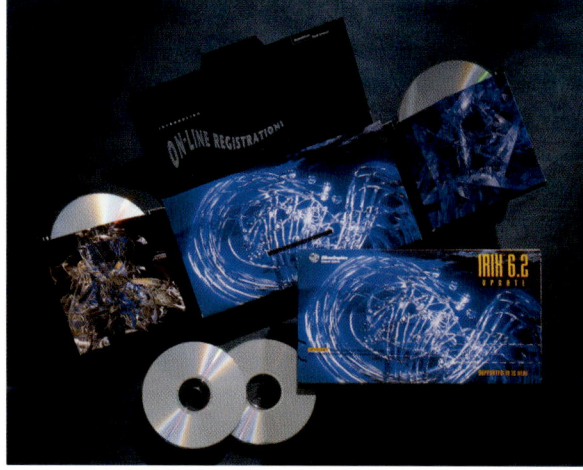

Client   SUPPORTFOLIO—SILICON GRAPHICS
Design Firm SILICON GRAPHICS CREATIVE
Art Director ELINOAR ALMAGOR
Designer JENNIFER SOUDERBY
Illustrator AYLIN UYSAL

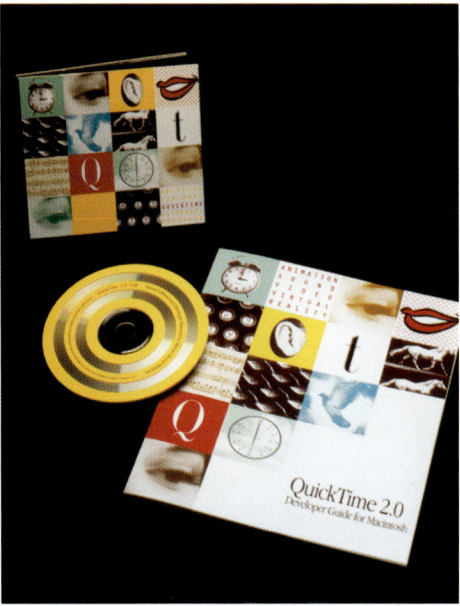

Client   GEMSTONE SYSTEMS, INC.
Design Firm COMMUNICATION BY DESIGN
Designer RICHARD ANDERSON
Photographer JASON KINCH

Client   APPLE COMPUTER
Design Firm MORLA DESIGN
Designers JENNIFER MORLA,
             CRAIG BAILEY

Client SHIMOKOCHI/REEVES
Design Firm SHIMOKOCHI/REEVES
Designers MAMORU SHIMOKOCHI, ANNE REEVES

Client GENERAL ELECTRIC LIGHTING—VALUE PACK
Design Firm ZEN DESIGN GROUP
Designer PAUL BURKE

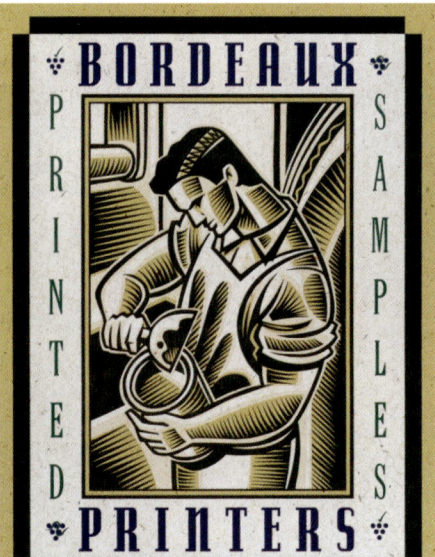

Client BORDEAUX PRINTERS
Design Firm MIRES DESIGN
Creative/Art Director JOSÉ A. SERRANO
Designers JOSÉ A. SERRANO, MIGUEL PEREZ
Illustrator TRACY SABIN

Client DELEO CLAY TILE
Design Firm MIRES DESIGN
Designer JOSÉ A. SERRANO

Client GE LIGHTING/CLARE FRISSORA
Design Firm STEIN AND COMPANY
Creative Director LES STEIN
Senior Art Director SUSAN LESKO YAKSICH
Designer DIANE ROBERTO
Illustrator MCRAY MAGLEBY

Client MOOG AUTOMOTIVE
Design Firm BRANDEQUITY INTERNATIONAL
Design Director JOE SELAME, IDSA
Design Team JOE SELAME, WILLIAM KENNEY,
GREG KOLLIGIAN

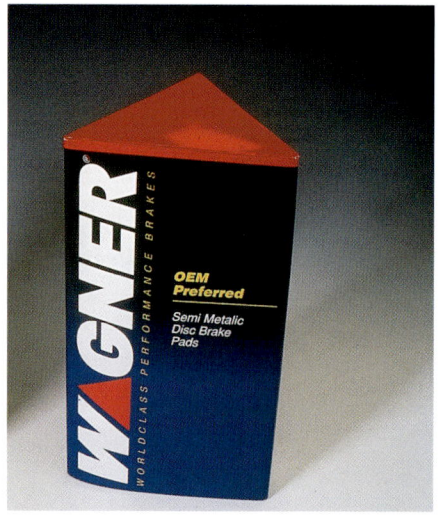

Client EASTMAN KODAK COMPANY
Design Firm MCELVENEY & PALOZZI
Designers JON WESTFALL, STEVE PALOZZI

Client HOMEDICS—FOOT PRO ULTRA
Design Firm ZEN DESIGN GROUP
Designers PAUL BURKE, DAVID YEE

Client EASTMAN KODAK COMPANY
    —DC 25 DIGITAL CAMERA & PICTURE CARD ADAPTER
Design Firm FORWARD DESIGN, INC.
Designers W. JAMES FORWARD, JONATHAN FORWARD,
    AARON SCHNITTMAN

Client OmniMedia
Design Firm AFTER HOURS
    CREATIVE
Designer AFTER HOURS
    CREATIVE

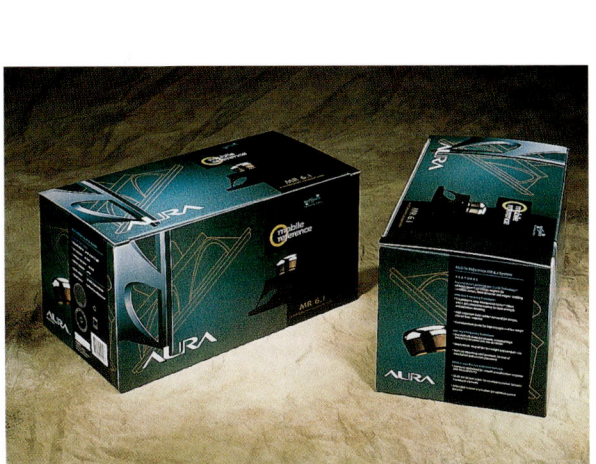

Client AURA SYSTEMS, INC.—MR SERIES
Design Firm CIRO DESIGN
Designers CHRIS RAGAINI, JOAN JUNG

Client CASIO PHONEMATE
Design Firm MARKETING AND
Designer JIM KELLEY

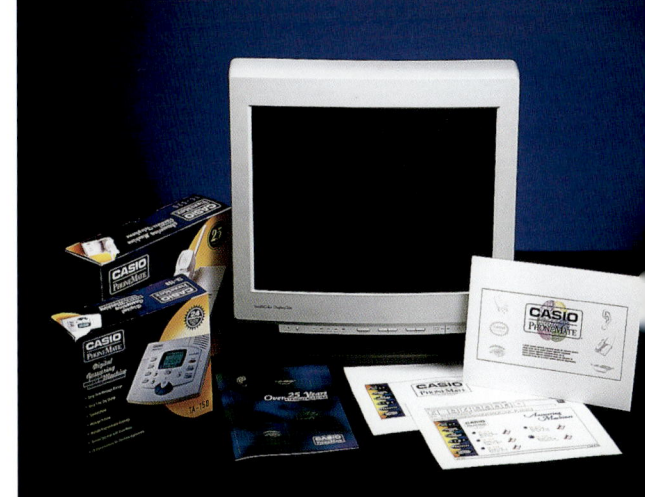

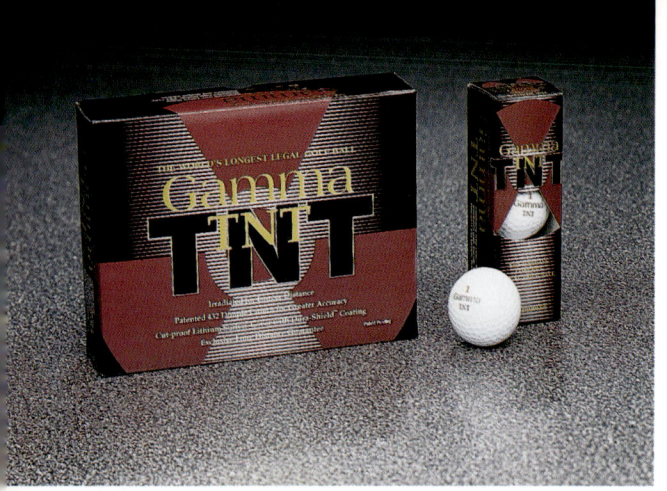

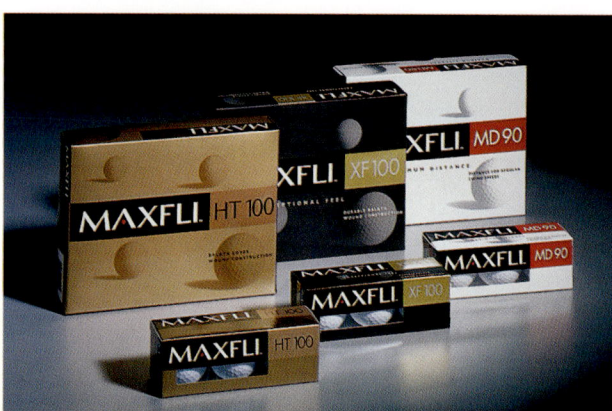

Client   GAMMA SPORTS
Design Firm   FAYE KLEIN DESIGN
Designer   FAYE KLEIN

Client   DUNLOP MAXFLI SPORTS CORPORATION
Design Firm   WALLACE CHURCH ASSOCIATES, INC.
Designers   STAN CHURCH, BOB RUSSELL, JOHN WASKI, DEREK SAMUEL

Client   DUNLOP MAXFLI SPORTS CORPORATION
Design Firm   WALLACE CHURCH ASSOCIATES, INC.
Designers   STAN CHURCH, DEREK SAMUEL, BOB RUSSELL

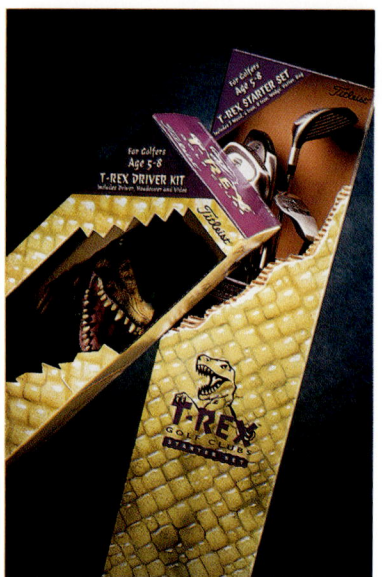

Client   TITLEIST AND FOOT-JOY
               WORLDWIDE—T-REX
Design Firm   LAURA COE
               DESIGN ASSOC.
Art Director   LAUREN BRUHN
Designer   DARRYL GLASS

Client   HOMEDICS—BODY BELT
Design Firm   ZEN DESIGN GROUP
Designer   PAUL BURKE

Client   CLARA'S FAMILY FARM
Design Firm   LOVE PACKAGING GROUP
Designer   TRACY HOLDEMAN

Client **BRAINWORKS**
Design Firm **PARHAM SANTANA, INC.**
Art Director/Designer **MILLIE HSI**

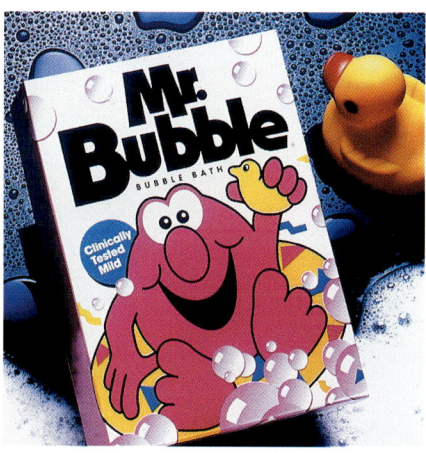

Client **PERSONAL CARE GROUP, INC.**
Design Firm **ZUNDA DESIGN GROUP**
Designer **CHARLES ZUNDA**

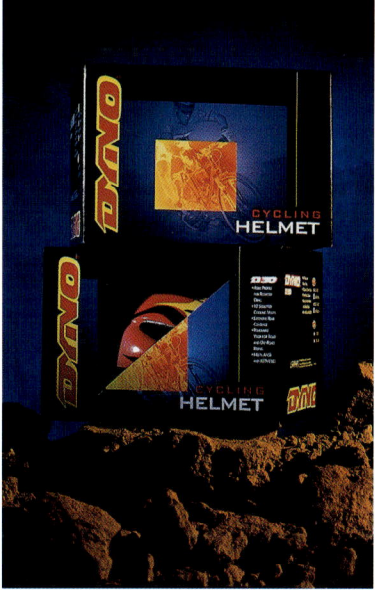

Client **G.T. BIKES**
Design Firm **RIECHES BAIRD**
Designer **CARRIE SANDOVAL**

Client **ODDZON PRODUCTS, INC.**
Design Firm **RILEY DESIGN ASSOCIATES**
Designers **DANIEL RILEY, CHA DIAZ, STEVE KU**

Client **DIXON TICONDEROGA**
Design Firm **GERSTMAN+MEYERS INC**
Creative Director **JUAN CONCEPCION**
Design Director **RAFAEL FELICIANO**

Client **PARIS, INC.**
Design Firm **THOMAS HILLMAN DESIGN**
Designer **THOMAS HILLMAN**

Client   LEVER BROTHERS CO.
Design Firm   HANS FLINK DESIGN INC.
Designers   GINA SPEARS, MARIANNE WALTHER

Client   LEVER BROTHERS CO.
Design Firm   HANS FLINK DESIGN INC.
Designers   CHANG MEI LIN,
              HANS FLINK,
              JAQUE AUGER

Client   COMPLIERS INC.
Design Firm   STEEL WOOL DESIGN
Designer   KRISTY LEWIS

Client   WESTERN WATER INTERNATIONAL—FRIGIPURE
Design Firm   STEVE TRAPERO DESIGN
Designer   STEVE TRAPERO

Client   PRESTONE (ANTIFREEZE/COOLANT)
Design Firm   HMS DESIGN
Designers   HUGH MONTGOMERY, PAUL BEICHERT

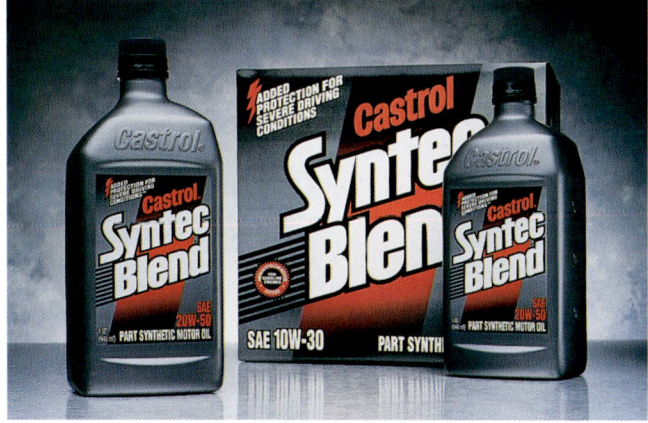

Client   CASTROL NORTH AMERICA—SYNTEC BLEND
Design Firm   BERNI DESIGN
Designer   MARK PINTO

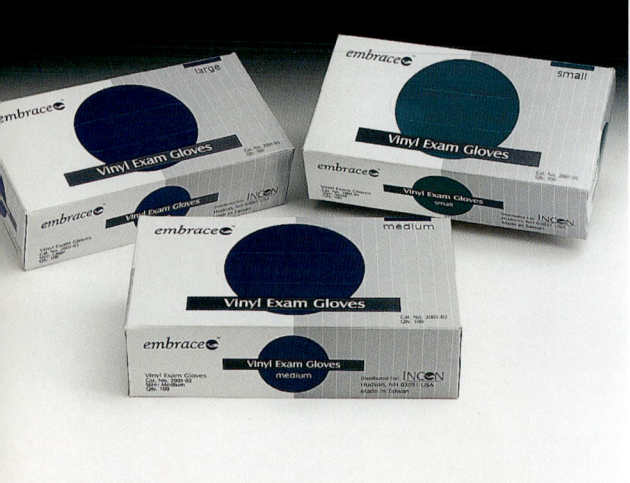

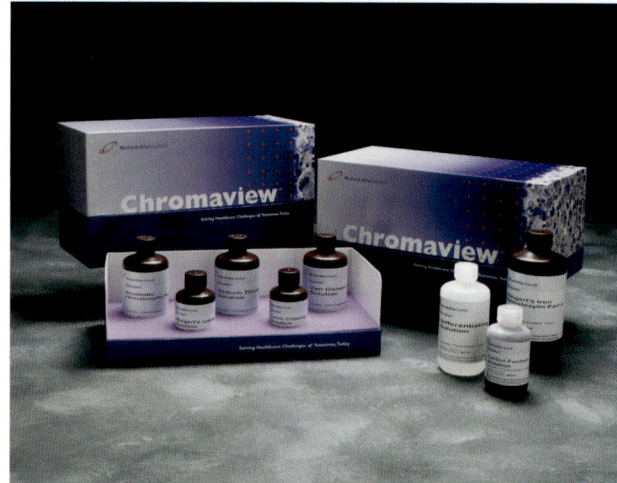

Client   RICHARD-ALLAN SCIENTIFIC
Design Firm   IN HOUSE DESIGN
Designers   JOEL SERVAIS, GARY WIEDERHOLD, JERRY FREDENBURGH

Client   INCON—EMBRACE HEALTHCARE
Design Firm   IMPACT DESIGN
Creative Director   ABBIE DEAN
Art Director   TRACY NEWMAN
Production Designer   MIKE RIDGE

Client   BAYER
Design Firm   WALLACE CHURCH ASSOCIATES, INC.
Designers   STAN CHURCH, DEREK SAMUEL

Client   SCHERING-PLOUGH HEALTHCARE PRODUCTS
Design Firm   SABAJ WILLIAMS & ASSOCIATES
Designer   JIM WILLIAMS

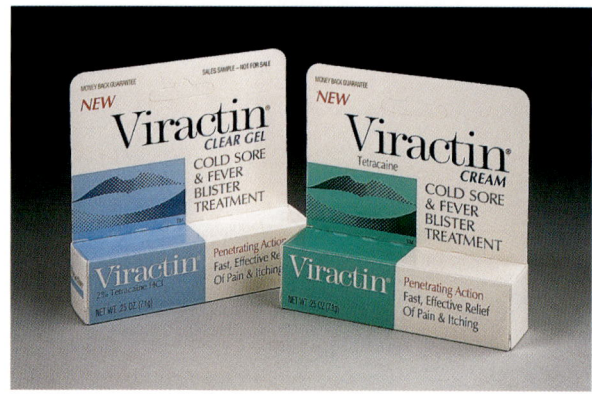

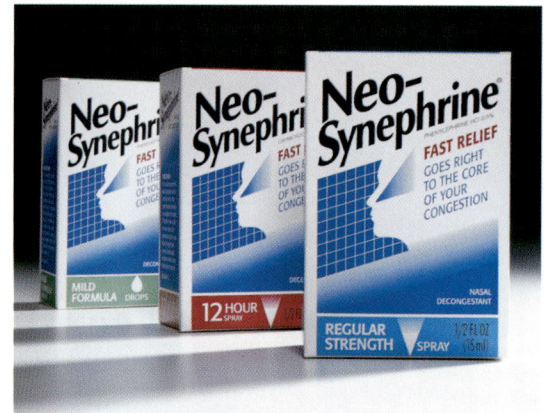

Client   BAYER CORPORATION
Art Director   HANS FLINK DESIGN INC.
Designers   MARK KRUKONIS, HANS FLINK

Client   W.F. YOUNG, INC. SPRINGFIELD MA
Design Firm   LUIS R. LEE & ASSOCIATES
Designers   HEATHER VAN LOAN, LUIS R. LEE

Letterheads

Client NAIMA
Design Firm A E R I A L
Designer TRACY MOON

Client JAE FEINBERG PHOTOGRAPHY
Design Firm TALBOT DESIGN GROUP
Designer CHRIS KOSMAN

111

619 E. Gutierrez Suite E, Santa Barbara, California 93103   Telephone 805-965-4455

Client   FAT CITY STUDIOS
Design Firm FAT CITY STUDIOS
Designer   JEFF WOODBURY

PO Box 344 Deer Harbor, WA 98243 Fax (360) 376-6091 Tel (360) 376-3037 VHF Channel 78

Client   DEER HARBOR MARINA
Design Firm   WIDMEYER DESIGN
Designer   DALE HART

Client   COBBLESTONE FILMS
Design Firm   KORN DESIGN
Designer   DENISE KORN

cobblestone films

THE MARGARET SANGER FILM PROJECT

26 west 17th street / 6th floor

new york city 10011

tel 212 / 647 / 1845

fax 212 / 647 / 0092

PALOMINO PARK

6700 PALOMINO PARKWAY
HIGHLANDS RANCH, CO 80126
PHONE 303-470-8400

Client   THE FELD COMPANY–WELLSFORD RESIDENTIAL PROPERTY TRUST
Design Firm   NOBLE•ERICKSON INC
Designers   JACQUELYN NOBLE, STEVEN ERICKSON, DAVID LANSDON

(510) 843-5555

1350 Addison Street
Studio 11
Berkeley
California
94702
design@fifthstreet.com
fax (510) 843-5395

FifthStreetdesign

Client   FIFTH STREET DESIGN
Design Firm   FIFTH STREET DESIGN
Designers   J. CLIFTON MEEK, BRENTON D. BECK

CONNELLY
DESIGN *for all dimensions*

444 N. Wabash
Suite 400
Chicago, IL 60611
312.595.9550
Fax 312.595.9559
pro@connellydesign.com

Client   CONNELLY DESIGN, INC.
Design Firm   CONNELLY DESIGN, INC.
Designer   DENNIS SCHEIBLE

Collector
Member ATCA & SBCCA

Matt Medeiros

11 Appian Way
Barrington
Rhode Island 02806
401-247-1477

Client   MATT MEDEIROS
Design Firm   CHAPMAN AND PARTNERS
Designers   ELEONORA HOUELLEMONT, DAVID CHAPMAN

Client **TUMBLE INTERACTIVE, INC.**
Design Firm **STREAMLINE DESIGN STUDIO**
Designer **KOUROSH GORJI**

Client **PROFESSIONAL MANAGEMENT GROUP**
Design Firm **HAFEMAN DESIGN GROUP**
Art Director **WILLIAM HAFEMAN**
Designer **GABRIELLE SCHUBART**

Client   REVOLUTION, HOLLYWOOD CA
Design Firm   PUSH
Designers   STEVE BARRETTO, TODD FOREMAN

Client   CERTAIN MIGHT
Design Firm   ADDISON WHITNEY
Designer   LORI EARNHARDT

301 South College Street · 2580 One First Union Center · Charlotte, North Carolina 28202
tel. 704 370-6500 · fax 704 370-6510
cmight@webserve.net

SPEAKERS EXCHANGE

Speakers Exchange
Post Office Box 77
Medford, Massachusetts 02153
[617] 422-1030 phone ■ [617] 787-1629 fax.

Client   SPEAKERS EXCHANGE
Design Firm   PANDAMONIUM DESIGNS
Designers   RAYMOND YU, STEVEN LEE

AMERICAN
MUSIC THEATRE

Client   AMERICAN MUSIC THEATRE
Design Firm   DEAN DESIGN/MARKETING GROUP, INC.
Designers   RUSS COX, LORI HESS

P.O. Box 10757 • Lancaster, PA 17605 • 717.397.7700 • FAX 717.397.7850

HealthGate DATA CORP.

380 Pleasant Street, Suite 230
Malden, Massachusetts 02148-8123

Tel: 617 321 6000
Fax: 617 321 2262
Web: http://www.healthgate.com

Client HEALTHGATE DATA CORP.
Design Firm STEWART MONDERER DESIGN, INC.
Designer STEWART MONDERER

NanoWave

180 Franklin Street

Cambridge, MA 02139

Tel 617 492 2323

Fax 617 497 6886

NANO WAVE

Client NANOWAVE TECHNOLOGY
Design Firm JOHNSON DESIGN GROUP
Designer JEFF JOHNSON

foglia
DESIGN ASSOCIATES

179 Boylston Street
Boston, Massachusetts
02130-4520
FAX 617 524 8809
TEL 617 524 8808

Client   **FOGLIA DESIGN ASSOCIATES**
Design Firm **FYFE DESIGN**
Designer   **ROBIN RATCLIFF**

F 310 204 1995 F 310 204 4879

edg
evenson design group

4445 overland avenue culver city california 90230

Client   **EVENSON DESIGN GROUP**
Design Firm **EVENSON DESIGN GROUP**
Designers   **STAN EVENSON, AMY HERSHMAN**

545 Concord Avenue, Suite 5
Cambridge, Massachusetts 02138
Telephone 617 876 8427

Sharon J. Esty-Tom
Naturopathy
Edgar Cayce Therapy
Hypnotherapy

Client   SHARON ESTY-TOM
Design Firm COMMUNICATION VIA DESIGN
Designer   VICTORIA ADJAMI

ABRAMS DESIGN GROUP

Client   ABRAMS DESIGN GROUP
Design Firm ABRAMS DESIGN GROUP
Designer   SANDER LEECH

100 View Street   Suite 203   Mountain View, CA   94041 1366   tel 415 964 2388   fax 415 964 5625

Client **:30 SECOND STREET**
Design Firm **A·HILL DESIGN**
Designer **SANDY HILL**

Client **DIG DESIGN**
Design Firm **DIG DESIGN**
Designer **AMY DECKER**

Creative Visions™ + 1405 Shefford + Wichita, KS 67212 Voice 316.729.6404 - Fax 316.729.6404 Web http://members.aol.com/bigweav

Client **CREATIVE VISIONS**
Design Firm **CREATIVE VISIONS**
Designers **CINDY WEAVER, VERN WEAVER**

GLOBALSERVE

The GlobalServe Corporation Park Plaza 1111 Chester Avenue Suite 800 Cleveland Ohio 44114 fax 216 579 0509 voice 216 579 1560

Client **THE GLOBALSERVE CORPORATION**
Design Firm **NESNADNY + SCHWARTZ**
Designer **GREGORY OZNOWICH**

Client   WEB ELITE
Design Firm   THE COMARK GROUP
Designer   ERIC LIVINGSTON

1700 Geddes Avenue

Suite C-7

Ann Arbor, MI 48104

P 313.998.3031

F 313.997.9177

www.webelite.com

PINNACLE ALLIANCE
Achieving Excellence Through
Global Teamwork

JPMorgan

CSC

ANDERSEN
CONSULTING

AT&T

Bell Atlantic

Client   COMPUTER SCIENCES CORPORATION
Design Firm   COMPUTER SCIENCES CORPORATION
   PRESENTATIONS AND PUBLICATIONS DEPARTMENT
Designer   RAMONA HUTKO

Advance Aqua Tanks

525 West 130th Street
Los Angeles, CA 90061-1134

310-538-4282 FAX 538-9249

Clear-for-life acrylic aquariums & accessories • Uniquarium

Clear for life

Client   ADVANCE AQUA TANKS
Design Firm   DEBORA LEM DESIGN
Designer   DEBORA V. LEM

---

business travel nw

phone 206 674 4400 | 2003 Western Avenue
fax 206 674 4444 | Seattle, WA 98121-2182

Client   BUSINESS TRAVEL NW
Design Firm   PHINNEY/BISCHOFF DESIGN HOUSE
Art Director LESLIE PHINNEY
Designer   DEAN HART

125

Client   **PEACHTREE CENTER**
Design Firm   **SKY DESIGN**
Designer   **DANA SABISTON**

Client   **SIMONS MICHELSON ZIEVE INC ADVERTISING**
Design Firm   **SIMONS MICHELSON ZIEVE INC ADVERTISING**
Designers   **HARVEY GABOR, LISA SABO, DONNA GILES**

We color a little bit outside the lines.

Simons Michelson Zieve · 900 Wilshire Dr. · Troy, MI 48084-5600 · (810) 362-4242 · FAX (810) 362-2044

55 Fifth Avenue • NY, NY 10003 • Ph: 212-463-9700 • Fax: 212-727-1716

eventive marketing

Client EVENTIVE MARKETING
Design Firm THE SLOAN GROUP
Designer WYNDY WILDER

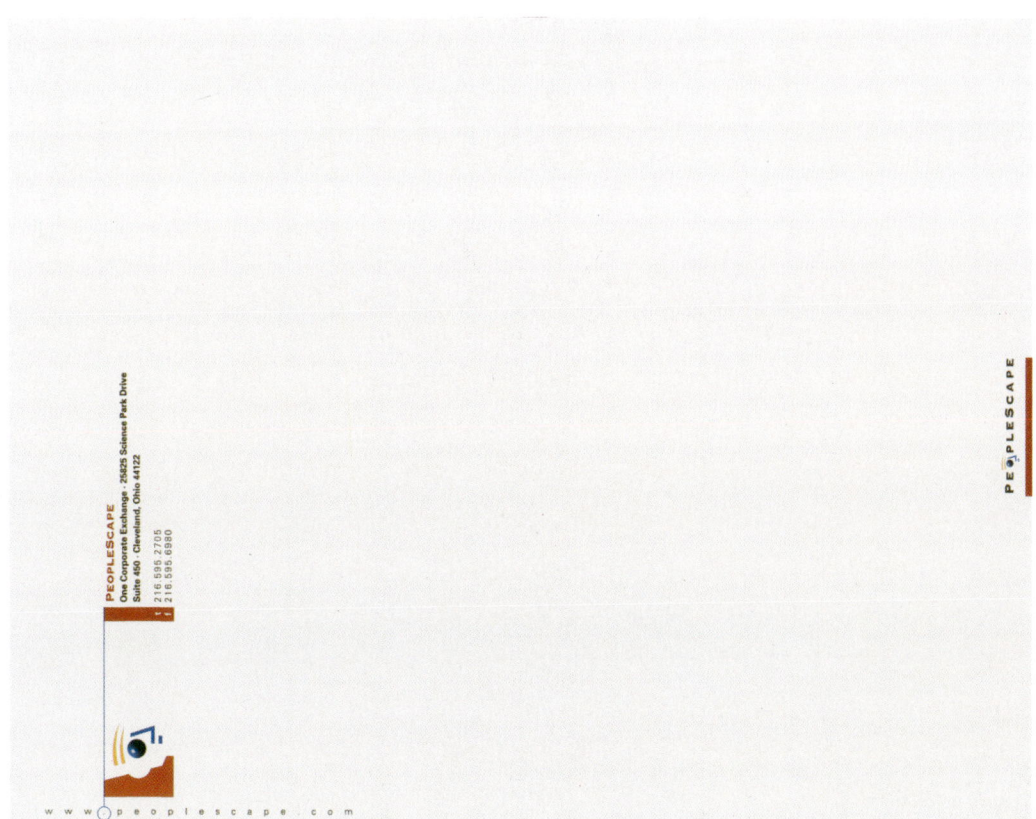

PEOPLESCAPE
One Corporate Exchange • 25825 Science Park Drive
Suite 450 · Cleveland, Ohio 44122
t 216.595.2705
f 216.595.6980

www.peoplescape.com

PEOPLESCAPE

Client PEOPLESCAPE
Design Firm VANTAGE ONE COMMUNICATIONS GROUP
Designer MIKE WOODCOCK

FARNET HART DESIGN STUDIO

822 Perdido Street, Suite 202 • New Orleans, LA 70112 • 504.522.6300 • fax 504.524.6359 • www.fhdesign.com

Client **FARNET HART DESIGN STUDIO**
Design Firm **FARNET HART DESIGN STUDIO**
Designers **WINNIE HART, GABY TILLERO**

STOTT & ASSOCIATES, Architects P.C.

600 Fifth Street
Ames, Iowa 50010
Ph. (515) 232-8447
Fax (515) 232-9521

Client **STOTT & ASSOCIATES—MICHAEL T. STOTT**
Design Firm **MICKELSON DESIGN & ASSOCIATES**
Designer **ALAN MICKELSON**

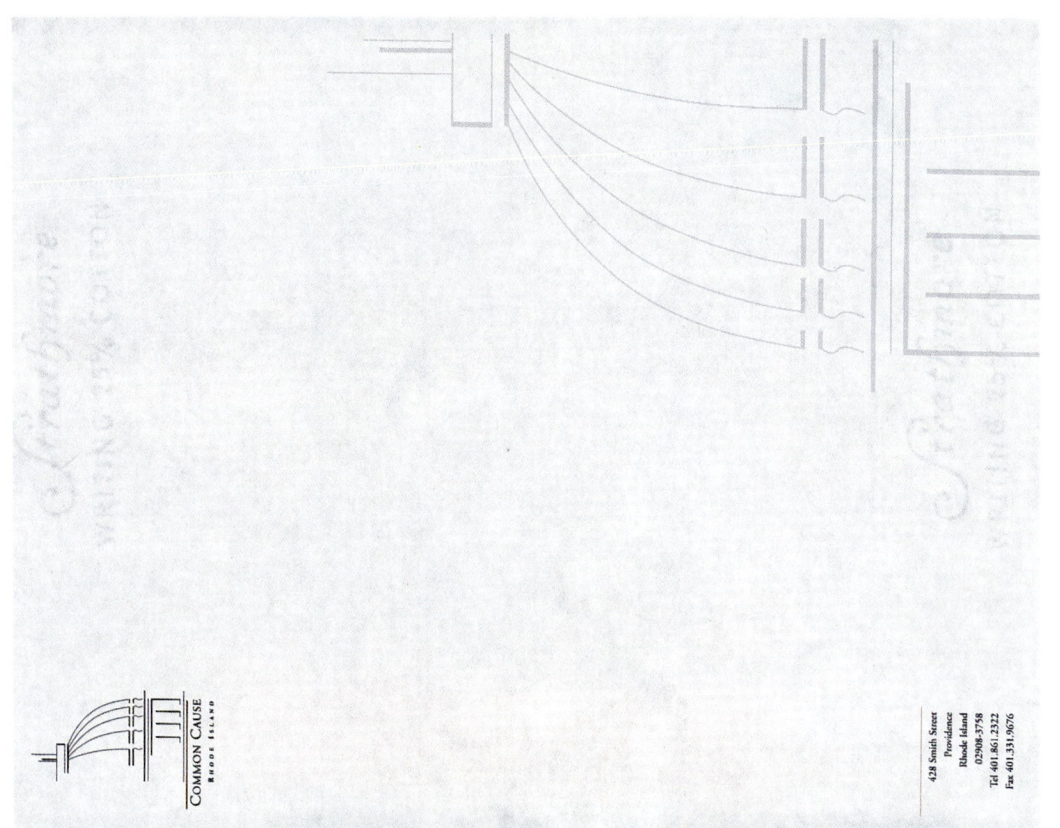

Client   **COMMON CAUSE OF RHODE ISLAND**
Design Firm   **COMMUNICATION & DESIGN MANAGEMENT**
Designer   **MARY TRODELLA**

Client   **DECISION SUPPORT SEARCH COMPANY**
Design Firm   **MCGAUGHY DESIGN**
Designer   **MALCOLM MCGAUGHY**

Warhaftig Associates, Inc.

361 Broadway, Suite 300, New York, NY 10013
Tel: 212·941·1700 Fax: 212·941·2490
E-mail: Warhaftig@aol.com

Client **WARHAFTIG ASSOCIATES, INC.**
Design Firm **WARHAFTIG ASSOCIATES, INC.**
Designer **REINER LUBGE**

Client **BETH FORER**
Designer **BETH FORER**

·D·E·S·I·G·N·S·T·U·D·I·O·
Beth Forer 243 Riverside Dr. NY, NY 10025 (212) 662-3716 FAX (212) 932-1522

Client   VON GAL ASSOCIATES
Design Firm VISUAL ASYLUM
Designer   AMY LEVINE

VON GAL ASSOCIATES

McDONAGH
BROTHERS
computer consultants

2205 california street ne
suite 312
minneapolis mn 55418-3351
tel 612.782.9939
fax 612.782.9855
http://www.mcdonagh.com/

Client   McDONAGH BROTHERS
Design Firm GARDNER DESIGN
Designer   BRUCE MACINDOE

131

Client   **BACK YARD DESIGN**
Design Firm **BACK YARD DESIGN**
Designer   **LORNA STOVALL**

Client   **MARSHALL WATSON INTERIORS**
Design Firm **TONI SCHOWALTER DESIGN**
Designer   **TONI SCHOWALTER**

Client
Design Firm   LOUIS & PARTNERS
                     LOUIS & PARTNERS

Louis+Partners
Marketing Design
1041 W Market Street
Akron, Ohio 44313
P. 330.836.8122
F. 330.836.1691

invisible

invisible HAND   8211 S. 77E Ave #202   Tulsa, Oklahoma 74133
918 631 2043   Fax 918 631 5008   steve@xpress.comm.utulsa.edu

Client   STEVE JONES
Design Firm   WALSH ASSOCIATES
Designer   TIM LANGENBERG

Client   INSOLROLL INC.
Design Firm POLLMAN MARKETING ARTS, INC.
Designer   JENNIFER POLLMAN

637 S. Pierce Avenue Louisville, CO 80027 TEL 800.447.5534 TEL 303.665.1207 FAX 303.665.1209

Client   WEBPA.COM
Design Firm W. RIMBELL DESIGN LAB
Designers   WAYNE KIMBELL, JEANNE SPENCER

The Web's Power Authority

610 Anacapa Street

Santa Barbara, CA 93101 USA

Tel. (805) 962-0222

Fax. (805) 730-3891

Email: info@webpa.com

Web: www.webpa.com

RIBOTSKYworldwide inc.

Client   **RIBOTSKY WORLDWIDE, INC.**
Design Firm   **RIBOTSKY WORLDWIDE, INC.**
Designer   **PETER HOFFMAN**

THINK

THINK *new ideas*

8522 NATIONAL BLVD., CULVER CITY, CA 90232   310 842.8063 FAX   310 842.8444

Client   **THINK NEW IDEAS**
Design Firm   **THINK NEW IDEAS**
Creative Directors **SCOTT MEDNICK. KEN ESKENAZI**
Designer   **KEN LOH**

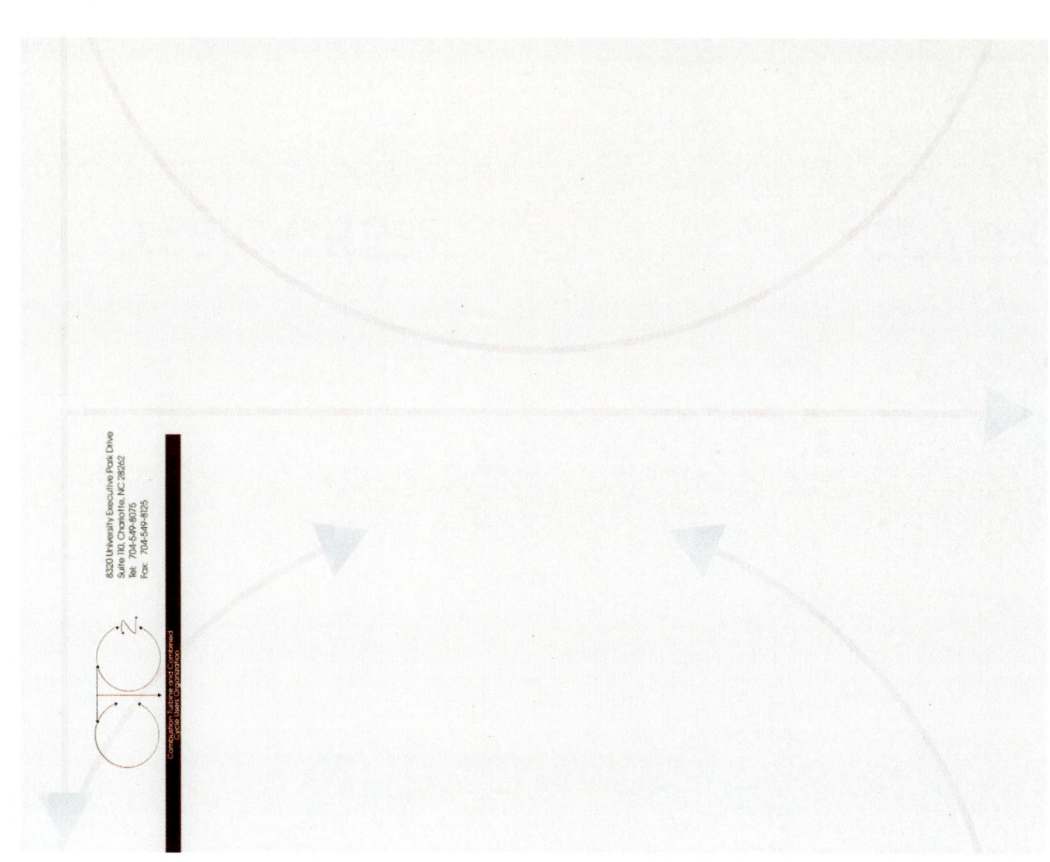

Client   COMBUSTION TURBINE AND COMBINED CYCLE USERS' ORGANIZATION
Design Firm   STEVE THOMAS MARKETING COMMUNICATIONS
Designer   STEVE THOMAS

Client   JAGER ASSOCIATES
Design Firm   JAGER ASSOCIATES
Designers   JEFF CONDON, GAYLE RAYMER, LEE JAGER

Robinson Advertising & Design

Client   ROBINSON ADVERTISING + DESIGN
Design Firm   ROBINSON ADVERTISING + DESIGN
Designer   DANA ROBINSON

2 Tunxis Rd., Tariffville, CT 06081, 860-651-9995, FAX 860-651-9188, E-Mail: DRobin 3633 @ aol.com

Esposito, Kiker and Associates

8755 West Higgins Rd.
Suite 250
Chicago, IL 60631

Telephone: 312/380-8700
Facsimile: 312/380-8905

EK&A

Client   ESPOSITO, KIKER AND ASSOCIATES
Design Firm   CLOSER LOOK CREATIVE
Designer   MARK JONES

1 East 53rd St. 10th fl. New York City 10022-4201

212-688-8280 / fax 212-688-0409

MUSE
Film and Television

Client   **KARL KATZ OF KATZLYST**
Design Firm **STUDIOWORKS**
Designer   **KEITH GODARD**

QUANTUM
COMMUNICATIONS

816 West Main Street · Louisville, Kentucky 40202

TEL 502·568·6628
FAX 502·568·2722

Client   **QUANTUM COMMUNICATIONS**
Design Firm **QUANTUM COMMUNICATIONS**
Designers   **PATTY MARGUET, JIM MILLER**

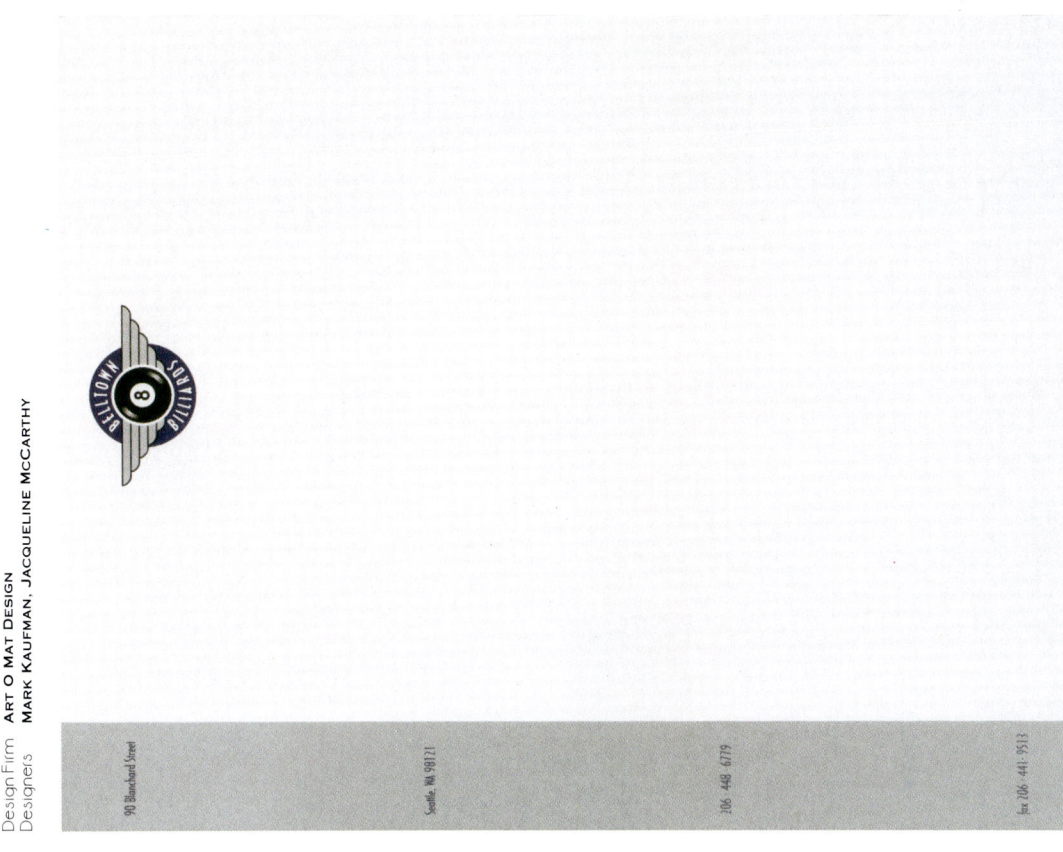

Client BELLTOWN BILLIARDS
Design Firm ART O MAT DESIGN
Designers MARK KAUFMAN, JACQUELINE MCCARTHY

90 Blanchard Street

Seattle, WA 98121

206 448 6779

fax 206 441 9513

Client THE JERMAIN COMPANY
Design Firm SOMA, INC.
Designers SARA ROGERS, STEVAN WITTENBROCK

Client   ZNETWORK (INTERNET ACCESS & WWW PROVIDER)
Design Firm L. BROOK FELLOWS DESIGN
Designer   L. BROOK FELLOWS

tel 800.336.1652   fax 600.353.3222   e-mail info@znetwork.net   url www.znetwork.net

625 broadway, suite 1020, san diego, ca 92101

get with it...

you want it...

Client   PUERTO RICO TOURISM COMPANY—LELOLAI
Design Firm GRAF, INC.
Designer   MARINA RIVÓN

Apartado Postal 4435, Estación Viejo San Juan, San Juan, PR 00902-4435
Teléfonos (787) 723-3135 / 723-3136 / 723-3132
Fax (787) 721-3878

PUERTO
RICO
Compañía de Turismo

Client   **EMI**
Design Firm   **ST. GEORGE GROUP**
Designer   **KEVIN POPOVIC**

Client   **TOLL-FREE CELLULAR**
Design Firm   **HORNALL ANDERSON DESIGN WORKS, INC.**
Designers   **JOHN HORNALL, HEIDI FAVOUR, JANA NISHI, JULIE LOCK,**
MARY CHIN HUTCHISON, BRUCE BRANSON-MEYER

Toll*Free*
c e l l u l a r

900 Fourth Avenue, Suite 3400 Seattle, Washington 98164   206.505.2200   206.505.2250 (F)   800.266.2125

33181 marina vista
dana point, ca 92629
714•493•4830

Client   JOE PAULICIVIC
Design Firm   FUSE, INC.
Designer   RUSSELL PIERCE

POLARIS

Polaris Associates, LLC

12804 Amaranth Street
San Diego, CA 92129

(619) 538-5254
(619) 538-5253 Fax

kdietz@fia.net

Client   POLARIS ASSOCIATES
Design Firm   CWA INC.
Designers   SYLVIE PUIG, CALVIN WOO

Client PRIMELINK
Design Firm WINTER GRAPHICS NORTH
Designers DEREK HOCKING, SIMON BISHOP-OLNEY

PRIMELINK

INTEGRATED NETWORK SOLUTIONS

11707 Fair Oaks Blvd. Suite 200. Fair Oaks, California 95628
916 965 5434 Fax: 916 962 3251 http://www.primelink.net email: info@primelink.net

Client FINATECH
Design Firm IMS
Designer JAMIE ANDERSON

SUMMIT CONSTRUCTION
QUALITY PUTS US ON TOP

910 EAST GREER STREET
HONEA PATH, SC 29654
PH 864-369-6466
FAX 864-369-6466

Client   SUMMIT CONSTRUCTION
Design Firm MJ DESIGN
Designer MARY JANE BATES

LAHONTAN

10815 TRUCKEE TAHOE AIRPORT ROAD ■ SUITE 410 ■ TRUCKEE, CALIFORNIA 96161-3325 ■ 916 582-9919 ■ FAX 916 582-7999

Client   LAHONTAN
Design Firm MÜHLHÄUSER & YOUNG
Designer BARBARA MÜHLHÄUSER

ALLIANCE BANK

120 TOWN SQUARE ▲ 444 CEDAR STREET ▲ ST. PAUL, MN 55101 ▲ (612)229-0070 ▲ FAX(612)229-0066

Client   ALLIANCE BANK
Design Firm   WELSH + ASSOCIATES
Designer   SUZANN BECK
Account Executive   FRED DRIVER

8265 COMMERCIAL STREET
LA MESA, CALIFORNIA 92042
(619) 464-0048

Client   CLEVELAND PRESS
Design Firm   MIRIELLO GRAFICO, INC.
Designer   RON MIRIELLO

CHILD & FAMILY **PROFILE**
Software for the information puzzle.

3737 N. Mozart
Chicago, Illinois 60618
Tel: 773-604-2252
Fax: 773-588-7762

http://www.sunmat.com/profile

Client　　　CHILD + FAMILY PROFILE
Design Firm　BULLET COMMUNICATIONS, INC.
Designer　　TIM SCOTT

Client　　　WORKHORSE DESIGN, INC.
Design Firm　WORKHORSE DESIGN, INC.
Designer　　CONSTANCE KOVAR

WORKHORSE
DESIGN, INC

432 AIRPORT ROAD, LEHIGHTON, PA 18235 TEL 610-377-5277 FAX 610-377-5453

Client   UD WEAR
DesignFirm   QUILL CREATIVE, INC.
Designer   STEVE M. UTLEY

UD-WEAR
CLOTHING COMPANY
4529 Atlanta Drive
Plano, Texas 75093
972.985.1744

Technology for the
Industrial Workplace
3413 Sullivan Trail
Easton, PA 18040-7823
Phone: 610.258.5161
Fax: 610.258.6217
tiwcorp@compuserve.com
http://www.tiwcorp.com

Client   ANDRA-HUYETT/TIW TECHNOLOGY
DesignFirm   GREENE & COMPANY
Designer   BARRY EDWARDS

Client PLAZA ALMERIA
Design Firm RIECHES BAIRD
Designer CARRIE SANDOVAL

PLAZA
ALMERIA

1372 Bolsa Chica Road
Huntington Beach, CA 92649
Commercial Leasing: (714) 897-7225
Residential Sales: (714) 891-2552
FAX: (714) 894-6321

Client BERTOLINI'S AUTHENTIC TRATTORIA
Design Firm ELIAS/SAVION ADVERTISING
Designer RONNIE SAVION

3500 Peachtree Road NE
Phipps Plaza
Atlanta, Georgia 30326
(404) 233-2333 • FAX (404) 233-7670

INTERPRISE
THE DESIGN RESOURCE

13455 Noel Road, Suite 2300 Dallas, Texas 75240
Tel 972.385.3991 | Fax 972.960.2519 | www.ntrpriz.com

Interior Design | Tenant Development | Strategic Planning | Retail Design

Client   INTERPRISE
Design Firm INTERPRISE
Designers   RITA RANDOLPH, SARAH HERRING

advertising & design

QUILL CREATIVE, INC.

1111 West Mockingbird Lane
Suite 830
Dallas, Texas 75247
214.688.3614
Fax:214.688.3673
Email: quill@onramp.net

Rochester, NY
716.256.0115
Fax:716.271.1083

Client   QUILL CREATIVE, INC.
Design Firm QUILL CREATIVE, INC.
Designer   STEVE M. UTLEY

BLUTOPIA
PICTURES, INC.

740 NORTH

LA CIENEGA BLVD.

LOS ANGELES

CA 90069

310.558.4434

Client   BLUTOPIA PICTURES
Design Firm   LORNA STOVALL DESIGN
Designer   LORNA STOVALL

Client   EPSTEIN DESIGN PARTNERS INC.
Design Firm   EPSTEIN DESIGN PARTNERS INC.
Designer   JOHN OKAL

Client HELLA EDICK (TRAVEL COORDINATOR AND TOUR GUIDE)
Design Firm HOLLAND & HOLLAND ADVERTISING
Creative Director STEPHANIE HOLLAND
Art Directors PAUL MAURINCE, ANGELA STIFF

Client CORPORATE APARTMENT SPECIALISTS
Design Firm JOHN VANCE
Designer JOHN VANCE

gym
adventures
for all
children

Gold's Gym
1 H.F. Brown Way
Natick, MA 01760

Telephone
508 936 2233

giant steps

Member of Named Center Marketing Network

Client   GIANT STEPS
Design Firm   KOR GROUP
Designers   MB SAWYER, ANNE CALLAHAN

CENTRI

C E N T R I I N C.
Academy House
1420 Locust Street
Philadelphia
P A   1 9 1 0 2
215-735-1600
FAX 215-735-6055
centri@pond.com

Client   CENTRI, INC.
Designer   MICHAEL CAVALLARO

StormshipStudios

call 617.646.9517

POST
641 Massachusetts Avenue
Arlington, Massachusetts 02174
fax 617.646.3623

POST
6927 Paseo del Serra
Los Angeles, California 90068
call 213.878.2609
fax 213.874.4754

Client   STORMSHIP STUDIOS
Design Firm STORMSHIP STUDIOS

Client   NORNET
Design Firm RILEY DESIGN ASSOCIATES
Designers   DANIEL RILEY, VONDRA DOHERTY

N O R N E T
INFORMATION SYSTEM INC

44 Montgomery Street
Suite 500
San Francisco
California 94104
Fax 510.944.9073
1.800.NORNET0 (667.6380)
Internet http://www.nor.net

153

Wilks + Frankey

MARKETING COMMUNICATIONS

P.O. BOX 465 · WILMINGTON, DE 19899 · PHONE:302.836.3880 · FAX:302.836.0369

Client **WILKS + FRANKEY**
Design Firm **WILKS + FRANKEY**
Designer **SARA-JO MATTHYS**

PEAPOD PROPERTIES LTD.

P.O. Box 2489 · Vashon Island, Washington 98070 · 206.463.3299 · Facsimile 206.463.3750

Client **PEAPOD PROPERTIES, LTD.**
Design Firm **HANSEN DESIGN COMPANY**
Designers **PAT HANSEN, JONATHON COMBS**

Client   DESIGNWRIGHTS INC.
Design Firm   DESIGNWRIGHTS INC.
Designer   ROSANNE ROMIGILIO

Client   ATHENA CREATIVE SERVICES
Design Firm   BARBARA RAAB DESIGN
Designer   BARBARA RAAB SGOUROT

Client   **TERPSICHORE SCHOOL OF DANCE**
Design Firm   **DESIGN RANCH**
Designers   **GARY GNADE, DANETTE ANGERER, KIMBERLY COOKE**

Client   **NETBOT**
Design Firm   **HANSEN DESIGN COMPANY**
Designers   **PAT HANSEN, KATE DODD**

156

Atlas

Atlas Carpet Mills, Inc. 2300 Saybrook Avenue Los Angeles, California 90040 Tel 213. 724. 9000 • 800. 372. 6274 Fax 900. 272. 8527

Client   ATLAS CARPET MILLS, INC.
Design Firm GENSLER
Designers LISA VAN ZANDT, PATRICIA GLOVER

PICTURE PALACE

CORPORATE OFFICE
3947 WITZEL DRIVE
SHERMAN OAKS
CA 91423-4609

PRODUCTION OFFICE
HOLLYWOOD CENTER STUDIOS
1040 N. LAS PALMAS AVE.
HOLLYWOOD, CA 90038

PHONE (818) 981-0252
FAX (818) 788-2759

Client   PICTURE PALACE
Design Firm DALTON DESIGN, INC.
Designer   ANNMARIE DALTON

Client   **WDBZ—THE BUZZ**
Design Firm   **JOHN SPOSATO DESIGN & ILLUSTRATION**
Designer   **J. SPOSATO**

Client   **SKLAR AND SECKINGER DESIGN ASSOCIATES**
Design Firm   **GRAPHITTI DESIGN GROUP**
Designer   **LAUREN HUGHES**

Client WOLFMAN PIZZA
Design Firm DELISLE & ASSOCIATES
Designer TIMOTHY DELISLE

Client COMMISSION FOR THE 2004 OLYMPIAD
Design Firm GRAF, INC.
Designer LYDIMARIE APONTE

a.c.c.i

american.cybernautics.construction.inc

"Providing Internet solutions for business"

m: 216·460·4401 | P.O. Box 501 | Northfield, Ohio 44067
t: 800·442·5135 | f: 216·468·4219 | e: sales@acci.com | w: acci.com

Client   AMERICAN CYBERNAUTICS CONSTRUCTION INC.
Design Firm   DESIGN ROOM
Designers   CHAD GORDON, MOLLY ZAKRAJSEK

Fabrications
Original Designs for the Interior

Judy A. Semrad
918.584.6558

Draperies • Slipcovers • Soft Furnishings

Client   JUDY A. SEMRAD—FABRICATIONS
Design Firm   WALSH ASSOCIATES
Designer   TODD PYLAND

PELE'S
HAWAIIAN PARTNERS, INC.

BOOMER'S
KIHEI

LAPPERT'S
LAHAINA

VILLAGE CAFE
KAPALUA

PELE'S CATERING CO.
LAHAINA

840 WAINEE STREET SUITE 125 LAHAINA MAUI HAWAII 96761 TEL: 808.661.1596 FAX: 808.661.5056

Client   PELE'S CATERING COMPANY
Design Firm   GOSS KELLER MARTINEZ, INC.
Designers   FERNANDO M. MARTINEZ, JERRY GOEN

design
L F Banks + Associates

voice 215.627.0555
fax 215.627.6724
banks@lfbanks.com

834 Chestnut Street Suite 425 Philadelphia PA 19107

Client   L.F. BANKS + ASSOCIATES
Design Firm   L.F. BANKS + ASSOCIATES
Designers   LORI F. BANKS, CESAR VARELA

RENT A WRITER

Why own when you can rent?

Karen Doornebos

1030 N. State • Suite 33I • Chicago, IL 60610
ph. 312.587.9694 fax: 312.587.9695

Client   **RENT-A-WRITER**
Design Firm   **IMS**
Designer   **JAMIE ANDERSON**

CONTRACT ∷ *Interiors*

10223 Barnes Canyon Road
Suite A203
San Diego, CA 92121
(619) 452-4342

Client   **CONTRACT INTERIORS**
Design Firm   **MIRIELLO GRAFICO, INC.**
Designers   **MICHELLE ARANDA, RON MIRIELLO**

645 Southcenter Mall
Suite 541
Seattle, WA 98188
(206) 539-4524

Client   PET FAIR PRODUCTIONS
Design Firm   SHEEHAN DESIGN
Designer   JAMIE SHEEHAN

516 3rd Street Suite 200
Des Moines, Iowa 50309
515.243.6010 phone
515.243.6011 fax
mauck@mauck.com e-mail
www.mauck.com internet

MAUCK + ASSOCIATES

Client   MAUCK AND ASSOCIATES
Design Firm   MAUCK AND ASSOCIATES
Designers   KENT MAUCK, SCOTT THORNTON, DAVIC JORDAN

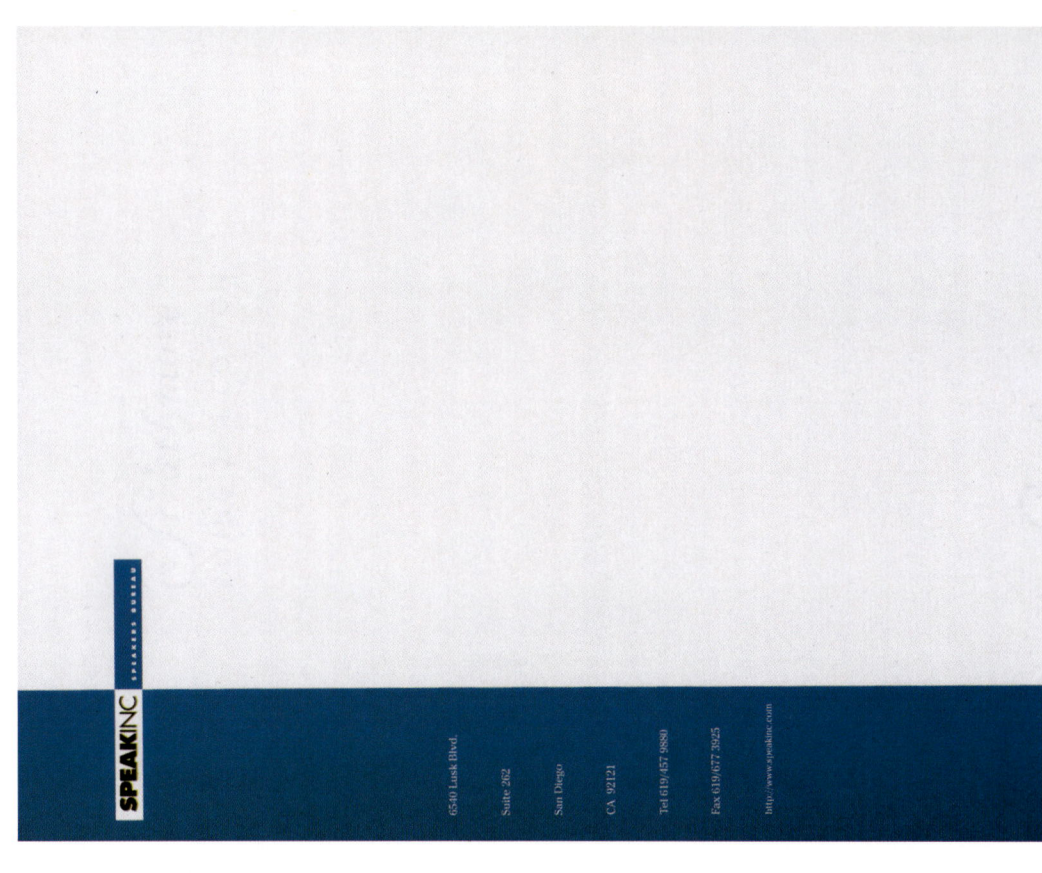

Client   SPEAKINC
Design Firm   VIADESIGN
Designers   STEPHAN DONCHE, MARK HAWKINS

Client   BERNSTEIN COMMUNICATIONS
Design Firm   JANE BERMAN GRAPHIC DESIGN
Designer   JANE BERMAN

Client   PRIZMA
Design Firm   MIRIELLO GRAFICO, INC.
Designer   RON MIRIELLO

Client   NEMZOFF & COMPANY, LLC
Design Firm   THOMAS RYAN DESIGN
Designers   THOMAS RYAN, STEVE GROVE

Client **SIGNORELLO GRAPHIC DESIGN**
Design Firm **SIGNORELLO GRAPHIC DESIGN**
Designer **MICHELLE SIGNORELLO**

Client **THE TRAVER COMPANY**
Design Firm **THE TRAVER COMPANY**
Designers **ANNE TRAVER, MARGO SEPANSKY**

80 Vine Street Suite 202 Seattle, Washington 98121

THE TRAVER COMPANY

· DESIGN STUDIO ·

TEL [206] 441-0611 FAX [206] 728-6016 E-MAIL studio@traver.com

Client CUBEWORKS, INC.
Design Firm KENDRA POWER DESIGN & COMMUNICATION
Designer KATHY KENDRA

CUBEWORKS, INCORPORATED

202 MEADOW ROAD ■ PITTSBURGH, PA 15116.2039 ■ PHONE 412.456.1250 ■ FAX 412.456.1250

Client BLUE HERON DESIGN
Design Firm BLUE HERON DESIGN
Designer REBECCA SIMONS

Client THE HARTWIG GROUP
Design Firm THE HARTWIG GROUP
Designer TOM HARTWIG

938 Lafayette Street   Suite 308   New Orleans   Louisiana   70113   [504] 524-8816

Client VISUAL PRODUCTIONS
Design Firm ZANDE NEWMAN DESIGN
Designers ADAM NEWMAN, MICHELLE ZANDE

Toni Schowalter Design

1123 Broadway

Suite 1600

New York, NY 10010

212 727 0072

Fax 212 727 0071

Client   TONI SCHOWALTER DESIGN
Design Firm   TONI SCHOWALTER DESIGN
Designer   TONI SCHOWALTER

Client   JOHN ROBBINS PHOTOGRAPHY
Design Firm   TED WILLIAMS DESIGN GROUP
Designer   TOM K. SIEU

john robbins

PHOTOGRAPHY

415 380 8588

Nealy Wilson Nealy Inc
visual communications

8650 Commerce
Park Place Suite D
Indianapolis
Indiana 46268

tel 317 879 9592
fax 317 879 9596

Client   NEALY WILSON NEALY INC.
Design Firm   NEALY WILSON NEALY INC.
Designers   NILA NEALY, STEVE NEALY, MIKE GARBER

ZENN GRAPHIC DESIGN
1637 McCollum Street
Los Angeles, CA 90026
Tel: 213-413-4369
Fax: 213-413-9668

Client   ZENN GRAPHIC DESIGN
Design Firm   ZENN GRAPHIC DESIGN
Designer   ZENGO YOSHIDA

Client   **ORDUÑA DESIGN**
Design Firm **BRD DESIGN**
Designer   **PETER KING ROBBINS**

Client   **MARY GRAND PRÉ (ILLUSTRATOR)**
Design Firm **ARMSTRONG GRAPHICS**
Designer   **R. BRUCE ARMSTRONG**

Client **RICAMIR**
Design Firm **DESIGN COUNCIL OF PUERTO RICO**
Designer **ASTRID FLORES**

Client **POTTS DESIGN**
Design Firm **KOR GROUP**
Designer **KAREN DENDY**

DESIGN MOVES, LTD.

10 23 GAGE STREET SUITE THREE WINNETKA, IL 60093

TEL: 847.441.6996   FAX: 847.441.6998

DSNMVS@AOL.COM or DSNMVS@INTERACCESS.COM

Client   DESIGN MOVES, LTD.
Design Firm   DESIGN MOVES, LTD.
Designer   LAURIE MEDEIROS FREED

2560 Ninth Street
Suite 312
Berkeley, CA
94710

tel: 510 845.0555
fax: 510 644.2680   e-mail: sales@xinet.com

Serve to the Macs

XINET

Client   XINET
Design Firm   GEE + CHUNG DESIGN
Designers   EARL GEE, ROBERT PASTRANA

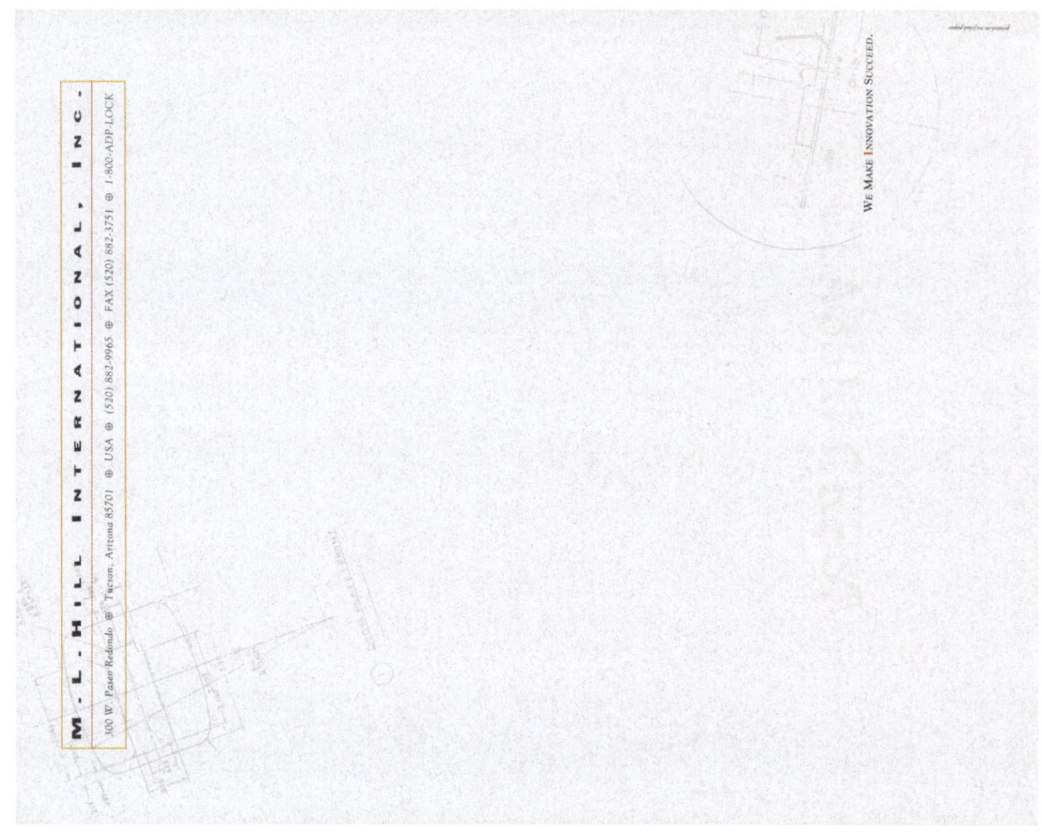

M.L. HILL INTERNATIONAL, INC.

300 W. Paseo Redondo ● Tucson, Arizona 85701 ● USA ● (520) 882-9965 ● FAX (520) 882-3751 ● 1-800-ADP-LOCK

WE MAKE INNOVATION SUCCEED.

Client   M.L. HILL INTERNATIONAL—HILL EUROPA AG
Design Firm   AIRE DESIGN COMPANY
Designer   CATHARINE M. KIM

HYPER think

info@hyperthink.com
www.hyperthink.com
P.O. BOX 520745
LONGWOOD, FLORIDA 32752
(407) 327-5200
(800) 336-0150

Client   HYPERTHINK MULTIMEDIA DESIGN
Design Firm   DELISLE AND ASSOCIATES
Designer   MICHAEL RUGE

Client THE WHITE ROCK COMPANY
Design Firm ZANDE NEWMAN DESIGN
Designers ADAM NEWMAN, MICHELLE ZANDE

able

Client ABLE DESIGN
Design Firm ABLE DESIGN
Designers MARTHA DAVIS, STUART HARVEY LEE
Consultant MARTIN PERRIN

Todo, Inc.
601 Union Street
Suite 220
Seattle, Washington
98101-2327

tel 206 340 1505
fax 206 340 1478

Todo

Client   **TODO WRAPS**
Design Firm **NBBJ GRAPHIC DESIGN**
Designers   **LEO RAYMUNDO, AMY LAM**

410 THIRD AVENUE SE • CEDAR RAPIDS IOWA 52401

319.366.7503

FAX 366.4111

ACCREDITED BY THE AMERICAN ASSOCIATION OF MUSEUMS

CEDAR RAPIDS MUSEUM *of* ART

Client   **CEDAR RAPIDS MUSEUM OF ART**
Design Firm **BASLER DESIGN GROUP**
Designers   **BILL BASLER, DREW DAVIES**

Client   DOINK INC.
Design Firm   DOINK INC.
Designer   CHARLIE CALDERIN

Client   PLAYWRIGHTS HORIZONS
Design Firm   STRAIGHTLINE INTERNATIONAL
Designer   MARTIN PERRIN

playwrights horizons

416 West 42nd Street New York NY 10036 68% TELEPHONE (212) 564 1235 FAX (212) 594 0296

1003 E. TRENT
SPOKANE, WA 99202
PHONE 509-484-4818 FAX 509-489-9572
[http://www.bayoubrewing.com]

Client   BAYOU BREWING COMPANY
Design Firm KLUNDT & HOSMER DESIGN ASSOCIATES
Designers   BRIAN GAGE, DARIN KLUNDT, SCOTT KNEESHAW

PORCELLI DESIGN
Lael Porcelli 24 Webster Place Port Chester NY 10573 914 934 1658

Client   PORCELLI DESIGN
Design Firm PORCELLI DESIGN
Designer   LAEL PORCELLI

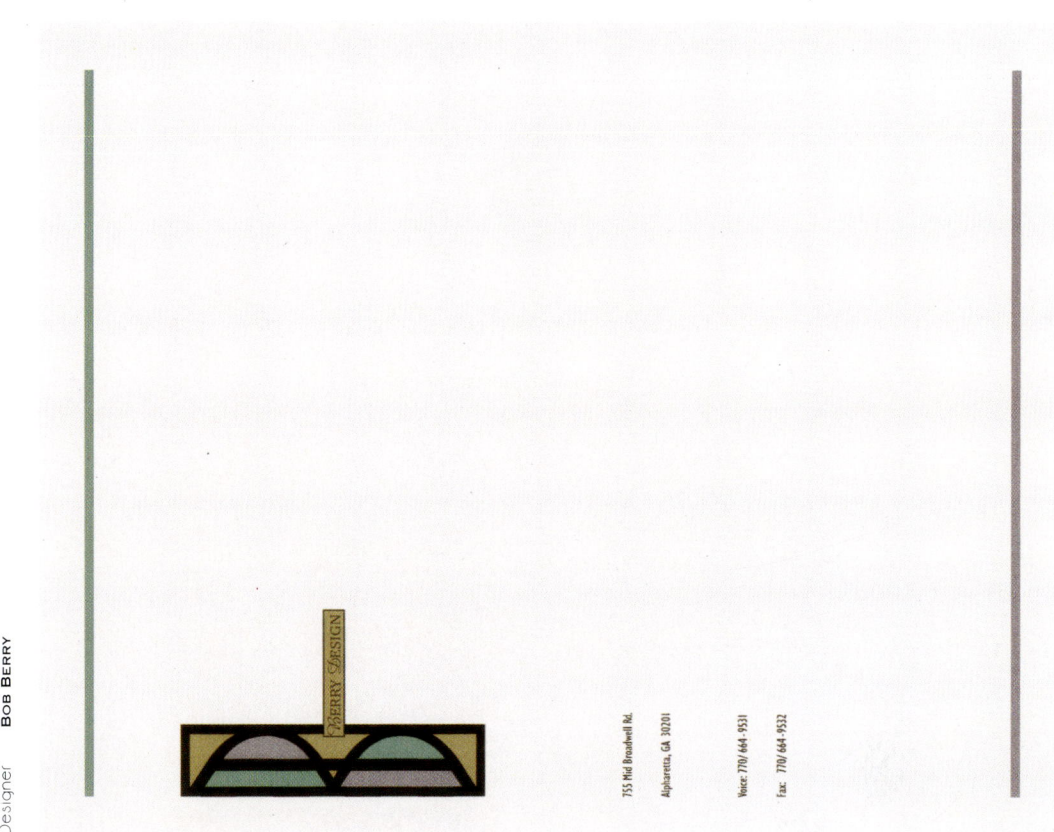

Client   **BERRY DESIGN, INC.**
Design Firm **BERRY DESIGN, INC.**
Designer   **BOB BERRY**

755 Mid Broadwell Rd.

Alpharetta, GA 30201

Voice: 770/ 664·9531

Fax: 770/ 664·9532

THE IMPACT GROUP INC

Client   **THE IMPACT GROUP**
Design Firm **SPANGLER ASSOCIATES**
Designer   **ALLEN WOODARD**

462 SUMMIT AVE
HAZELWOOD
MISSOURI 63042
314 731 8181
FAX 314 731 1044

Quality From The Ground Up!

Client   CLAYCO TILT-UP
Design Firm CUBE ADVERTISING & DESIGN
Designers   DAVID CHIOW, BRIAN BARCLAY

805 Scott Street • Madison, Wisconsin • 50103 • Phone 6087378344

Client   MAD CITY CAFE
Design Firm Z•D STUDIOS INC
Designer   MARK SCHMITZ

KILMER, KILMER & JAMES
DESIGN & ADVERTISING

191 TRUMAN NE, SUITE 200
ALBUQUERQUE, NEW MEXICO

zip 87108.1330

tel 505.260.1175
fax 850.260.1651
fax 505.260.1555

Client   KILMER & KILMER, INC.
Design Firm KILMER & KILMER, INC. DESIGN & ADVERTISING
Designers   RICHARD KILMER, BRENDA KILMER, RANDALL MARSHALL

Jane Terzis

Art Boy Inc.
119 Seward Street Sta 5
Juneau Alaska 99801
tel 907 586 4076
fax 907 586 0859

Client   ART BOY INC.
Design Firm ART BOY INC.
Designer   JANE TERZIS

Huckleberry's Fresh Markets
P.O. Box 9000
1815 West Garland
Spokane, Washington
99209-9000
509-326-8900
Fax: 509-328-2483

HUCKLEBERRY'S

Client   HUCKLEBERRY'S FRESH MARKET
Design Firm KLUNDT + HOSMER DESIGN ASSOCIATES
Designers   BRIAN GAGE, DARIN KLUNDT, RICK HOSMER
Illustrator CHARLES WALTMIERE

Printed with soy based inks on 100% recycled floor content paper.

VISTAMONTE

2682 Santa Ynez Avenue
Simi Valley CA 93063

805-579-7004
Fax: 805-579-7081

Client   STANDARD PACIFIC OF VENTURA
Design Firm MUSTANG MARKETING & ADVERTISING
Designer   EDWARD SCULLY

Client   CITYNET INC.
Design Firm   H2 DESIGN GROUP INC.
Art Director   TIMOTHY HUSNI
Designer   GINO TAVOLETTI

Client   GST INTERNET
Design Firm   GST INTERNET
Designer   KEITH SASAKI

183

ccwriter

Cheri Choudoir **Wordsmith**
1678 N.Humboldt Ave., Milwaukee, WI 53202
tel/fax 414.278.0399

Client   **CHERI CHOUDOIR**
Design Firm   **ART HAUS CREATIVE INC.**
Designer   **LEE PLANK**

SOUTHERN COMPANY
Energy to Serve Your World™

A.W. Dahlberg
Chairman, President and
Chief Executive Officer

270 Peachtree Street NW
Suite 2200
Atlanta, Georgia 30303
Tel 404.506.0500
Fax 404.506.0504

Client   **SOUTHERN COMPANY**
Design Firm   **LIPPINCOTT & MARGULIES**
Designers   **CONNIE BIRDSALL, MICHELLE CASSUTO**

NOT DESIGNED!

JMU TRUDY COLE-ZIELANSKI

James Madison University
School of Media Arts and Design

Harrisonburg, Virginia 22807
(540) 568-7000

Client   TRUDY COLE-ZIELANSKI
Design Firm   TRUDY COLE-ZIELANSKI DESIGN
Designer   TRUDY COLE-ZIELANSKI
Original Design   PUBLICATIONS DEPARTMENT AT JAMES MADISON UNIVERSITY

Pathlore

Pathlore Software Corporation

Corporate Headquarters   Suite 300   7965 North High Street   Columbus, Ohio 43235   800.829.9088   Fax: 614.781.7200

Client   PATHLORE SOFTWARE CORP.
Design Firm   GRAPHICA
Designer   DREW CRONENWETT

TRACY PORTER
The Home Collection

N5373 County W   Princeton, WI 54968   (414) 295 0142   Fax (800) 713 4756

Client   TRACY PORTER THE HOME COLLECTION
Design Firm   JCNB DESIGN
Designer   JANE NASS BARNIDGE

e-Tribe
electronic media

4011 WestChase Blvd.   Suite 120   Raleigh NC 27607   919.856.0094   fx 919.856.0084

Client   E-TRIBE
Design Firm   ADDISON WHITNEY
Designers   LORI EARNHARDT, KIMBER FLYNN

Client **CAFE 222**
Design Firm **VISUAL ASYLUM**
Designers **JOEL SOTELO, MAELIN LEVINE**

CAFE 222

222 ISLAND AVENUE · SAN DIEGO, CA 92101 Phone 619.236.9902 Fax 619.236.8191 e-mail terryl.@cafe222.com url www.cafe222.com

chameleon creative inc

2820
wilderness
place · suite f
boulder, co
80301

303.444.8667
303.444.5007 fax
jrc@usa.net e-mail

Client **CHAMELEON CREATIVE, INC.**
Design Firm **CHAMELEON CREATIVE, INC.**
Designer **MONA CORNWELL**

Client GEIGER DESIGN/BEVOLO CREATIVE
Design Firm GEIGER DESIGN/BEVOLO CREATIVE
Designers SCOTT GEIGER, CHRIS BEVOLO

GEIGER DESIGN
BEVOLO CREATIVE

322 First Avenue North
Suite 201
Minneapolis, MN 55401
612.672.9842 (Geiger)
612.305.0916 (Bevolo)
(fax.376.7976

155 STEUART STREET, SAN FRANCISCO, CALIFORNIA 94105 TELEPHONE 415.495.6500 FAX 415.495.3522

Client REAL RESTAURANTS, INC.
Design Firm RUSSELL LEONG DESIGN
Designer RUSSELL LEONG

11940 Riverside Drive Suite B North Hollywood CA 91607

Telephone 818.769.5510 Facsimile 818.345.2254

HUFF
INDUSTRIES

HUMIDOR ORIGINALS

Client   HUFF INDUSTRIES
Design Firm   MARK DESIGNS
Designers   MARK LEROY, INSUNG KIM, HIDEKO YAMAMATO

FULLER

Fuller Designs, Inc.
8150 Leesburg Pike, Suite 513
Vienna, Virginia 22182

Phone 703.760.0061
Fax 703.760.0065
designfull@aol.com

Client   FULLER DESIGNS, INC.
Design Firm   FULLER DESIGNS, INC.
Designers   DOUG FULLER, AARON TAYLOR

THREE BAGS FULL

825 RIVER ROAD · NORTH TONAWANDA · N.Y. 14120 · © · PHONE: (716) 694-4990

Client   THREE BAGS FULL (WOOLEN GOODS)
Design Firm LOURAGE DESIGN
Designer   ALAN KEGLER

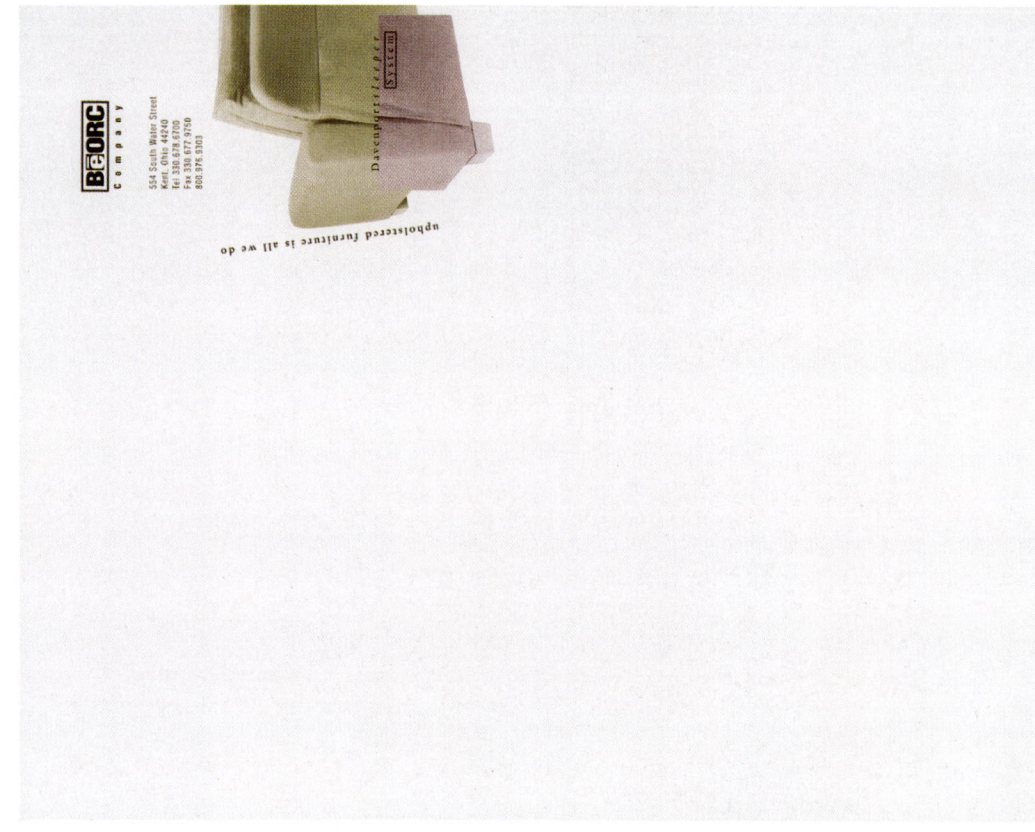

BēORC
Company

554 South Water Street
Kent, Ohio 44240
Tel 330.678.6700
Fax 330.677.9750
800.976.9303

upholstered furniture is all we do

Client   BēORC COMPANY
Design Firm TIM LEIHER DESIGN
Designer   TIMOTHY LEIHER

Client JENGA CONSULTING
Design Firm KNOX DESIGN
Designer LUTHER KNOX

Client STEVEN DINBERG
Design Firm FINE PRINT, INC.
Designer CRAIG FORD

Client THE FELD COMPANY—BRIDGWATER
Design Firm NOBLE • ERICKSON INC
Designers JACQUELYN NOBLE, STEVEN ERICKSON, CHELSEA ERICKSON

Client MEDIA VISTA PRODUCTIONS
Design Firm THE VISUAL GROUP
Designer ARK STEIN

192

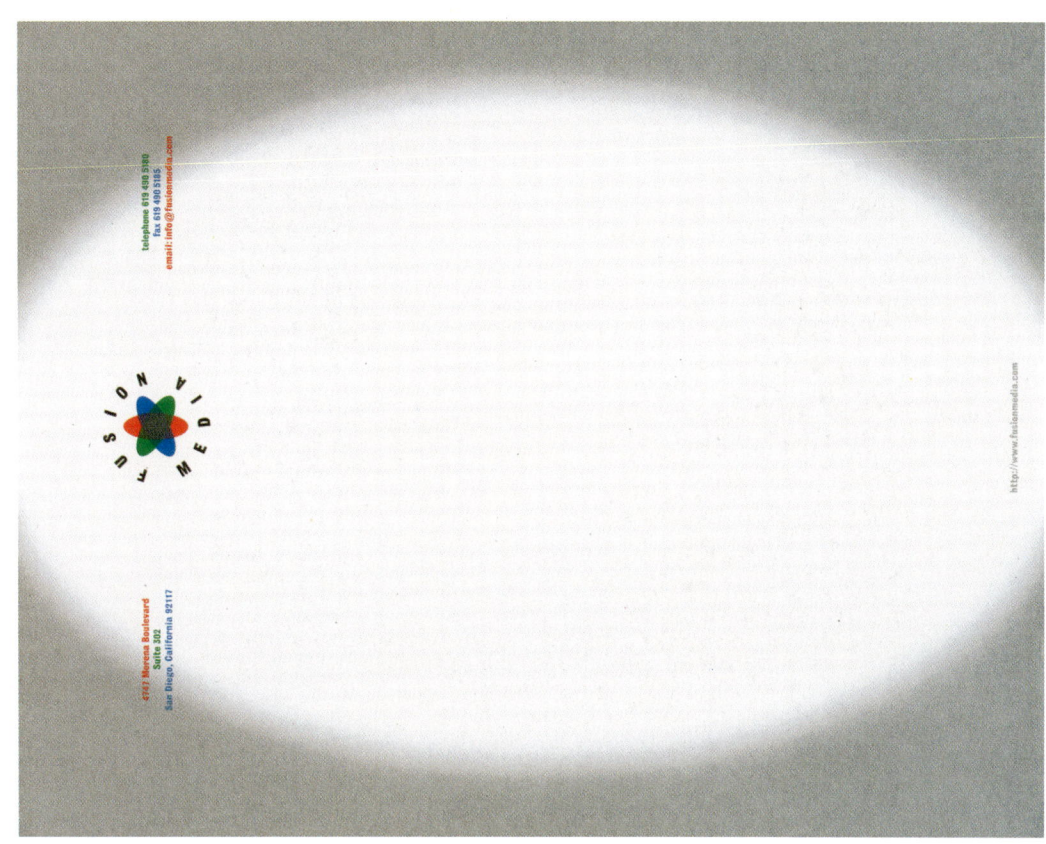

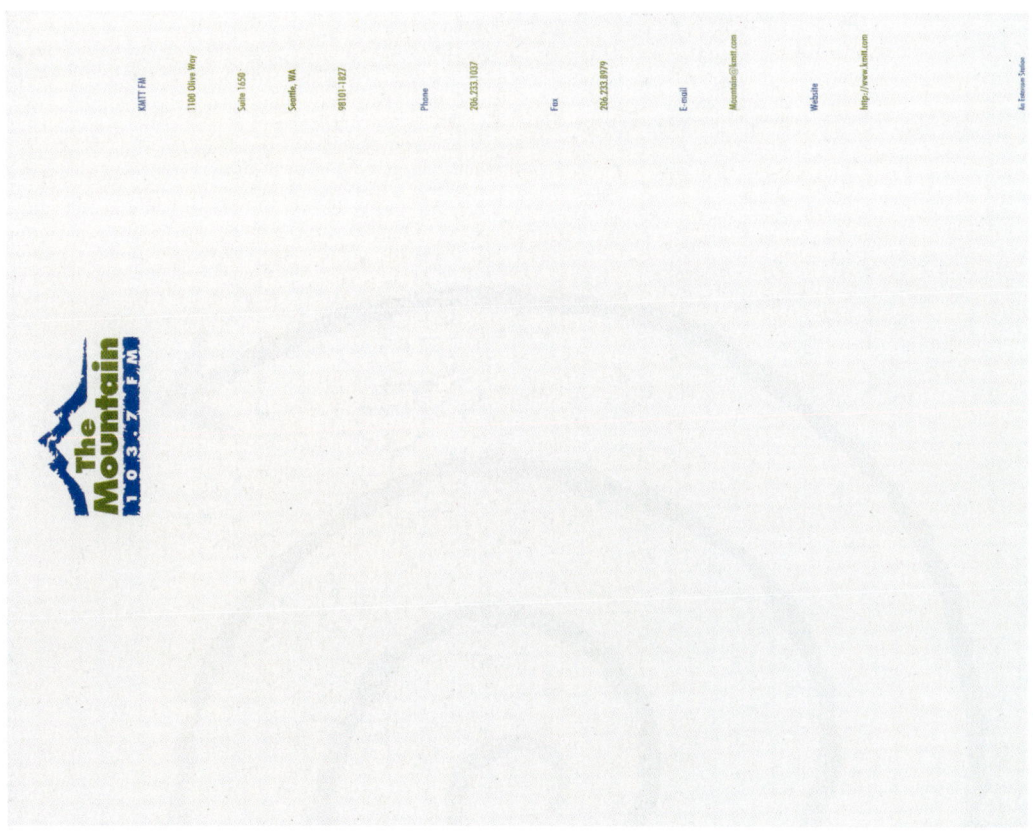

Client **FUSION MEDIA**
Design Firm **MIRES DESIGN**
Art/Creative Director **JOHN BALL**
Designers **JOHN BALL, DEBORAH HORN**

Client **THE MOUNTAIN RADIO**
Design Firm **ART O MAT DESIGN**
Designers **MARK KAUFMAN, JACKI MCCARTHY**

KIMURA DESIGN

500 W. 41st Avenue, Suite 202A
Anchorage, AK 99503

Phone 907.563.4948
Fax   907.563.0032
E-Mail kidesign@alaska.net

Client   KIMURA DESIGN
Design Firm   KIMURA DESIGN
Designer   CAREY KIMURA

Client   J.J. RAKETICH & COMPANY
Design Firm   H2 DESIGN GROUP INC.
Art Director TIMOTHY HUSNI
Designer   GINO TAVOLETTI

Client BARRY FISHLER (DIRECT RESPONSE COPYWRITER)
Design Firm DAVID LEMLEY DESIGN
Designer DAVID LEMLEY

Client FLORAL IMAGES
Design Firm FIFTH STREET DESIGN
Designers J. CLIFTON MEEK, BRENTON D. BECK

195

Client   **DE WITT/WOLF CONSULTANTS**
Design Firm **WATERWORK ART**
Designer   **JIM RUDOLPH**

Client   **DIGITAL MINDS**
Design Firm **MODERN DESIGN**
Designer   **CHRISTOPHER B. FOOTE**

IMAGE ALCHEMY

Client   IMAGE ALCHEMY (BUSINESS PRINTING BROKERAGE)
Design Firm SHAUN HUBBARD GRAPHIC DESIGN
Designers   SHAUN HUBBARD, PAULETTE EICKMAN

Mail: 2442 NW MARKET STREET #47   SEATTLE WA 98107   Office: 3429 FREMONT PLACE N #107
Phone: (800) 545-1787   (206) 547-6225   Fax: (206) 545-1886   (206) 632-0967

1505 fourth st
studio 220
santa monica
california
90421

Axolotl
art&science

310 †
458 0650
f a x
458 0730

Client   AXOLOTL ART&SCIENCE
Design Firm AXOLOTL ART&SCIENCE
Designer   JENNIFER BOOSE

Client INKTOMI CORPORATION
Design Firm CALIFORNIA DESIGN INTERNATIONAL
Designers TOM LAMAR, LINDA KELLEY

2168 Shattuck Avenue S.210
Berkeley California 94704
fax 510.883.7399
tel 510.883.7300
www.inktomi.com

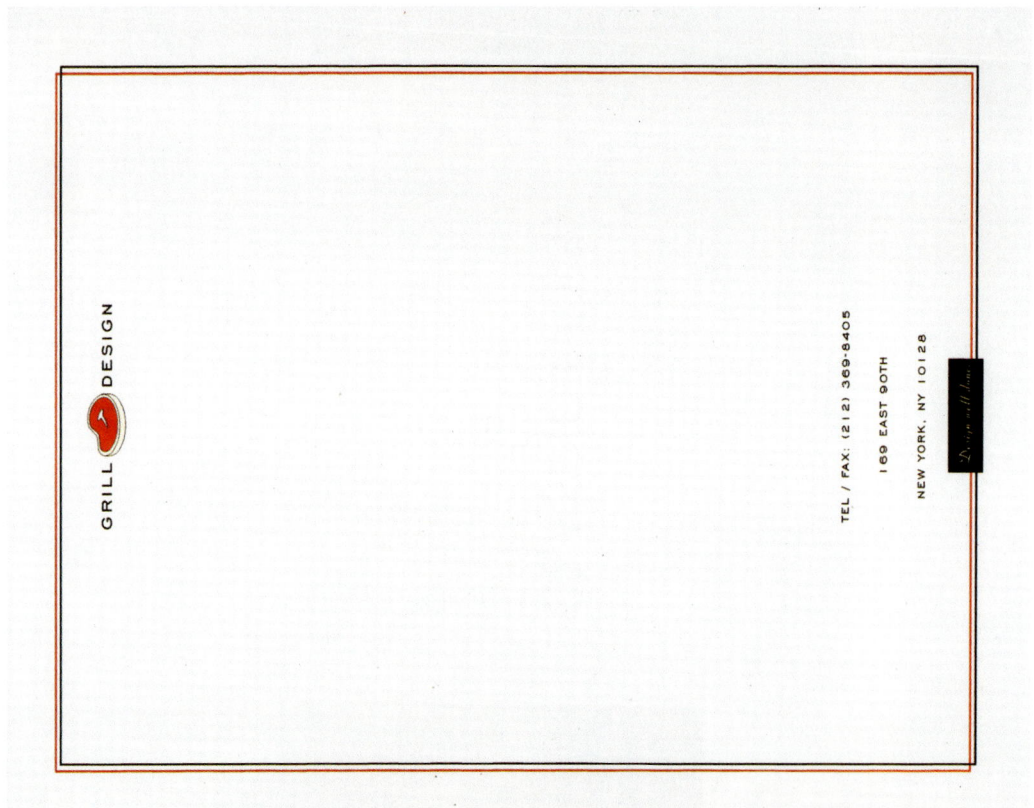

Client GRILL DESIGN
Design Firm GRILL DESIGN
Designers WENDY HALITZER, MIGUEL SANTANA

GRILL DESIGN

TEL / FAX: (212) 369-8405

169 EAST 90TH

NEW YORK, NY 10128

Client **LEVEL 7 COMMUNICATIONS**
Design Firm **YOUNG & ROEHR, INC.**
Designer **AMY KECK**

LEVEL SEVEN
COMMUNICATIONS

2B SW First Avenue, Suite 410
Portland, Oregon 97204-3597
(503) 223-4242 FAX 223-4442
http://www.level-seven.com

Firm Design
Environmental Graphics
Architectural Presentation

RUEMMELE DESIGN
1825 North Pennsylvania Street
Indianapolis, IN 46202
317.924.0606

Client **RUEMMELE DESIGN**
Design Firm **RUEMMELE DESIGN**
Designer **STEVE RUEMMELE**

199

Client **WILD CANARY PRODUCTIONS**
Design Firm **MATOUSEK DESIGN**
Creative Director **LORI PRECIOUS**
Designer **MICHAEL MATOUSEK**

8210 Melrose Avenue
Los Angeles, CA 90046
fax: 213|951-1495 | tel: 213|951-1494
email: WILDCANPROD@aol.com

CORPORATE VIDEO
ANIMATION
POST PRODUCTION

9338 GEHARTE DRIVE
CENTERVILLE OH 45459
PHONE 513 436 0900
fax 513 436 9968

Client **CLOONAN & ASSOCIATES**
Design Firm **KEARNS DESIGN, INC.**
Designer **B. COX**

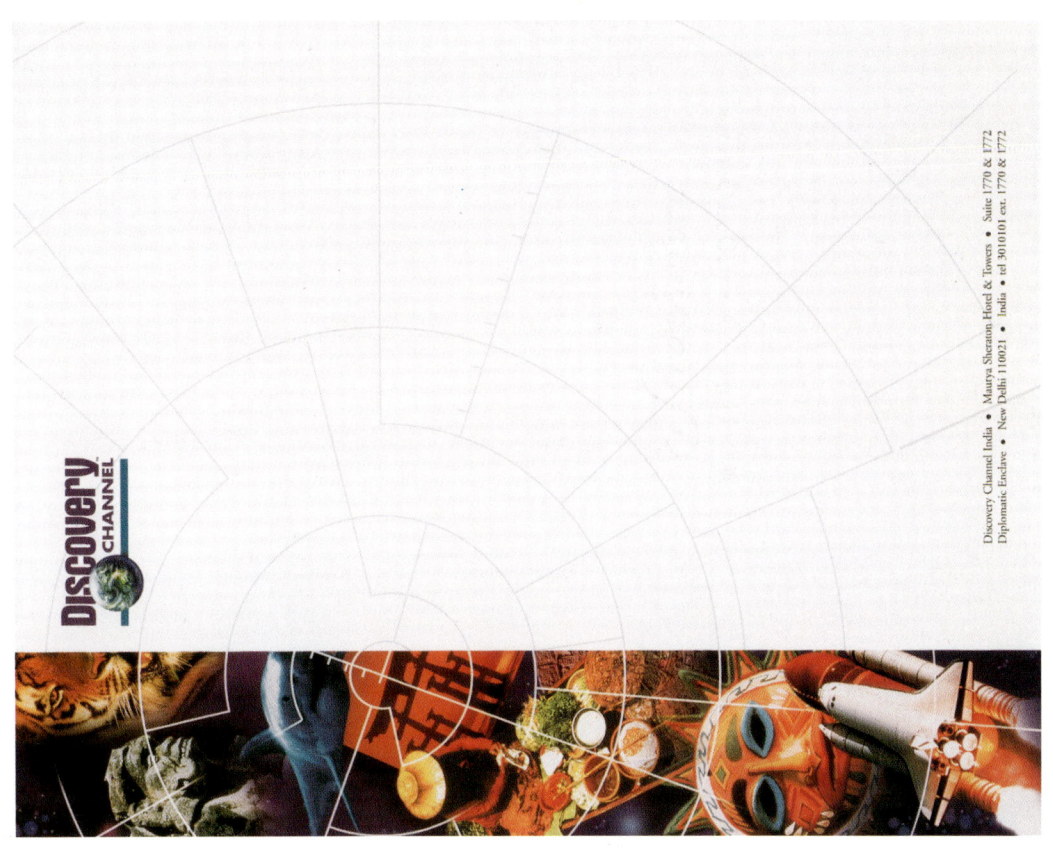

Client **DISCOVERY COMMUNICATIONS**
Design Firm **SUPON DESIGN GROUP.**
Designer **KHOI VINH**

Discovery Channel India • Maurya Sheraton Hotel & Towers • Suite 1770 & 1772
Diplomatic Enclave • New Delhi 110021 • India • tel 3010101 ext. 1770 & 1772

Client **THEA KOVAC**
Design Firm **STEVE HORVATH DESIGN, INC.**
Designer **STEVE HORVATH**

2623 EAST BELLEVIEW PLACE, MILWAUKEE, WI 53211 414-961-0908

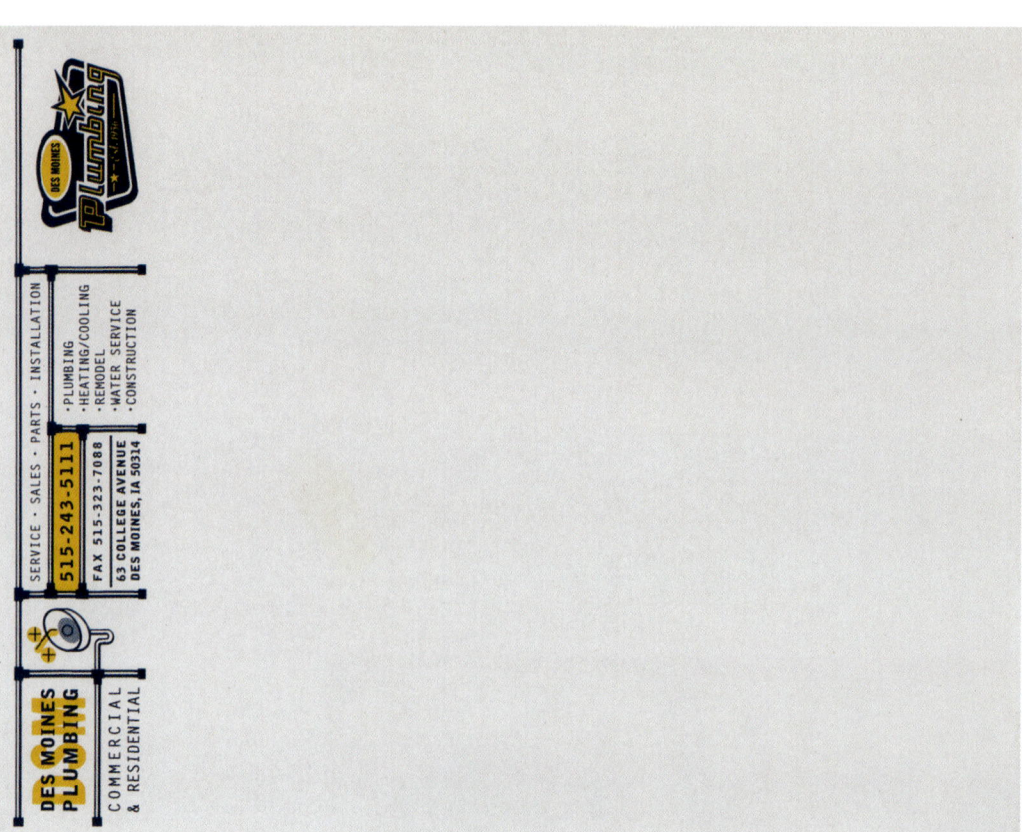

Client   DES MOINES PLUMBING
Design Firm   SAYLES GRAPHIC DESIGN
Designer   JOHN SAYLES

Client   WASHINGTON SOFTWARE & DIGITAL MEDIA ALLIANCE
Design Firm   TEAM DESIGN, INC.
Designers   ROSS HOGIN, PAULA RICHARDS

Client   MILLENNIUM MARKETING
Design Firm   SULLIVAN MARKETING & COMMUNICATIONS
Designer   JACK SULLIVAN

8776 EAST SHEA BOULEVARD
BLDG B3A, SUITE 500
SCOTTSDALE, AZ 85260

TELEPHONE: 602.661.6858
FACSIMILE: 602.991.7949

MILLENNIUM MARKETING

Zitzloff Training Resources, Inc
325 Barry Avenue So., #302
Minneapolis, MN 55391
Phone: 612.473.7576
Fax: 612.473.7094
Email: ztraining@aol.com

Zitzloff
TRAINING RESOURCES

Directions for Business Success

Client   ZITZLOFF TRAINING RESOURCES
Design Firm   KRUEGER WRIGHT DESIGN
Designers   BOB TEMA, KAREN KRUEGER WRIGHT

Client **C&C Sales, Inc.**
Design Firm **Words and Pictures**
Designer **Smita Aggarwal**

Client **T3 Media, Inc.**
Design Firm **T3 Media, Inc.**
Designer **Ellen Diamant**

HORIZON
BENEFITS, INC.

HORIZON BENEFITS, INC. 2432 N. SHARON AMITY RD. CHARLOTTE, NC 28205 (704)531-2911 FAX:(704)531-6911

Client HORIZON BENEFITS, INC.
Design Firm LYERLY AGENCY
Designer GALE HARUTA

Fraser Papers Inc.
9 West Broad Street
PO Box 10055
Stamford CT 06904
203 359 2544 Tel
203 965 7197 Fax

FraserPapers

A Noranda Forest Company

Client FRASER PAPERS
Design Firm LIPPINCOTT & MARGULIES
Designers JERRY KUYPER, MICHELLE CASSUTO

Jeana Lautigar, CPA
SMALL BUSINESS SPECIALIST

2800 WEST 44TH STREET
MINNEAPOLIS, MN 55410
PHONE: 612 928.3871

Client   JEANA LAUTIGAR
Design Firm TILKA DESIGN
Designers   JANE TILKA, MARK MULARZ

Client   INTELECT COMMUNICATIONS SYSTEMS LIMITED
Design Firm METZDORF, INC.
Designers   LYLE METZDORF, ROBERT VAN LENTEN

Intelect

Intelect Communications Systems Limited ● Reid House, 31 Church St, Hamilton HM 12 Bermuda ● Telephone 441.295.8639 ● Facsimile 441.292.5560

Client TIP TOP CREATIVE
Design Firm TIP TOP CREATIVE
Designers DEBBIE CAMPBELL, DAVID DAY

1306 WESTERN AVENUE • SUITE 307 • SEATTLE, WASHINGTON 98101 • TEL (206) 682·9840 • FAX (206) 682·9844

TIP TOP CREATIVE

WORKER BEES, INC.

Client WORKER BEES, INC.
Design Firm WORKER BEES, INC.
Designer ANN RHODES
Photographer ROBIN LAUGHLIN

Client   RESOLUTION GRAPHIC RESOURCES
Design Firm WILLOUGHBY DESIGN GROUP
Designer   MICHELLE SONDEREGGER

China Basin 185 Berry St Suite 5400 San Francisco CA 94107   phone 415.546.0331   fax 415.546.7821

Battery St   724 Battery St   San Francisco CA 94111   phone 415.788.0300   fax 415.788.3331

Client   VIDEO ARTS
Design Firm WATERWORK ART
Designer   BRENDA PHILIPS

Cooperstown
GRADUATE ASSOCIATION

PO Box 4
Cooperstown, New York 13326

Client   THE COOPERSTOWN GRADUATE PROGRAM
Design Firm   TWO TWELVE ASSOCIATES
Designers   ELLEN CONANT, PATRICIA KELLEHER

Swiss Skin Care Clinique

13401 Bel-Red Road Suite B-12   Bellevue WA 98005   206-746-0446

Client   SWISS SKIN CARE
Design Firm   GREG WELSH DESIGN
Designer   GREG WELSH

11921 Freedom Drive • Reston, VA 22090
TEL: 703.742.0951 • FAX: 703.742 0953

Client   PARADISE WILD
Design Firm   SUPON DESIGN GROUP.
Designer   ANDY DOLAN

Client   NATIONAL CITY
Design Firm   SCHULTZ/CAGLEY/KROSSCHELL/INC.
Designer   MICHAEL IRELAND

PRIVATE CLIENT GROUP

National City.

AZALEA FILMS

9821 cherokee road

richmond, virginia 23235

tel : 804 . 323 . 5740

fax : 804 . 320 . 5461

Client   AZALEA FILMS
Design Firm CADMUS/O'KEEFE MARKETING
Designer   BRIAN THOMSON

Inter-Sphere
M E D I A G R O U P

human 714.722.9910
fax 714.722.9951
629 TERMINAL WAY,#25
COSTA MESA, CA 92627
HTTP://WWW.NOTHING-BUT.NET

Client   INTERSPHERE
Design Firm RIECHES BAIRD
Designer   RAY TARQUINIO

Client **STEVENS DESIGN**
Design Firm **STEVENS DESIGN**
Designers **JEAN STEVENS, KAREN NOMURA**

STEVENS DESIGN · 500 AIRPORT BOULEVARD · SUITE 360 · BURLINGAME, CA 94010 · PHONE: 415-579-5840 · FAX: 415-579-5902

BRUTON|STROUBE

38 NORTH VANDEVENTER ST.LOUIS, MO 63108 FAX 533.8061

314 533.6665

Client **BRUTON/STROUBE STUDIOS**
Design Firm **PHOENIX CREATIVE**
Designer **ERIC THOELKE**

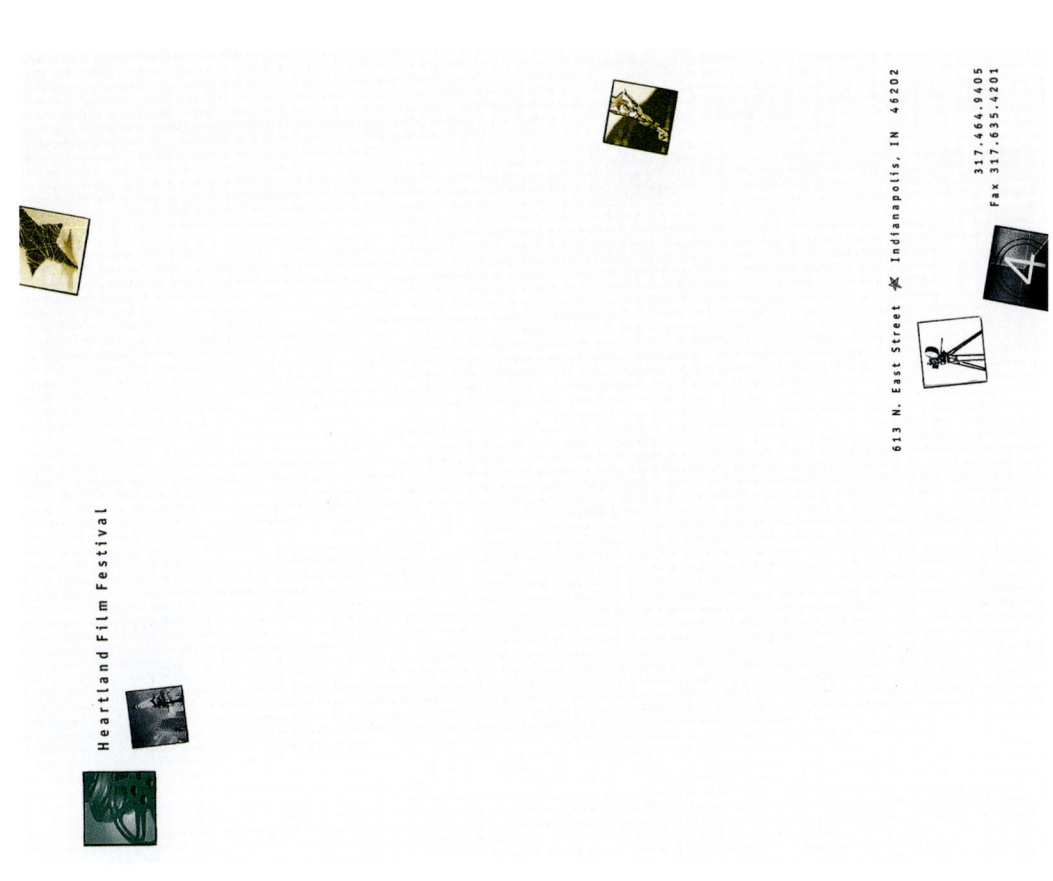

Heartland Film Festival

Client   PETER SCHMIDT PHOTOGRAPHY
Design Firm SUSAN REED DESIGN
Designer   SUSAN REED

Client   HEARTLAND FILM FESTIVAL
Design Firm   TRACY REA & ASSOCIATES, INC.
Designers   TAMMY LUTZE, TRACY REA

613 N. East Street ✈ Indianapolis, IN 46202

317.464.9405
Fax 317.635.4201

1. Peter Schmidt Photography
2. 411 East Hennepin Avenue
   Minneapolis, MN 55414
3. 612/378-9454 phone
   612/623-7654 fax

BEST CELLARS INC
1291 LEXINGTON AVE
NEW YORK NY 10128
TEL 212.426.4200
FAX 212.426.9597

BEST CELLARS™

Client   BEST CELLARS
Design Firm   HORNALL ANDERSON DESIGN WORKS, INC.
Designers   JACK ANDERSON, LISA CERVENY, JANA WILSON

Client   DISCOVERY COMMUNICATIONS
Design Firm   SUPON DESIGN GROUP.
Designer   EDDIE SAIBUA

http://www.discovery.com

online

DISCOVERY CHANNEL ONLINE

7700 Wisconsin Avenue · Bethesda, MD 20814-3579 · 301.986.0444 · http://www.discovery.com

214

SIMPLY CRUISES

Call Us At Any Time
314 832-8880

384 Hampton Avenue
Saint Louis
Missouri 63109-2499

Telephone:
314 832-8880

Facsimile:
314 832-8282

Toll Free:
1 888 307-9398

Client   SIMPLY CRUISES
Design Firm   PHOENIX CREATIVE
Designer   ED MANTELS-SEEKER

creative
works
· advertising · design · photography

CreativeWorks
5280 Claremont Avenue, Suite 242
Stockton, California 95207
Phone · 209 472 3680
Fax · 209 472 3780

Client   CREATIVEWORKS
Design Firm   CREATIVEWORKS
Designers   BEVERLY PHARR, BRUCE PHARR

SALEM AREA TRANSIT

3140 Del Webb Avenue NE
Salem, OR 97303-4165

503-588-2885   Fax 588-0209

Client   CHERRIOTS
Design Firm   CREATIVE COMPANY, INC.
Designer   CHRIS NOUD

14400 Doolittle Drive
San Leandro, CA 94577
510.895.1300 Fax 895.1320
E-Mail: dakota@crl.com

DakotaPress

Client   DAKOTA PRESS
Design Firm   SHAWVER ASSOCIATES
Designers   MARK SHAWVER, KYLE OGDEN, TERI GANE

META QUEST
t e c h n o l o g i e s

2513 McVeary Court • Suite E • Silver Spring, MD 20906 • 301-598-6611 • F 301-598-6608
74443.1152@compuserve.com • www.mqt.com/metaquest

Client   META QUEST TECHNOLOGIES
Design Firm   SUPON DESIGN GROUP.
Designer   BRENT ALMOND

AFTER HOURS
DESIGN•ADVERTISING

Client   AFTER HOURS DESIGN & ADVERTISING
Design Firm   AFTER HOURS DESIGN & ADVERTISING
Designer   BETH SHOTT

16593 SPRINGDALE DRIVE
CANYON COUNTRY, CA 91351
PHONE 805 252-9543
FAX 805 252-9543

address ~ 1804 *Fifth* Street Berkeley CA 94710   TELEPHONE ~ [510 845 2000]   facsimile ~ *510 644 2889*   Email ~ smedias@smedias.com

SMETTS STAFFORD MEDIA

Client   SMETTS STAFFORD MEDIA
Design Firm   BONNIE SMETTS DESIGN
Designer   BONNIE SMETTS

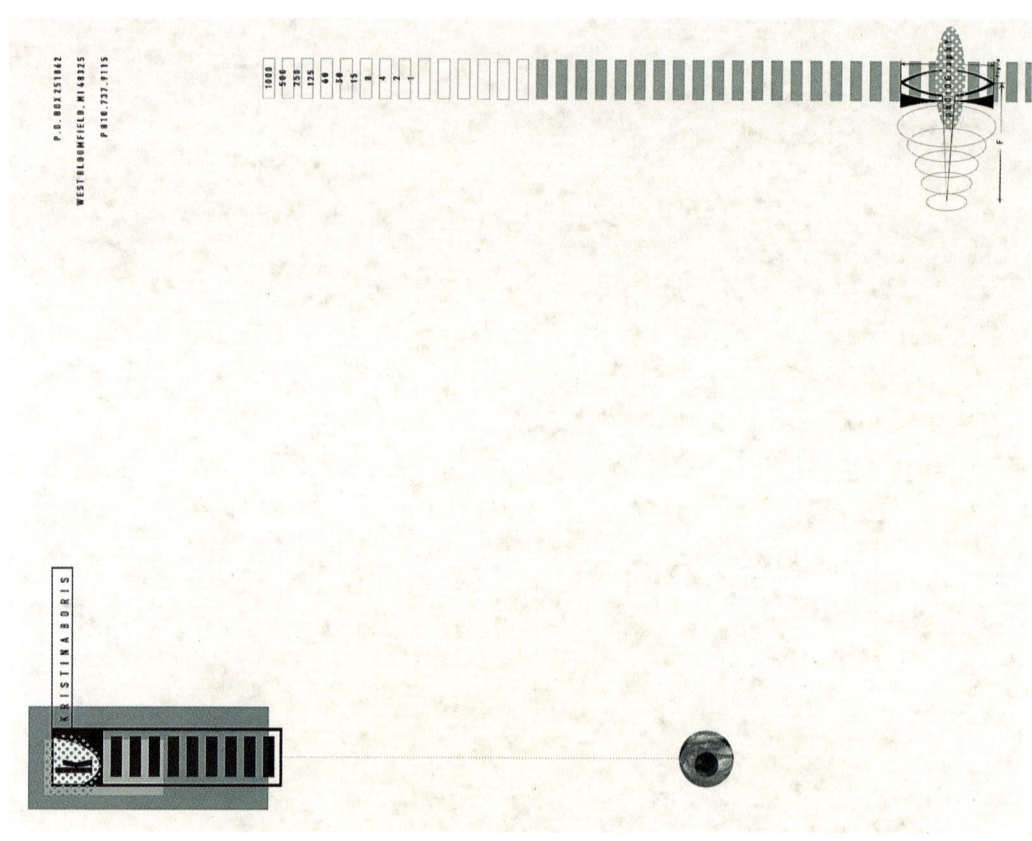

P.O. BOX 251862
WEST BLOOMFIELD, MI 48325
P 810.737.9115

KRISTINA BORIS

Client   KRISTINA BORIS PHOTOGRAPHY
Design Firm   CELLAR 8 DESIGN
Designer   ERIC LIVINGSTON

Client   HOUSEWORKS HOME
Design Firm   D-ZINE INC.

A HouseWorks Home LLC

1111 Route 110, Suite 220 ■ East Farmingdale, NY 11735
516-694-6009 ■ Fax 516-420-0352

Computer Friendly™

Learning to feel at home
with your computer

Client   COMPUTER FRIENDLY
Design Firm   OPTIONS BY DESIGN
Designers   JEFF WRIGHT, SUSAN NEUHAUS

115 Adams Dam Road
Wilmington, DE 19807
302.428.6077 • Fax 302.427.3567
ComFriend@aol.com

Client   JOHN SCHULZ PHOTOGRAPHY
Design Firm   LAURA COE DESIGN ASSOC.
Designers   DARRYL GLASS, LAUREN BRUHN

Client   KILTER INDUSTRIES
Design Firm   KILTER INCORPORATED
Designer   TIM SCHUMANN

Corporate
Identity
Manuals

Client   TOWN OF FRAMINGHAM, MASSACHUSETTS
Design Firm   B+B DESIGN, INC.
Designer   BENJAMIN DEMPSTER

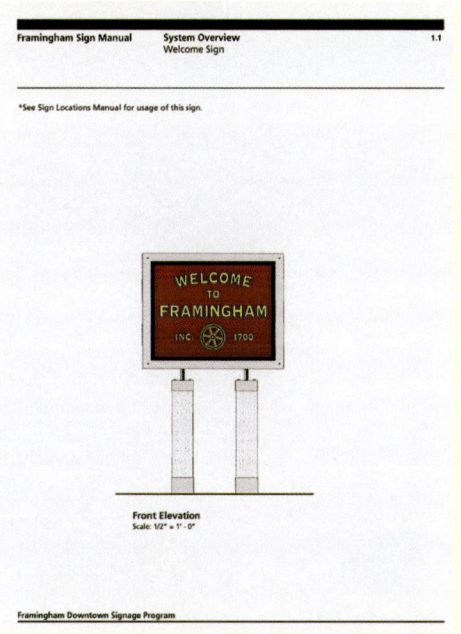

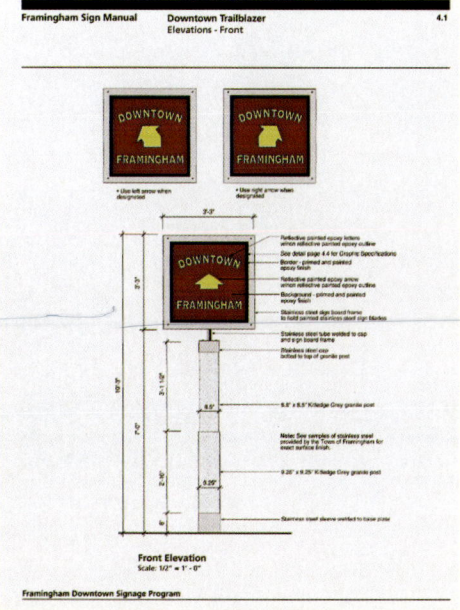

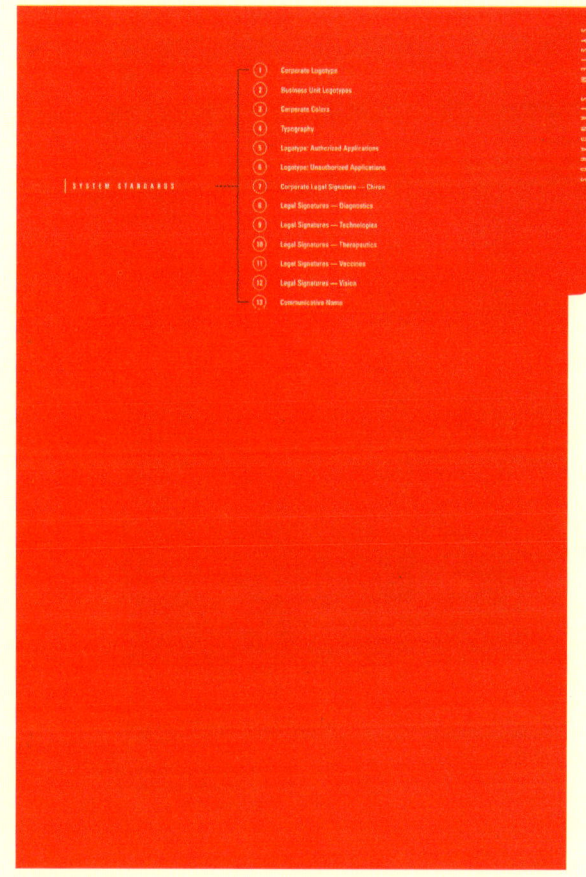

CHIRON

Client   CHIRON CORPORATION
Design Firm   COREY MCPHERSON NASH
Art Director PHYLLIS KIDO
Designers   TIM CHAN, CAROL WINTERBOURNE,
              PHYLLIS KIDO, BOB POTTS

221

Client　　　　NATIONAL SEMICONDUCTOR
Design Firm　CASPER DESIGN
Designer　　　CHARLENE TIANI

Client　　　　AMGEN INC.
Design Firm　AMGEN COMMUNICATIONS SERVICES
Designers　　FRITZ KOCH, JANE LUPER

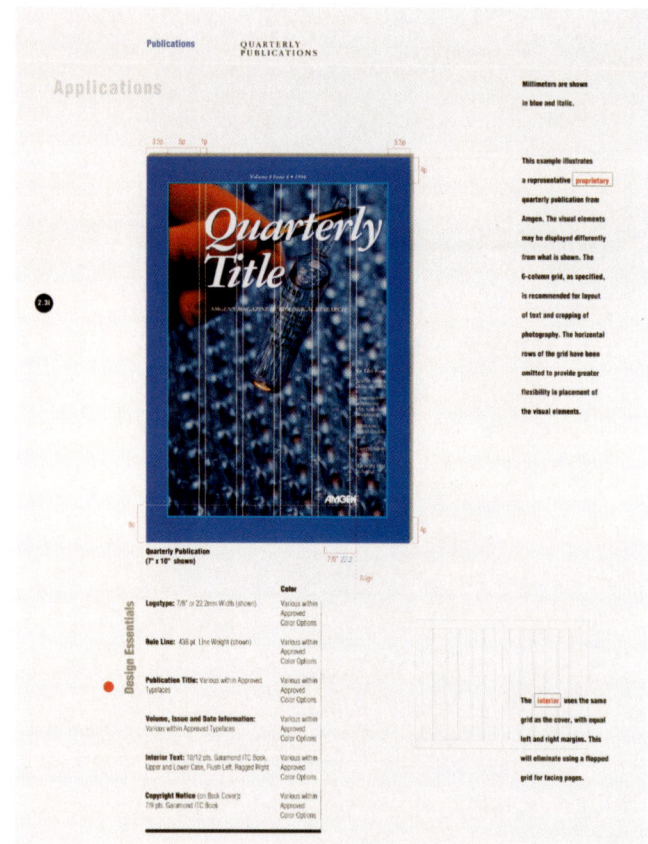

Guidelines for Using the Corporate Trademark

Alcoa Identity

Multi-media: Slide/Video/Film

If the three-color format trademark is chosen for a slide presentation, video production, or television commercial, version A can also appear in Alcoa blue, Alcoa red, and white, provided the trademark appears on a black background. Otherwise, use a single solid color format for presenting the trademark in a slide, video, or film production.

Multi-media: Computer

If the Alcoa trademark is used on graphic materials generated by electronic publishing techniques, its appearance must meet or exceed the professional standards of conventional photographic reproduction methods. To achieve this required level of quality, the trademark should be scanned only from original reproduction proofs and its final output resolution should not be less than 1200 dpi (dots per inch). An exception to final output resolution is made when using a low resolution printer to produce a document inhouse.

For your convenience the Alcoa trademark has been formatted as a font file on disk for either IBM compatible or Macintosh computers. The disks can be obtained from the Corporate Literature Warehouse.

The version A trademark is the preferred configuration for usage on all media.

13

Client   ALCOA, ALUMINUM COMPANY OF AMERICA
Design Firm   INFORMATICS STUDIO INC.
Designers   ROSS LEVINE, TODD CAVALIER

CORPORATE SIGNATURE

Clear-Space Requirements

The logotype and corporate signatures should be allowed a clean visual separation from all other elements.

The height of the 'N' serves as a measurement for minimum clear-space requirements around the signatures. This space should be flat and unpatterned, clear of type or any other element, as well as the edge of the page.

Large-scale uses of the Novell logotype are inherently bold and solid, and will command a clean visual separation from surrounding elements. Use 1/2 the 'N' height for clear-space around the logotype only version when used 18 picas wide or larger. When used smaller than 18 picas wide, adhere to the typical 'N' height clear space.

Minimum Reduction

The minimum reduction for the signature should be no smaller than those shown below. There are no maximum-size restrictions. Large-scale uses – such as banners, signs, trade show exhibits, etc. – require accurate enlargements and attention to retain the integrity of the signature. In these large-scale uses, the size of the ® and TM should be reduced to an appropriate size in each situation and should never be used larger than 3 inches (76mm) in height.

Client   NOVELL, INC.
Design Firm   HORNALL ANDERSON DESIGN WORKS
Designers   JACK ANDERSON, BRUCE BRANSON-MEYER,
       LARRY ANDERSON, DON STAYNER

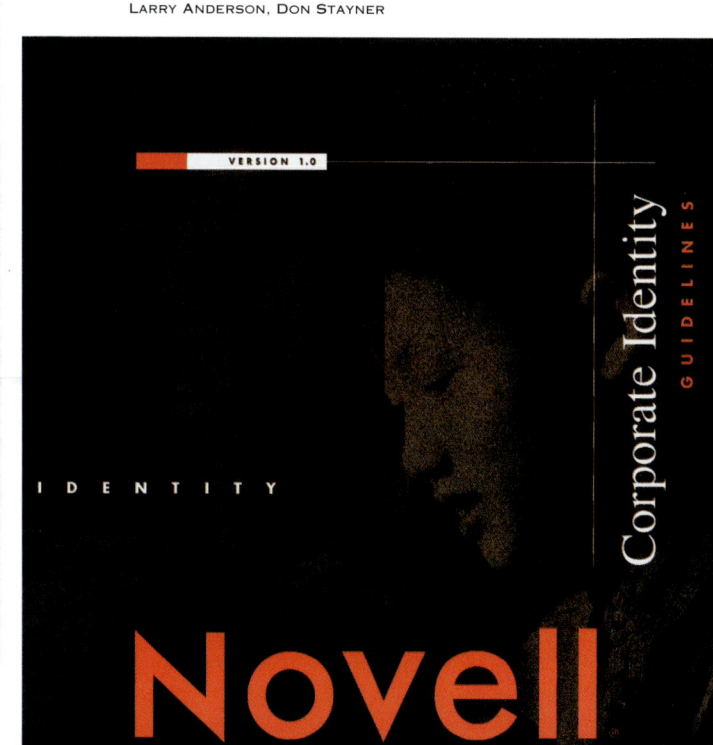

In the RS/6000 visual system, there are two types of trapezium shapes. The primary - or visual - trapezium is a photograph, illustration or other graphical element that is cropped or designed in a trapezium shape. The secondary - or solid-color-trapezium is a flat, solid color. These shapes may be used together on a

white background with the primary trapezium on top and the secondary trapezium extending out from under it. This allows the two shapes to act in counter-point and create visual interest, while providing a great deal of design flexibility.

For the visual trapezium, the sides and corners should be adjusted so that the trapezium's shape calls attention to key attributes of the photograph or other image. This image should also be colorful and vibrant, and reflect color planes or motion where possible.

When viewed as a unit, the two shapes work together to create an integrated, balanced image. For this reason, the solid-color trapezium should never overpower or distract attention from the visual trapezium.

The solid-color trapezium which extends out from under the top layer creates contrasting lines and angles to frame the visual. This adds depth, enhances the visual and helps direct viewer attention to key aspects of the image.

By presenting the viewer with images in different and dynamic forms, the design represents the RS/6000 family as a system without boundaries. As such, the combination of trapezium shapes should be 'free' that is, parallel lines or rapetitious corners should be avoided as these look less dynamic. In addition, the colors selected for the secondary trapezium should be flat colors. Color gradations, shading and other variations should never be used.

This is the primary, or visual trapezium. It should contain a photograph or illustration that is exciting and pertinent to the overall contents of the piece being developed. Excitement can be achieved through color, motion, soft-focus photography or angle. The photograph shown here reflects the tone of an executive overview brochure.

This is the secondary, or solid-color trapezium. An overall balance should be maintained with the overlapping trapezium shapes.

Trapezium corners and angles should be varied for impact and dynamism.

RS/6000

6

Design Firm **BYER AND MCGUGGART**
Designers **MARTY CARRICHNER,
PETER MCGUGGART**

*What's included
in the RS/6000
design color palette*

RS/6000

Colors

Color is the third design element in the new RS/6000 family look. It is used in the secondary, solid-color trapezium shape as a contrasting frame to highlight the photographs, illustrations and graphic images in the primary trapezium. This contrasting color frame heightens the impact of these images and further conveys the power, vitality and flexibility that are inherent in the RS/6000 family. Color also provides a consistent visual vocabulary that is specific to RS/6000 brand deliverables. In order to make the most of this important design element, an RS/6000 family color palette has been developed. It is a palette that has been designed to provide a great range of flexibility for use across all types of deliverables.

Colors selected from this palette should always be vibrant and rich, as an expression of RS/6000 brand power and strength. This can be accomplished by specifying 100% of a selected color, which also leads to the most satisfactory printing of these colors. However, the color palette can be extended by adding 10% to 70% (exact percentages are indicated on page 12) black tints on 100% of a selected palette color. This allows for a variety of color tones to complement a wide range of photography or illustrations.

Color tints that range from 60% to 80% of a selected palette color are also appropriate when being used behind typography or as an optional color field. However, color tints can present problems during printing, so this option should be cho-

sen selectively. For process color printing, the process color (CMYK) equivalent of a selected palette color should be used.

You may substitute inks indicated from the PANTONE Matching System™ or Toyo Color System. Appropriate process-color simulations are also acceptable. Please note that usage of yellow should be avoided in instances where photocopying or transmitting by fax is likely. Colors shown here are not intended to match PANTONE Matching System or Toyo Color System standards; refer to those companies' publications for exact matches.

13

Client **VISIO CORP. MKTG. DEPT.**
Design Firm **IN HOUSE CREATIVE SERVICES**
Designer **LORI ZENTNER**

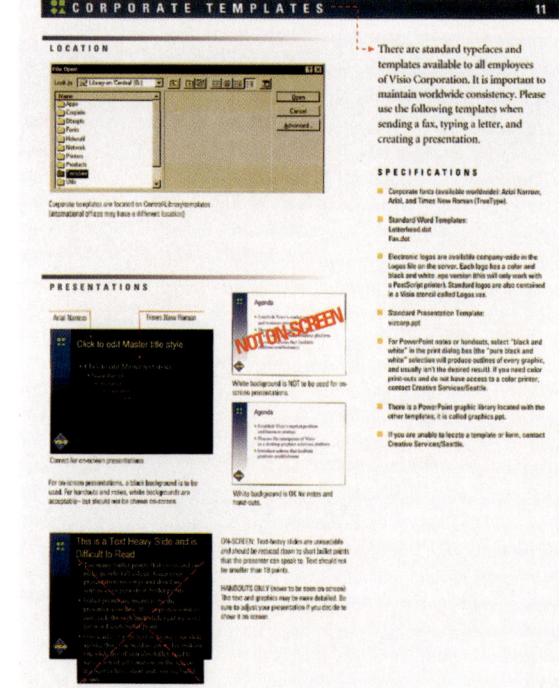

Identity Strategy And Basic Identity Standards

Second Edition
June 1996

Client   3M
Design Firm   RUSTEN MARKETING GROUP
Designer   DAVE BRADLEY

What You Should Know About 3M Brand Loyalty Management.

The 3M Brand Promise
3M promises innovative, quality products and services that make our customers' lives easier and better from a company they can trust.

Creating and reinforcing brand loyal customers is the key to sustained, profitable growth. This all-important task requires constant and diligent management throughout the life of the brand.

Managing The Total Brand Experience
• The brand loyalty management process is the day-by-day process of bringing together separate functions (namely sales, marketing, service, laboratory, manufacturing and communications) into a Total Brand Experience – in order to best deliver a brand promise to the customer.

Brand Promise
• Each brand's promise is a statement of the relevant and distinctive benefit that it delivers to the customer. It is what we want our customers to think and feel when they see each brand, purchase a product or hear about the brand in any context. Its brand promise must be reinforced in all we say and do.

• To effectively communicate each brand promise in a unique and meaningful way, design is used to create a visual language using form, our logo, typography, visuals and color. This language is incorporated in a system that includes all forms of communication from product and packaging to sales literature and trade shows. With our use of this visual language consistently over time, each brand promise comes to life in the mind of the customer and becomes a real and valuable asset to the company.

The 3M Brand
• The 3M Brand stands for Trust, Leadership and Quality (TLQ). To the customer, it is a guarantee of quality and reliability. When we use the 3M Brand, we are leveraging our "TLQ" and creating distinctive, relevant differentiation through our products' unique features and benefits.

For Further Assistance
For further information, contact your Global Brand Coordinator or the Brand Loyalty Management Hotline at 612 733-8641.

UNISYS CORPORATE IDENTITY
Our Fingerprint in World Markets

Client   UNISYS CORPORATION
Design Firm   JOEL KATZ DESIGN ASSOCIATES
Designers   JOEL KATZ, DAVID SCHPOK,
              KIM MOLLO, JENNIFER LONG

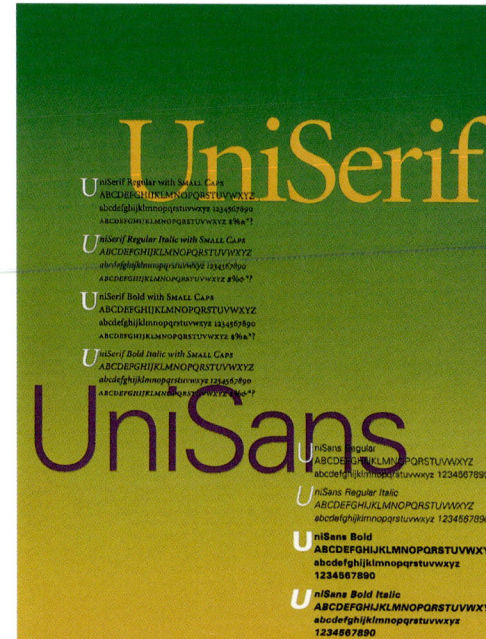

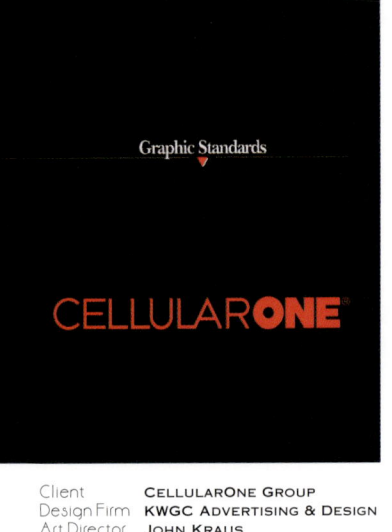

Graphic Standards

CELLULARONE®

Client | CELLULARONE GROUP
Design Firm | KWGC ADVERTISING & DESIGN
Art Director | JOHN KRAUS
Designer | TONY GHANEM

COLOR COMBINATIONS—THE PREFERRED OPTION

You have the option to use any one of only three authorized color combinations when applying the Cellular One® logotype to interior signage and displays (see examples).

1. The logotype in CELLULAR Red on a white background.

2. The logotype in white on a CELLULAR Red background.

3. The logotype in CELLULAR Red on a black background.

NOTE

The logotype in black on a CELLULAR Red background is NOT an authorized combination.

CELLULARONE®

CELLULARONE®

CELLULARONE®

SECTION 2   PAGE 3

Client | LEVI STRAUSS & COMPANY
Design Firm | MÜHLHÄUSER & YOUNG
Designer | BONNIE MATZA

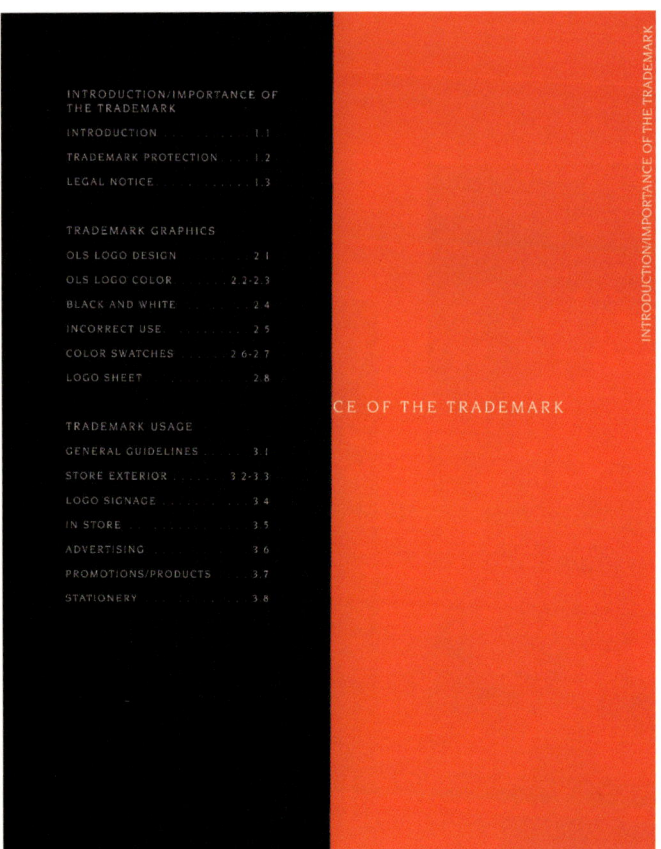

INTRODUCTION/IMPORTANCE OF THE TRADEMARK

...CE OF THE TRADEMARK

OLS LOGO COLOR

ORIGINAL **Levi's** STORE®

Use the color version of the logo whenever possible. The **Original Levi's Store™** logo design may be reproduced in color using the Pantone Matching System or four color process as follows.

Pantone Matching System:
Top and bottom elements: Pantone #2757 Blue. Center element, Pantone #485 Red. Type reverses out of the solid colors (prints white).

Four Color Process:
Top and bottom elements, 100% Cyan, 60% Magenta, 65% Black. Center element, 100% Magenta and 91% Yellow. Type reverses out (prints white).

Two Color Printing: Black and Red is NOT an acceptable 2 color application. You must print the logo using the 2 approved colors (blue and red) or print the logo in black and white.

2.2

Stationery System

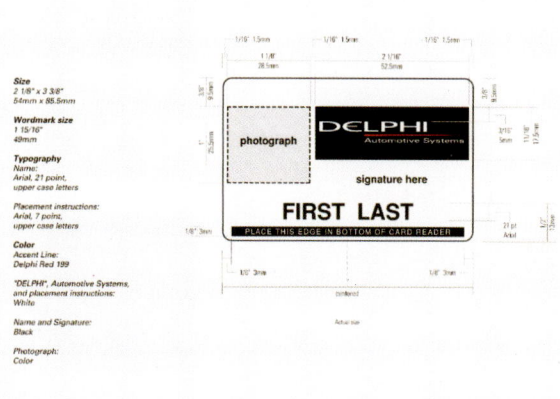

Illustrated below is the Delphi *Identification Badge*.

Size
2 1/8" x 3 3/8"
54mm x 85.5mm

Wordmark size
1 15/16"
49mm

Typography
Name:
Arial, 21 point,
upper case letters

Placement instructions:
Arial, 7 point,
upper case letters

Color
Accent Line:
Delphi Red 199

"DELPHI", Automotive Systems,
and placement instructions:
White

Name and Signature:
Black

Photograph:
Color

Client **DELPHI AUTOMOTIVE SYSTEMS**
Design Firm **FORD & EARL ASSOCIATES**
Designer **PETER REED**

The corporate **signature** is the most visible and recognisable element of the Oracle corporate identity. Just as it is illegal for someone to use your signature, it is improper for anyone to use our corporate signature in any manner that has not been approved. When used in accordance with the corporate identity program, the signature effectively links all Oracle products and services.

Client **ORACLE CORPORATION**
Design Firm **CAHAN & ASSOCIATES**
Designer **MICHAEL VERDINE**

Signature Staging
Staging refers to the area directly surrounding the signature. To ensure its visibility and integrity, the Oracle signature staging area must be clear of other elements such as type, images, or other signatures.

Signature Clearspace
The clearspace surrounding all sides of the signature is equal to the distance between the top of the logotype and the baseline of the tagline. In cases when the logotype is used alone, the clearspace is determined by the height of the logotype.

The example on this page highlights the major components of the inside spread of Invacare® brand product literature. Both specific and general guidelines are included.

Product Title Bar Specifications

Follow height, width and copy alignment based on the front cover format outlined on the previous page, 5.4.

Intro Text

All type prints black.
- Initial cap: 14 pt. Univers 55
- Body copy: 10 pt. Palatino Book; 15 pt. leading

Head and Subhead Text

- Head and subhead copy is set in all caps. Both print the solid color of the designated business unit. For detailed color guidelines, refer to Corporate Guidelines, pp. 2.4 - 2.5.
- Head copy: 10 pt. Univers 55 Regular with an applied forced bold.
- Subhead copy: 9 pt. Univers 45 Light; 9 pt. leading.
- Body copy: 9 pt. Palatino Book; 11 pt. leading
- Footnotes: 8 pt. Palatino Book; 9 pt. leading

Product Visual Guidelines

- The product is featured in four-color photographs.
- The picture box sizes will vary.
- If included, color palettes which show product color selections are composed of four-color process screen combinations.

Production Specifications

The production specifications follow that of the front cover. Refer to the previous page, 5.4. However, gloss varnish is applied to title bar, all four-color photographs, screened match color bars and bullet points.

Standard publication size is 8½" x 11". This example is 70% of the final size.

Client	INVACARE CORPORATION
Design Firm	KAREN SKUNTA & COMPANY
Designers	KAREN A. SKUNTA, CHRISTOPHER SUSTER, BARBARA CHIN

Client	BROWN PRINTING
Design Firm	LARSEN DESIGN OFFICE, INC.
Art Director	MIKE HAUG
Designers	PETER DE SIBOUR, TODD NESSER

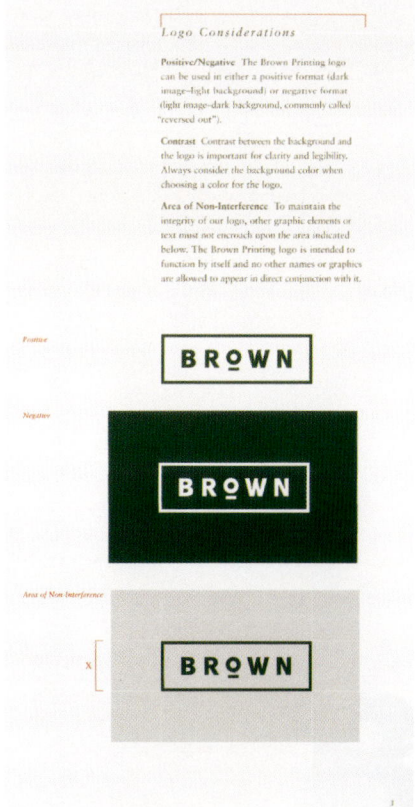

Client   FIRST INTERSTATE
Design Firm   LANDOR ASSOCIATES
Designers   MARGARET YOUNGBLOOD,
                JENNIFER BOSTIC

Contents
One Banking Company

Part 1 The Basic Identity

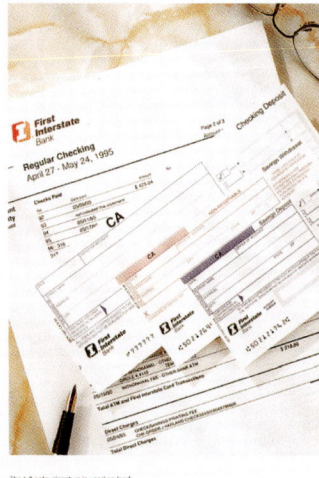

The full-color signature is used on bank statements, and the typography size and position are standardized for consistency as well as for automated reproduction requirements. On most in-bank papers, the signature is reproduced in black.

2.27

Raritan Computer Inc.   Corporate Standards Manual   Alternate   3
                                                                     Identifier Standards

Client   RARITAN COMPUTER INC.
Design Firm   HENRY DREYFUSS ASSOCIATES
Project Manager JOHN BETTS
Designer   FRANCISCA SHERIF

Alternate Identifier

This version is used only in cases where the standard identifier cannot be used, for example, in restricted vertical areas or on small products. In all cases, the standard identifier is preferred over this alternate identifier. The Raritan Alternate Identifier consists of the same symbol and logotype as the standard Raritan Identifier, however, it is composed in a vertical orientation with the symbol dominant in relation to the logotype. The logotype appears below the symbol with its width aligned to the inner square that is formed by the symbol.

Alternate Identifier Lock-up

The Raritan Alternate Identifier lock-up is the relationship between the symbol and logotype, stacked in relation to one another. The distance and proportion of the logotype to the symbol is fixed and cannot be altered.

Symbol   Alternate Identifier

Logotype

Raritan Computer Inc.   Corporate Standards Manual   Color Standards   5

Identifier Color

The color of the Raritan Identifier is Pantone 235C. This color should be specified for all printed materials. To insure consistency in color reproduction, use the swatches provided in the back of this manual.

Pantone 235C   Black

Example

Color Printing. The Raritan Identifier is Pantone 235C and should be printed against a white background for color printing. The nomenclature should print black.

Example

Black and White Printing (Black background). The Raritan Identifier should print 50% tint of black against a black background for black and white printing. The nomenclature should print white.

Example

Black and White Printing (White background). The Raritan Identifier should print 70% tint of black against a white background for black and white printing. The nomenclature should print black.

Client   H.P. Hood Inc.
Design Firm   The Coleman group
Designers   Larry Aaron,
              Stephanie Simpson

Client   Informix Software, Inc.
Design Firm   Mortensen Design
Designer   Gordon Mortensen

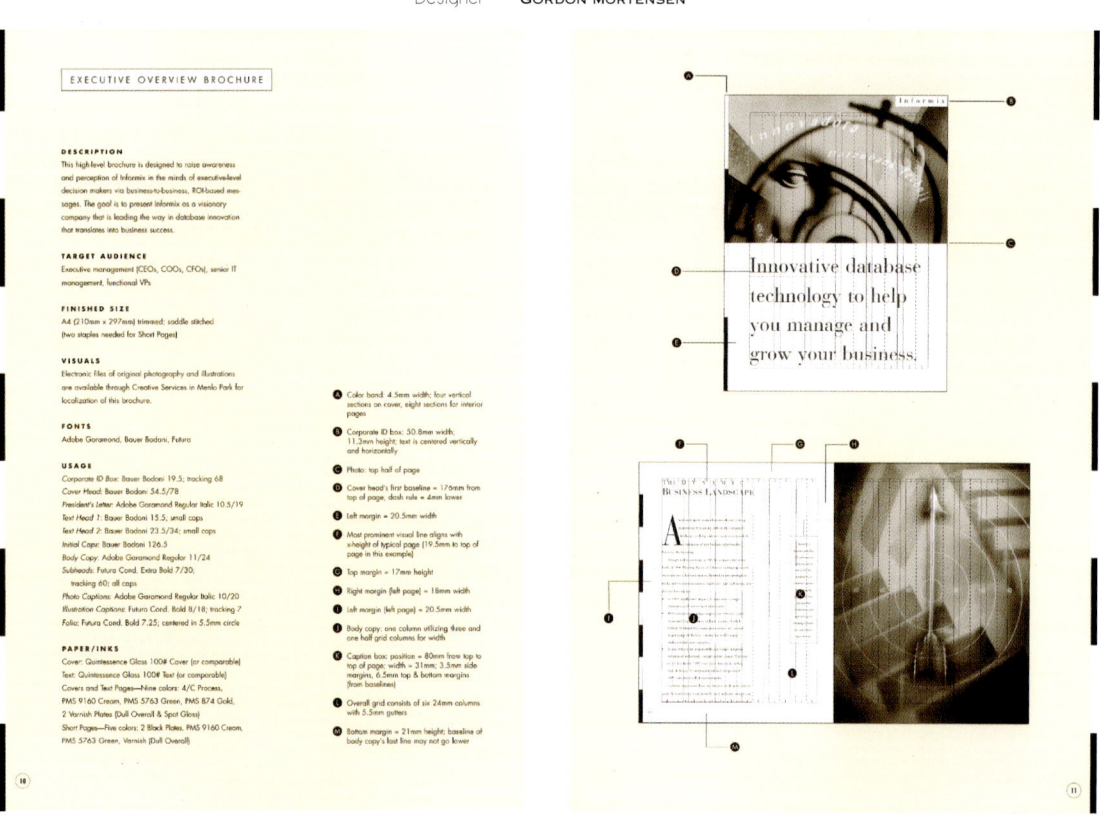

We sell solutions, but our customers buy brands

Brand	Sub-brand	Descriptor	Model
Cisco		Systems	
Cisco	Cisco IOS		
Cisco		Connection Online	
Cisco	Catalyst	Workgroup Switch	WS-C1201
Our company name functions as the umbrella brand. The Cisco name forms the basis for customer preference and receives the largest focus of our advertising and promotional efforts.	Major hardware product families or long-term corporate initiatives such as Cisco IOS will retain their proprietary sub-brand names or receive new ones. With the difficulty of trademarking new software names, software product lines will usually use the Cisco brand rather than a sub-brand name.	Most products within a product family will receive industry-standard descriptive names. These names will not be trademarked nor are they trademarkable.	These model designators should be numeric or alphanumeric, and whenever possible indicate product specs such as power or hierarchy in the product line.

Purchasing decisions are not always based simply on cost, quality, and service comparisons. Often customers buy products because they recognize and trust a particular brand. People buy Cisco products and services based on our innovation, reliability, quality, and expertise.

Proper branding ensures that Cisco and its products are recognized by our customers, enabling them to make buying decisions easily. Branding represents name recognition, consistent messages, and product integration throughout the company.

A good brand name is easy to remember and follows a coherent structure. Brands provide consistent, clear messages that make our products stand out in the marketplace.

A unified brand name strategy is key in establishing a consistent voice at Cisco. We have developed a four-tiered system to provide an orderly naming framework as illustrated here.

Without the Cisco logo, it isn't Cisco

PROMOTIONAL MERCHANDISE

Coats, pens, hats, t-shirts, sweatshirts, cups, and plaques all spell recognition and reward. Please follow the guidelines for logo usage and make certain a Cisco logo appears in a prominent place on all promotional items, such as on the left front pocket of a t-shirt, sweatshirt, or jacket or on the front of a cap. Logo placement on a sleeve, the back of a shirt or the visor of a cap is not acceptable.

If using embroidery, the minimum size is 1¾" wide, an exception to the previous rule. In the case of smaller items such as pens, the logo will need to be less than .75". Please work with a representative from the Corporate Identity organization to ensure acceptability of the size and quality of the logo on these items.

Our key merchandising vendors have a complete palette of approved colors available and will help you select quality items that fit your budget and time frame.

Client	CISCO SYSTEMS
Design Firm	1185 DESIGN
Designers	PEGGY BURKE, MEHDI ANVARIAN

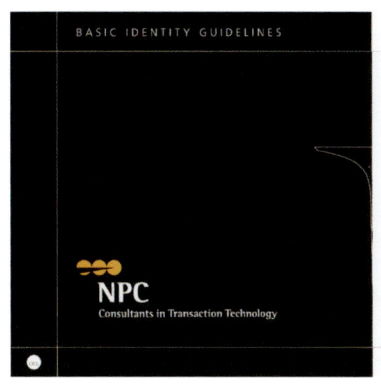

Client	NPC
Design Firm	LANDOR ASSOCIATES
Art Director	VASSOULA VASILIOU
Designer	DAVID GARCIA

Client	O'NEILL, INC.
Design Firm	IN-HOUSE ADVERTISING DEPT.
Designers	ANNE ENDRUSICK, ANDREW JONES, MIKE BERTONI

O'Neill is pleased to introduce our updated worldwide brand identity. This comprehensive system projects our determination to enter the twenty-first century remaining a leader in the concept, design, and manufacturing of wetsuits, sportswear, and accessories.

This system, and the way we use it, constitutes something every bit as valuable to our company as the products we sell, our brand identity. It brings immediate credibility and worldwide recognition on everything it appears. It's one of the most powerful marketing tools we possess. Unfortunately, it's also quite fragile. Easily imitated, compromised, and sometimes abused.

Therefore, we have set out to clearly define and guide the use of our brand identity. I urge you to follow these guidelines to the benefit of us all. As we continue to capitalize on O'Neill's equity, it becomes vitally important that we work together by consistent use of this mark in all internal communications, advertising, retail, and promotions.

Take a few moments to study the guidelines described here and refer to them as you develop your advertising and marketing tools.

We anticipate a strongly successful implementation of this program.

Pat O'Neill
President and
Chief Executive Officer
August 10, 1995

A complete line of internal communications have been developed for worldwide use. These pieces are shown on the left at a reduced size. These pieces should be reproduced in the approved colors, Pantone 185 Red and Pantone Black 6.

Specifications for the design of these pieces will be included in the Brand Identity Guidelines available soon from O'Neill.

To the right are examples of advertising and promotional materials containing the new wave graphic and the wordmark. Specifications for the design of these pieces will also be included in the Brand Identity Guidelines.

For print advertising purposes, the italics may be reproduced in additional colors providing there is enough contrast between the photography and the brand identity.

Brand Signatures

O'Neill's brand signature consists of the wave graphic and the wordmark. There are two lockups — that is, the positioning and sizing of these two elements, which are available for use. Shown at left: Italics, Italics and wave, center position.

Italics

Italics and wave, center position

Logo Background Colors

For internal communications purposes, the logo should appear on a white background. In print advertising and collateral materials, the use of color, photography, or illustration must be directed to insure enough contrast between the brand identity and the background on which it appears.

Logo/Color Variations

Again, there is only one color combination for the O'Neill logo. For black and white reproductions, there are three options: solid black, reverse the entire logo to white, or separate it to black and 50% gray, as shown at left.

Logo History

Everyone knows that O'Neill has been in the wetsuit business since 1952. But have you noticed the changes that have been made to the logo along the way? Each step in our logo's evolution was appropriate for its time, but those early logos look dated today. Be sure you're using the current version, and not a relic.

1952
1963
1966
1972
1989
1993
1995

Trademark Identity

O'Neill has spent considerable time to build equity in the O'Neill name throughout the past 43 years. That name is put into jeopardy when we fail to use trademarks properly. By following these simple guidelines, we will be assured of worldwide seamless communications.

Brand Identity Guidelines

O'Neill is currently developing *Brand Identity Guidelines* which will be available for use in the next few months. These guidelines are designed to be simple and easy to follow. If the information you need is not contained in these interim guidelines, you can bet it will be in the official guidelines.

Logo and Color Standards

This wordmark has been designed to carry forward the character of the original surf logo, in the overall weight, proportion, and speed of the characters.

It will be linked across all worldwide internal communications, advertising, sporting wetsuit lines, sportswear apparel, and accessories.

Pantone 185

Pantone Black 6

The bold, simplified line weights work well for reduction purposes.

Developing this system has afforded us the opportunity to streamline use of this trademark. It is crucial that these guidelines are adhered to in the following 3 areas:

First, the spacial relationship between the wave graphic and wordmark must not be changed.

Second, for all internal communications, the identity's colors must be matched to Pantone 185 Red and Pantone Black 6. Do not alter these colors in any way.

Third, the logo is not to be modified by additional outlines or other photographic effects when the logo appears for branding identification purposes. Save your creativity for whatever the logo will be applied to.

231

Images in the library should address most needs. For additional requirements, do not attempt to imitate the AS/400 photographic style. Instead, use a conventional photographic approach, and combine those images with ones from the library.

Do not adapt special images created for a specific layout or purpose, for example, advertising photography should not be used in printed and promotional materials.

When necessary, images may be cropped, so long as cropping is careful and logical, and visual communication is preserved. Images are not intended to wrap around covers.

Application screen from the AS/400 image library

Stock photography used in picture frames from image library

Theme objects used to illustrate application development

Situational photography demonstrating small business environment

23

Covers

Four variations show how to address different markets and selling needs. Two are appropriate for the general family of products, one for members of the product line, and one for software products and applications.

Grids used to create the cover (and interior formats) are based on the IBM Sales Promotion Design Guide. Templates are available in QuarkXpress® and PageMaker®, complete with artwork files for the IBM logo. These can be obtained from Corporate Identity and Design.

For European booklet usage, please follow A4 specifications found in the brochure section of this manual (pages 3.1 - 3.3).

Client · IBM Corporation AS/400 Division
Design Firm · C3 Incorporated
Creative Director · Randall Hensley
Senior Designer · Sylvia Chu

Client · Motorola
Design Firm · Karnes Prickett Design
Designer · Dave Prickett

MOTOROLA CORPORATE SIGNATURE

The Motorola Corporate Signature, sometimes referred to as the Motorola Identity, is the visual symbol that represents the company's brand name. Worldwide recognition of the Corporate Signature is the result of significant, long-term investment and a rigorous effort to present a uniform and consistent graphic image. Consistent presentation is essential if we are to leave a lasting impression with consumers and maintain the value of the Motorola brand.

The Motorola Corporate Signature is a registered trademark and is the primary element in the Motorola Wireless Data Group identity program. The Motorola Corporate Signature is a single element made up of two parts:

A symbol, which is called the emsignia, located within a ring.
The logotype, which is the name Motorola in a unique letter style. This letter style is a custom design. It can not be executed from any computer font. It is not Helvetica Bold Italic.

The Motorola Corporate Signature is always used as a complete unit and must not be altered from its approved form.

Graphic Controls Neither the emsignia symbol or the logotype may be used alone. The Motorola name, Corporate Signature or emsignia symbol cannot be used as part of another company's trade name or business identity. The Motorola Corporate Signature must be reproduced from the reproduction artwork provided in this manual only or from an approved electronic file.

Signature Format There are two primary approved signature formats, a horizontal and a vertical format. The relation between the emsignia symbol and logotype for both is indicated. The horizontal format is always the preferred format of the corporation. The vertical format may be used on everything except stationery.

Consistent application and precise reproduction of the symbol/logotype is critical to conform to all legal and graphic requirements specified in the Motorola Corporate Identity Manual.

Area of Isolation The Motorola Corporate Signature should not be positioned close to distracting design elements. In addition, it should not become part of a larger design element or pattern. The Corporate Signature should always be separated from any other graphic element by a "free space" or area of isolation equal to, at a minimum, the diameter of the emsignia symbol (1X) for the horizontal format. The 1/2 the diameter of the symbol (1/2X) for the vertical format. This isolation area should surround the entire signature.

Signature
Symbol · Logotype

Horizontal Format
Symbol and Logotype relation

Vertical Format
Symbol and Logotype relation

MOTOROLA

Area of Isolation

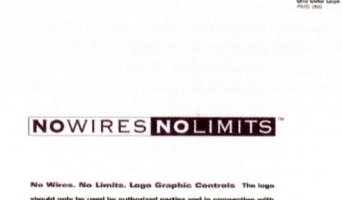

NOWIRES NOLIMITS™

No Wires. No Limits. Logo Graphic Controls The logo should only be used by authorized parties and in connection with the promotion of No Wires. No Limits.™ Use of the logo must be in accordance with the following guidelines:

Logo Format, Size and Positioning The logo is to be positioned horizontally only and must not be altered in any way through the addition of graphics or versions of part(s) of the logo from the approved format shown in the reproduction art on the following pages. The logo should be reproduced from the reproduction artwork provided in this manual or electronically from an approved disk only. The logo should never appear smaller than 1.5 inches (38 mm) in length in print. The logo should not be positioned on a screened or patterned background.

Area of Isolation The logo should have a clear area of at least 3/8-inch (9.25 mm) surrounding the logo in which there can be no print, graphics or other illustration.

Color Specifications Color treatment for the logo must be one color in black or purple PMS 268 (4/C process mix: C-91; M-94; Y-0; K-23.5). The logo is a complete unit and all elements must appear in the same color. The logo can also be produced in white out of black or any dark color, using the reverse versions.

Trademark Statement: The following statement should always be included on any approved artwork or marketing communications, advertising and promotional materials where the No Wires, No Limits logo mark is included. ® and Motorola are registered trademarks and No Wires, No Limits is a trademark of Motorola, Inc.

Approval: Prior to printing or publication, use of the logo must be approved by Motorola. Allow a minimum of two days for approval/turnaround by faxing representative layouts, comps and/or mechanicals to: Motorola, WDG Marketing Communications, fax: 847.538.4405.

One Color Logo
PMS 268

One Color Logo Reverse
PMS 268 Background

Signage &
Environmental
Graphics

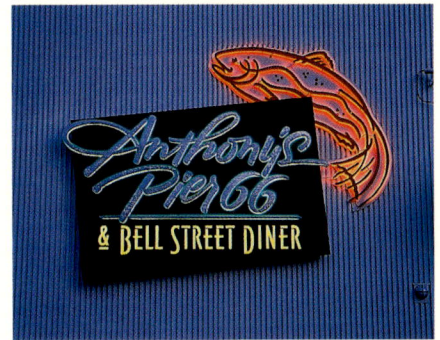

Client   BROOKLYN CHILDREN'S MUSEUM
Design Firm RUSSELL DESIGN ASSOCIATES
Designers ANTHONY RUSSELL,
          PO-WEN SHAW

Client   PUERTO RICO TOURISM COMPANY
          UNDERWATER ADVENTURES
Design Firm GRAF, INC.
Designer LYDIMARIE APONTE

Client   ANTHONY'S
Design Firm TIM GIRVIN DESIGN, INC.
Designers TIM GIRVIN,
          GRETCHEN WEGNER

Client   LIPPOLAND
Design Firm THE GNU GROUP
Designers NANCY DANIELS,
          MELISSA LACOUNTE

Client   POWERTEL
Design Firm COPELAND HIRTHLER
          DESIGN + COMMUNICATIONS
Creative Directors BRAD COPELAND,
          GEORGE HIRTHLER
Designer MICHELLE STIRNA
Environmental Designers JEFF HAACK,
          ERIK BROWN
Producers LAURA PERLEE,
          DONNA HARRIS,
          TOR GUNDERSON
Account Executive SARAH HUIE

Client   WEST END MARKETPLACE
Design Firm TL HORTON DESIGN, INC.
Designer TONY L. HORTON

Client   FORD MOTOR COMPANY
Design Firm FORD & EARL ASSOCIATES
Designer FRANCHESKA GUERRERO

Client   CONSOLITE CORPORATION
Design Firm TRACY SABIN GRAPHIC DESIGN
Designer TRACY SABIN

Client FUKUOKA URBAN DESIGN & DEVELOPMENT
Design Firm CLIFFORD SELBERT DESIGN COLLABORATIVE
Designers ROBIN PERKINS, CLIFFORD SELBERT

Client THE HAHN COMPANY
Design Firm COMMUNICATION ARTS, INC
Designers HENRY BEER,
MICHAEL DOYLE,
BRYAN GOUGH,
KELAN SMITH

Client LUCENT TECHNOLOGIES
Design Firm LANDOR ASSOCIATES
Creative Director SCOTT DRUMMOND
Designers SCOTT DRUMMOND, DAVID ZAPATA, DAVID ROCKWELL

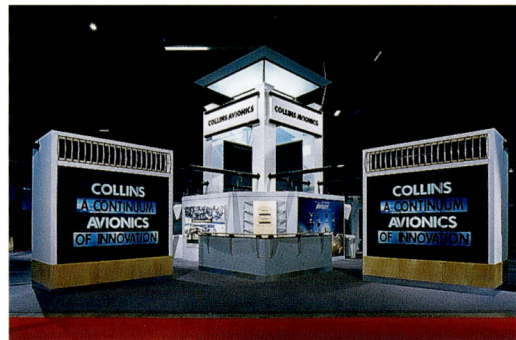

Client ROCKWELL/COLLINS AVIONICS
Design Firm TL HORTON DESIGN, INC.
Designer TONY L. HORTON

Client TEXACO REFINING AND MARKETING
Design Firm ANTISTA FAIRCLOUGH DESIGN
Designers TOM ANTISTA, THOMAS FAIRCLOUGH

Client DICTAPHONE CORPORATION
Design Firm DICTAPHONE CREATIVE SERVICES
Designers VINCENT MASOTTA, TOM PENDLETON,
MARK COLBERT, JEFF COLLIER,
BARRY MORGAN, SANDY WEISZ

Client GREAT LAKES SCIENCE CENTER
Design Firm KIKU OBATA & COMPANY
Designers KIKU OBATA, JOHN SCHEFFEL,
KAY PANGRAZE, KATHLEEN ROBERT

Client EMERALD DOWNS THOROUGHBRED RACETRACK
Design Firm TRA, LTD/MAESTRI
Designers JON BENTZ, SCOTT SOUCHOCK, PAULA REES,
LINDA SOUKUP, JANA REKOSH, KEN SHAFER

Client OGILVY & MATHER
Design Firm EVA MADDOX
ASSOCIATES, INC.

Client WEST VIRGINIA PARKWAYS ECONOMIC DEVELOPMENT
& TOURISM AUTHORITY—TAMARACK
Design Firm CHUTE GERDEMAN
Designer SUSAN HESSLER

Client CLEVELAND
BICENTENNIAL
COMMISSION
Design Firm EPSTEIN DESIGN
PARTNERS INC.
Designers ANNE TOOMEY,
JOHN OKAL

Client LASER PACIFIC
Design Firm VISUAL ASYLUM
Designers AMY LEVINE, MaeLIN LEVINE

Client ICON
Design Firm ICON
Designers JAMES ELLSWORTH,
KUOMARS KARAMI,
JAN SZUBIAK

Client MEPC AMERICAN PROPERTIES
Design Firm RTKL ASSOCIATES INC.
Designers SUZANNE SCHWARTZ, CODY CLARK,
LYNN BARNARD

Client HILTON HOTELS CORP.—FLAMINGO HILTON
Design Firm COMMUNICATION ARTS, INC
Designers RICHARD FOY, BRYAN GOUGH,
MICHAEL RIGGS, MICHELLE WENTWORTH,
KEVIN MEQUET, AMY SCHROEDER

Client CHILDREN'S
HOSPITAL
MEDICAL CENTER
Design Firm EVA MADDOX
ASSOCIATES, INC.

Client   HANCOCK NATURAL RESOURCE GROUP
Design Firm   GRISWOLD, HECKEL & KELLY ASSOC., INC.
Project Manager   FRANCINE MERCADANTE
Director of Design   WILLIAM O. SMITH
Job Captain   DANNY THOMPSON
Project Designer   CORNELL GRIGORIU

Client   CHICAGO STATE UNIVERSITY
Design Firm   EVA MADDOX ASSOCIATES, INC.

Client   MCKAY INVESTMENT COMPANY
Design Firm   OSLUND DESIGN INCORPORATED
Designers   CARL OSLUND, CINDY UESATO

Client   MB EXPLORATION, LLC
Design Firm   INTERPRISE
Designers   RITA RANDOLPH, SARAH HERRING, RUSS PETERS

Client   CORE STATES BANK— NETWORTH CAFÉ
Design Firm   DSI • LA
Designers   ROD PARKER, BRYAN MURPHY, LONNIE CARNAGGIO, CHRIS STEINER

Client   WATERSTONE'S BOOKSELLERS
Design Firm   KOR GROUP
Designers   MB SAWYER, KAREN DENDY

Client   SPORT TRUCK MAGAZINE
Design Firm   DENNIS S. JUETT & ASSOCIATES INC
Designer   DENNIS SCOTT JUETT

Client   OTIS SPUNKMEYER, INC.
Design Firm   PROFILE DESIGN
Designers   THOMAS MCNULTY, BRIAN JACOBSON, EILEEN CAREY, PHILIP SALSBURY, LIZ WHEATON

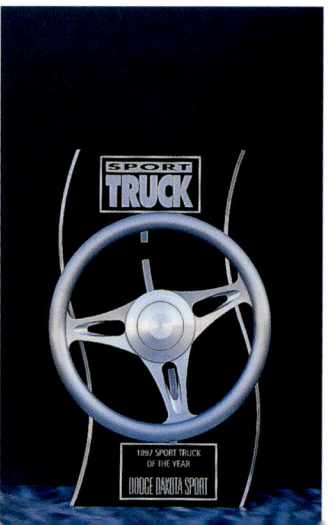

Client	America's Smithsonian
Design Firm	Supon Design Group.
Designers	Supon Phornirunlit,
	Kathleen Tobin,
	Richard Law,
	Maria Sese Paul,
	Nigel Briggs

Client	Genesco
Design Firm	Communication
	Arts, Inc.
Designers	Doug Stelling,
	David Stein,
	David Dute Jr.,
	John Ward,
	Richard Foy

Client	Zap at Stratosphere
Design Firm	TL Horton Design, Inc.
Designer	Tony L. Horton

Client	West Hollywood
	Chamber of Commerce
Design Firm	Smullen Design
Designers	Maureen Smullen,
	Mary Cay Walp

Client	Seattle Center
Design Firm	TRA, Ltd/Maestri
Designers	Jon Bentz,
	Scott Souchock,
	Paula Rees,
	Linda Soukup,
	Jana Rekosh

Client	Chronicle Books
Design Firm	Gee + Chung Design
Designer	Earl Gee

Client	MEPC American Properties
Design Firm	RTKL Associates Inc.
Designers	Suzanne Schwartz, Cody Clark,
	Lynn Barnard

Client	McKay Investment Company
Design Firm	Oslund Design Incorporated
Designers	Carl Oslund, Jenny Gray

Client   360° COMMUNICATIONS
Design Firm   SIEGEL & GALE

Client   CROSSROADS ARENA CORP.
Design Firm   COMMUNICATION ARTS, INC
Designers   RICHARD FOY,
                PATRICIA VAN HOOK,
                JASON HOWARD,
                LEONARD THOMAS

Client   OUT ON MAIN
                (RESTAURANT)
Design Firm   CHUTE GERDEMAN
Designer   ALAN JAZAK

Client   AMOCO
Design Firm   LANDOR ASSOCIATES
Creative Director SCOTT DRUMMOND
Designers   SCOTT DRUMMOND,
                JEAN LOO

Client   UNITED PARCEL SERVICE
Design Firm   ROLAND GEBHARDT DESIGN
Designer   ROLAND GEBHARDT

Client   THE MILLS CORPORATION
Design Firm   COMMUNICATION ARTS, INC
Designers   BRYAN GOUGH, PAUL MACK, KARL HIRSCHMANN,
                KELAN SMITH, HENRY BEER

Client   ACT THEATRE
Design Firm   MICHAEL COURTNEY DESIGN
Designer   MICHAEL COURTNEY

Client   CLAIRE'S STORES, INC.
Design Firm   555 DESIGN FABRICATION MANAGEMENT, INC.
Principal   JAMES GEIER

Corporate
Image
Brochures

Client   SPIRIT ROCK MEDITATION CENTER
Design Firm IDEAS FOR ADVERTISING & DESIGN
Designer   ROBIN BRANDES

Client   ZURICH KEMPER INVESTMENTS, INC.
Design Firm BRIERTON DESIGN, INC.
Designers   MICHAEL BRIERTON, KIRK HITSCHEL

Client   CORPIS CORPORATION
Design Firm HORNALL ANDERSON
             DESIGN WORKS, INC.
Designers   JACK ANDERSON,
             JOHN ANICKER,
             MARGARET LONG

Client   CONDÉ NAST SPORTS FOR WOMEN
Design Firm THE SLOAN GROUP
Designer   JANETTE EVSEBIO

Client   OASIS, INC.
Design Firm PINK COYOTE DESIGN, INC.
Designer   JOEL PONZAN

Client   JOHN W. HENRY & COMPANY, INC.
Design Firm SCHNEIDER GRAPHICS
Designer   ELLIOT SCHNEIDER

Client   METRO CONTRACT
             GROUP, INC.
Design Firm KNOX DESIGN
Designer   LUTHER KNOX

Client THE GUNLOCKE COMPANY
Design Firm MICHAEL ORR + ASSOCIATES, INC.
Designers GREGORY DUELL,
MICHAEL R. ORR

Client ANTISTA FAIRCLOUGH DESIGN
Design Firm ANTISTA FAIRCLOUGH DESIGN
Designers TOM ANTISTA, THOMAS FAIRCLOUGH

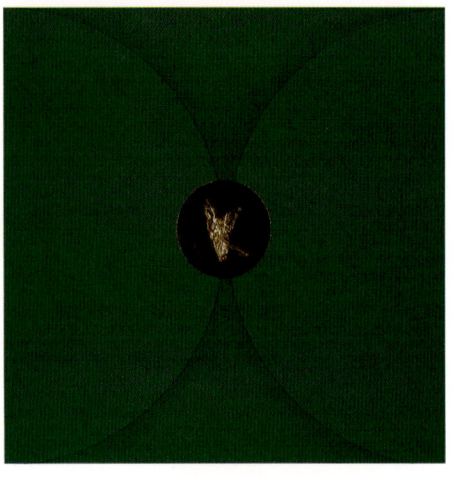

Client BAXTER FENTRISS & CO.
Design Firm CADMUS O'KEEFE MARKETING
Designer BRIAN THOMSON

Client THE KITANO NEW YORK HOTEL
Design Firm GIOVANNI PELLONE AND BRIDGET MEANS, INC.
Designers GIOVANNI PELLONE, BRIDGET MEANS

Client ATLANTA COMMITTEE FOR
THE OLYMPIC GAMES
Design Firm COPELAND HIRTHLER
DESIGN + COMMUNICATIONS
Creative Directors BRAD COPELAND,
GEORGE HIRTHLER
Art Director MELANIE BASS POLLARD
Designers MELANIE BASS POLLARD,
MICHELLE STIRNA
Copywriter GEORGE HIRTHLER
Producers LAURA PERLEE,
TOR GUNDERSON
Account Executive WARD COPELAND

Client GEORGIA-PACIFIC CORP.
Design Firm LESLIE EVANS DESIGN ASSOCIATES
Designers LESLIE EVANS, TERESA OTAL-CUMMINGS,
TOM HUBBARD

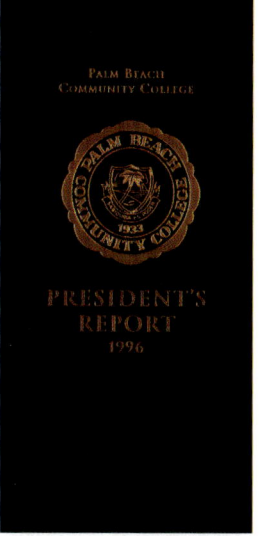

Client LEE HECHT HARRISON, INC.
Design Firm LINCOLN DESIGN
Designer TOM LINCOLN

Client WINDIGO
Design Firm WINDIGO
Creative Director JAMES B. GUBELMANN
Client Supervisor MARY LOU FERRIS
Account Executive JANET RALLI

Client PALM BEACH
COMMUNITY COLLEGE
Design Firm FISHER GRAPHICS
Designer AMY FISHER

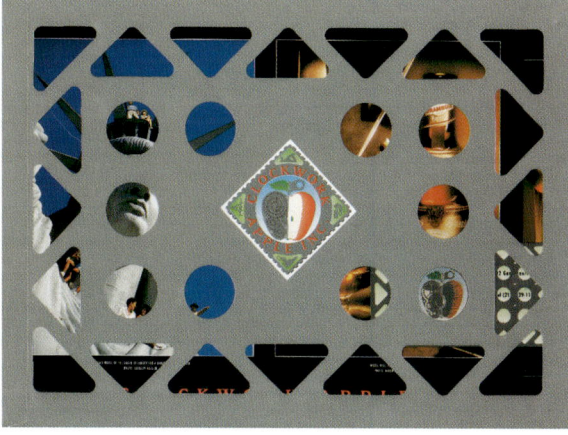

Client CLOCKWORK APPLE INC.
Design Firm CLOCKWORK APPLE INC.
Designer CHRISTO HOLLOWAY

Client SPIRTAS
WRECKING
COMPANY
Design Firm KIKU OBATA
& COMPANY
Designer RICH NELSON
Copywriter CAROLE JEROME

Client NATWEST MARKETS
Design Firm PAGANUCCI DESIGN, INC.
Designers BOB PAGANUCCI, FRANK PAGANUCCI

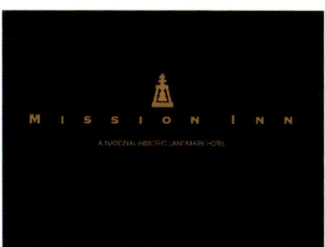

Client THE MISSION INN
Design Firm WINTER GRAPHICS SOUTH
Designer MARY LARUE WINTER

Client MERRILL LYNCH
Design Firm PAGANUCCI DESIGN, INC.
Designers BOB PAGANUCCI,
FRANK PAGANUCCI

CHANCES THAT
THERE IS LIFE ON
ANOTHER PLANET:
1 IN 1,000,000,000

Client   GVO
Design Firm   CAHAN & ASSOCIATES
Designers   KEVIN ROBERSON,
              BOB DINETZ

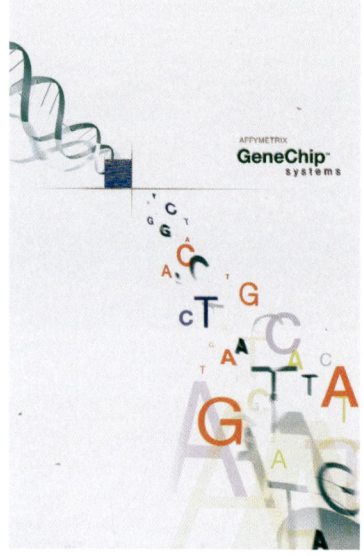

Client   AFFYMETRIX
Design Firm   CURTIS DESIGN
Designer   JOAN BITTNER

Client   ROCKWELL
              INTERNATIONAL
Design Firm   SPANGLER ASSOCIATES
Designers   SUSAN MENDENHALL,
              DAVID KENDALL

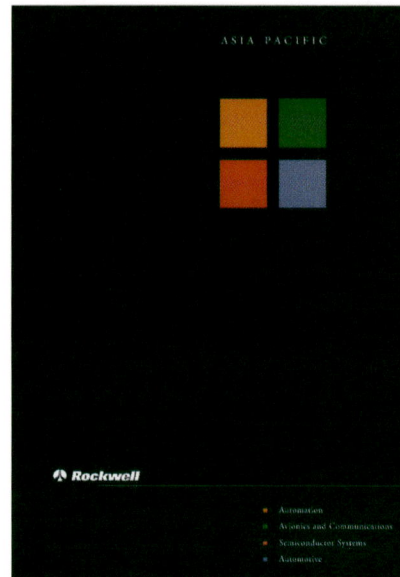

Client   MONSANTO
              CORPORATION
Design Firm   TDC/THE DESIGN
              COMPANY SAN
              FRANCISCO
Designers   SANDRA KOENIG,
              CRAIG FRAZIER

A NEW COMPANY TAKES FLIGHT

Client   TARMAC, INC.
Design Firm   CADMUS O'KEEFE
Designer   BRIAN THOMSON

Client   BACARDI LIMITED
Design Firm   WATERS DESIGN ASSOCIATES, INC.
Design Manager JOHN WATERS
Designer   CAROL BOUYOUCOS

Transforming the Landscape

Client WATTS WACKER, SRI CONSULTING
Design Firm WAYMAN PRODUCTIONS, INC.
Designer BILL WAYMAN

Client KPMG PEAT MARWICK
Design Firm NED STEELE
     COMMUNICATIONS
Designers SUSAN HODGES,
     RAFAEL HOLGUÍN

Client ANTISTA FAIRCLOUGH DESIGN
Design Firm ANTISTA FAIRCLOUGH DESIGN
Designers TOM ANTISTA, THOMAS FAIRCLOUGH

Client AMERICAN HEART ASSOCIATION
Design Firm SAYLES GRAPHIC DESIGN
Designers JOHN SAYLES, JENNIFER ELLIOTT

Client SPANGLER DESIGN TEAM
Design Firm SPANGLER DESIGN TEAM
Designers LAURA BARTLEY,
     MARK SPANGLER

**MAYBE GOOD DESIGN
ISN'T PRETTY**

Client SEASONAL SPECIALTIES LLC.
Design Firm SEASONAL SPECIALTIES LLC.
Creative Director JENNIFER SHEELER
Designer LISA MILAN

Client GVO
Design Firm CAHAN & ASSOCIATES
Designers KEVIN ROBERSON,
     BOB DINETZ

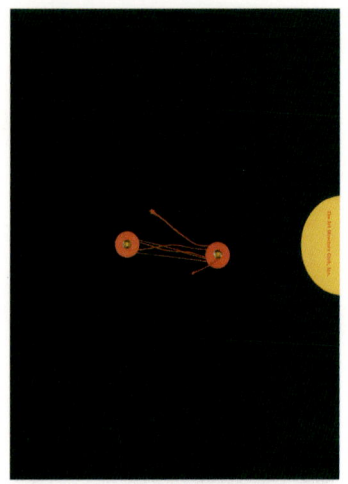

Client **ANDERSEN CONSULTING**
Design Firm **OH BOY, A DESIGN COMPANY**
Art Director **DAVID SALANITRO**
Designer **MIKE KRAINE**

Client **ART DIRECTORS CLUB**
Design Firm **PLATINUM DESIGN INC.**
Designer **KATHLEEN PHELPS**

Client **PRETTY GOOD PRIVACY**
Design Firm **HORNALL ANDERSON DESIGN WORKS, INC.**
Designers **JACK ANDERSON, DEBRA HAMPTON,**
HEIDI FAVOUR, MICHAEL BRUGMAN,
JANA WILSON, KATHA DALTON

Client **ERIC SCOTT**
Design Firm **G.W. GRAPHICS**
Art Director **GLENN WHALEY**
Designer **KEVIN KAMPWERTH**

Client **PARBEL GROUP**
Design Firm **ORIGINAL IMPRESSIONS**
Designer **MICHAEL BLOUNT**

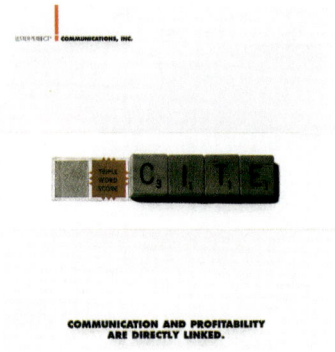

Client **LETTERPERFECT**
Design Firm **GREENFIELD/BELSER LTD.**
Designer **BURKEY BELSER**

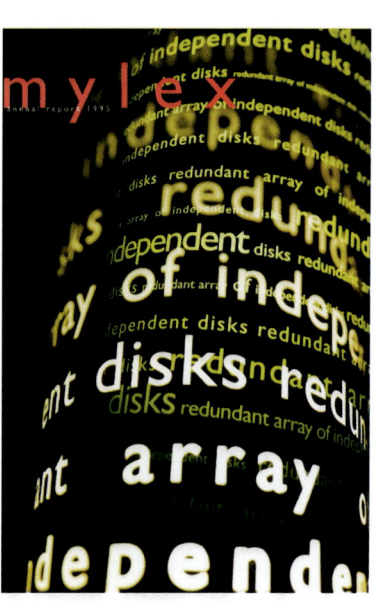

Client **MYLEX**
Design Firm **HAUSMAN DESIGN**
Designers **LAURIE CARRIGAN, SABINE GRÜNWALD**

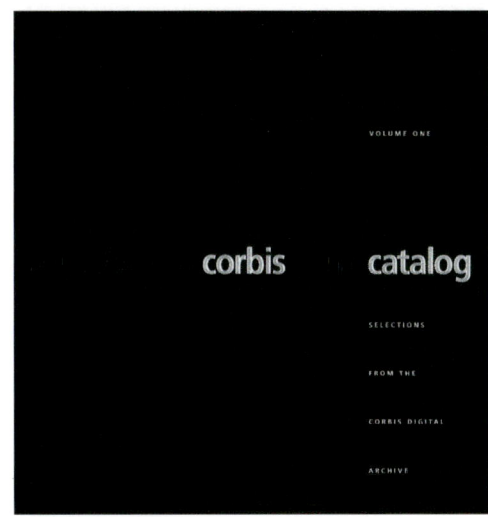

Bob Kolbrener Photographs
Twenty-Five Years In The American West

The Saint Louis Art Museum

Client   THE FELD COMPANY
             WELLSFORD RESIDENTIAL PROPERTY TRUST
Design Firm NOBLE•ERICKSON INC
Designers   JACQUELYN NOBLE, STEVEN ERICKSON,
             DAVID LANSDON, BRITTA ERICKSON

Client   OXO INTERNATIONAL
Art Director JENNIFER MARIOTTI WILLIAMS
Designer   THERESA O'LOUGHLIN

Client   NEENAH PAPER
Design Firm   COPELAND HIRTHLER DESIGN + COMMUNICATIONS
Creative Directors BRAD COPELAND, GEORGE HIRTHLER
Art Directors   TODD BROOKS, MELISSA JAMES KEMMERLY,
                RAQUEL C. MIQUELI
Designers   TODD BROOKS, DAVID CRAWFORD,
                SEAN GOSS, MICHELLE STIRNA
Illustrators   ELIZABETH BRADY, JEFFERY FISHER
Photographers   MARY ANNE MITCHELL,
                JERRY BURNS,
                JOHN GROVER
Copywriter   MELISSA JAMES KEMMERLY
Producers   LAURA PERLEE, DONNA HARRIS
Account Executive SHENNA PRICE

Client   CALYPSO
Design Firm AERIAL
Designer   TRACY MOON

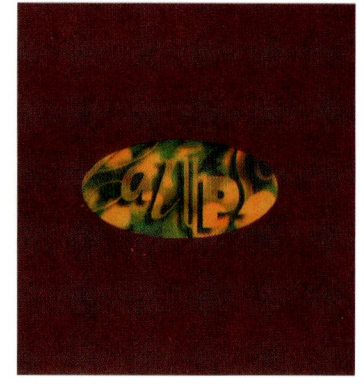

Client   ONSET VENTURES
Design Firm 1185 DESIGN
Designers   PEGGY BURKE,
             JENNIFER HARDY,
             JULIA FOUG

Client   GOLDWELL COSMETICS
Design Firm GRAFIK
             COMMUNICATIONS, LTD.
Design Team JOHN VITOROVĬCH,
             JUDY KIRPICH,
             GREGG GLAVIAWO

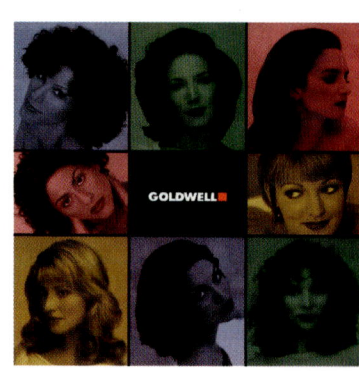

246

Client FREYER WOOD WORKS
Design Firm KILMER & KILMER, INC. DESIGN & ADVERTISING
Designers RICHARD KILMER, BRENDA KILMER,
RANDALL MARSHALL

Client SEASONAL SPECIALTIES LLC.
Design Firm SEASONAL SPECIALTIES LLC.
Creative Director JENNIFER SHEELER
Art Director BARBARA ROTH
Producer DEB LEE

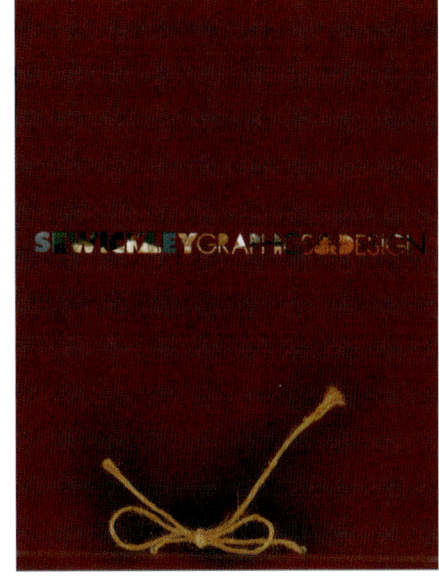

Client ENSR REMEDIATION
& CONSTRUCTION
Design Firm SEWICKLEY
GRAPHICS &
DESIGN, INC.
Designers DARREN MILLER,
BETH GRIMES

Client KATSIN-LOEB
ADVERTISING
Design Firm MORLA DESIGN
Designers JENNIFER MORLA,
PETRA GEIGER

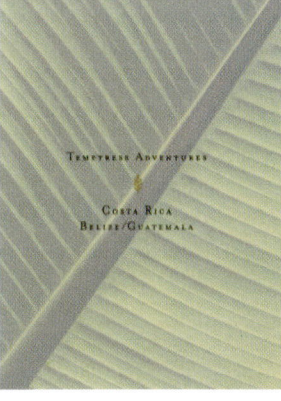

Client KILMER, KILMER & JAMES
Design Firm KILMER & KILMER, INC.
DESIGN & ADVERTISING
Designers RICHARD KILMER, BRENDA KILMER,
RANDALL MARSHALL

Client TRIDENT, INC.
Design Firm KEILER DESIGN GROUP
Designers JEFF LIN, MIKE SCRICCO

Client MICROSOFT CORPORATION
—MUNGO PARK
Design Firm THE LEONHARDT GROUP
Designer GREG MORGAN

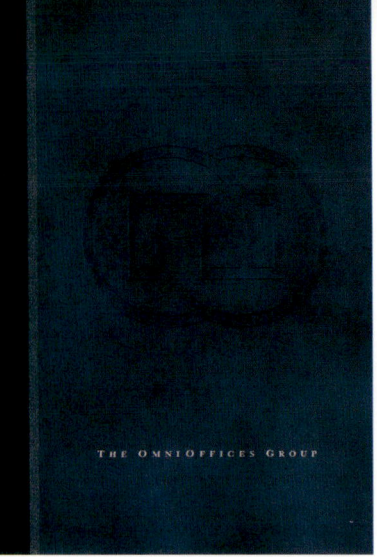

Client   OMNI OFFICES GROUP
Design Firm   ROUSSO + ASSOCIATES
Designer   STEVE ROUSSO

Client   THE EVENT NETWORK
Design Firm   LOMANGINO STUDIO INC.
Designer   ALAIN DELILLE BLUNT

Client   ATRIX LABORATORIES
Design Firm   COONTS DESIGN GROUP
Designer   GREG RATTENBORG

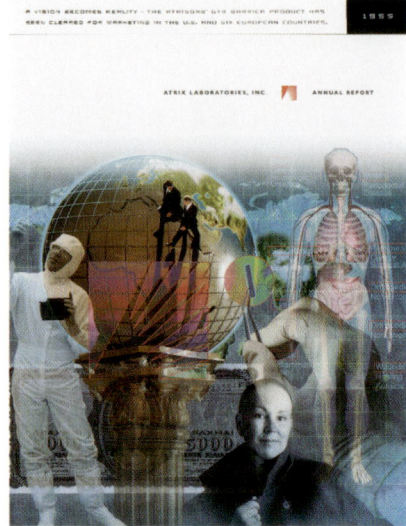

Client   FOLLETT
                SOFTWARE
                COMPANY
Design Firm   ESDALE
                ASSOCIATES,
                INC.
Designer   ILSE KRAUSE

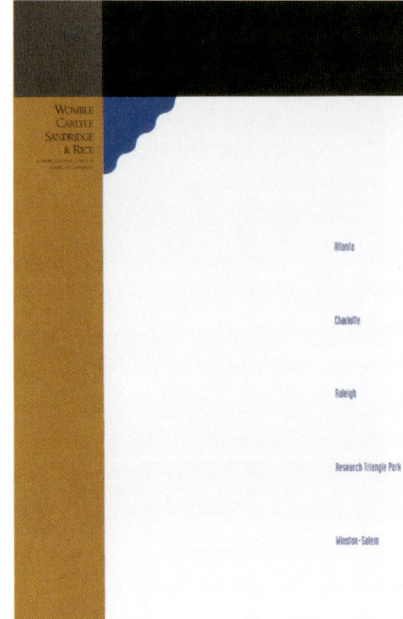

Client   WOMBLE
                CARLYLE
Design Firm   GREENFIELD/
                BELSER LTD.
Designer   AMY DARRAGH

Client   YOUNG & RUBICAM
Design Firm   LANDOR ASSOCIATES
Creative Director NANCY HOEFIG
Designers   CLARK RICHARDSON, CINTHIA WEN

Client   SAAB CARS USA, INC.
Design Firm   RMI, INC.
Creative Director LEE EINHORN

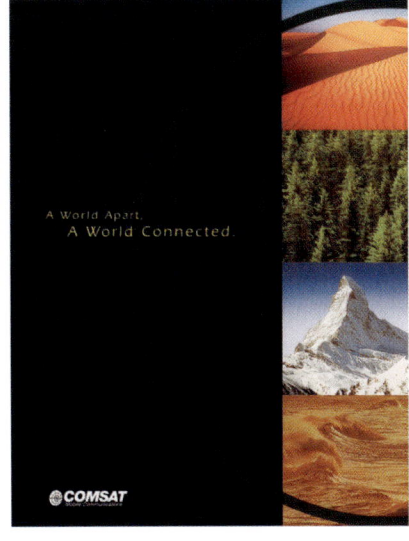

Client   STARBUCKS COFFEE COMPANY
Design Firm   HORNALL ANDERSON
              DESIGN WORKS, INC.
Designers   JACK ANDERSON, JULIE LOCK,
              HEIDI FAVOUR, ALAN FLORSHEIM,
              JOHN ANICKER, MICHAEL BRUGMAN

Client   BARRINGTON CONSULTING GROUP
Design Firm   WHITE DESIGN, INC.
Designers   JOHN WHITE,
              JAMIE GRAUPNER,
              ALEXANDRA
              MORNELL

Client   COMSAT COMMUNICATION
Design Firm   SULLIVAN & COMPANY
Creative Director GIGI LEUNG
Designers   HIEN IM, JUNE HWANG

Client   HITACHI DATA
              SYSTEMS
Design Firm   HDS CREATIVE
              SERVICES
Designer   MICHAEL MCCANN

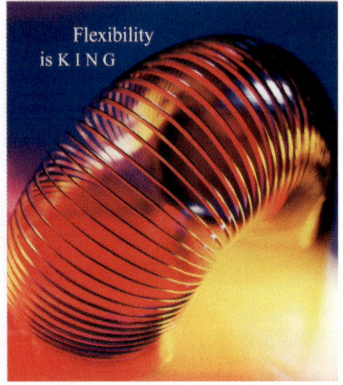

Client   AIRBORNE
              EXPRESS
Design Firm   HORNALL
              ANDERSON
              DESIGN WORKS,
              INC.
Designers   JOHN HORNALL,
              LISA CERVENY,
              HEIDI FAVOUR,
              BRUCE BRANSON-MEYER

Client   ANTISTA FAIRCLOUGH DESIGN
Design Firm   ANTISTA FAIRCLOUGH DESIGN
Designers   TOM ANTISTA,
              THOMAS FAIRCLOUGH

Client   KNIGHT-RIDDER, NEW MEDIA
Design Firm   PATT MANN BERRY DESIGN
Designer   PATT MANN BERRY

Client STRATEGY MANUFACTURING, INC.
Design Firm PROFILE DESIGN
Designers RUSSELL BAKER, ANTHONY LUK,
   JEANNE NAMKUNG, GARY SIU, KEVIN NG

Client CADENCE
Design Firm OH BOY, A DESIGN COMPANY
Designer DAVID SALANITRO

Client LANDOR ASSOCIATES
Design Firm LANDOR ASSOCIATES
Creative Director NANCY HOEFIG
Designers NANCY HOEFIG, CINTHIA WEN

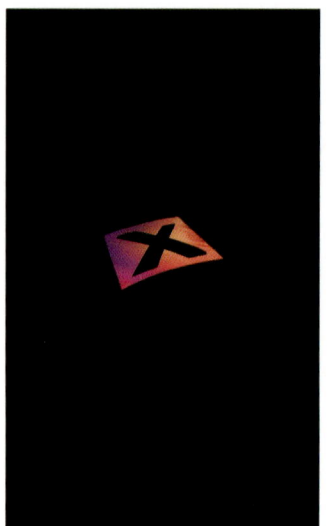

Client CONSUMER
   CREDIT
   COUNSELING
   SERVICE
Design Firm COLEMAN
   DESIGN
   GROUP, INC.
Designer AMANDA GRUPE

Client NEXTLINK
   CORPORATION
Design Firm HORNALL ANDERSON
   DESIGN WORKS, INC.
Designers JACK ANDERSON,
   MARY HERMES,
   DAVID BATES,
   MARY CHIN HUTCHISON

Client PEOPLESOFT
Design Firm CASPER DESIGN GROUP
Designer ANDERSON GIN

Client QUESTAR-NETQUEST
Design Firm TIM GIRVIN DESIGN, INC.
Designers STEPHEN PANNONE,
   MARC GREEN,
   BRIAN MATHIS

HDS Professional Services —
Making IT Work for You.

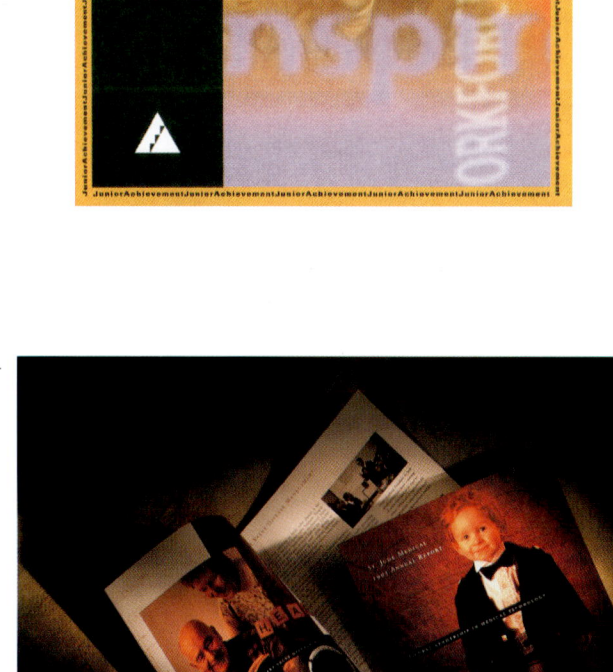

Some Choices
In Life Are
Perfectly Clear.

Client   APPLIED THEORY COMMUNICATIONS, INC.
Design Firm   DE PLANO DESIGN
Designer   JAKOB FIELDHAUER

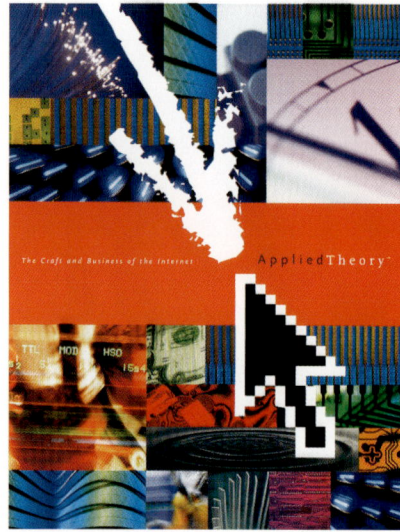

Client   NAMALE RESORT
Design Firm   ROBERT MOTT & ASSOCIATES
Designers   ROBERT MOTT, KATHY WISE

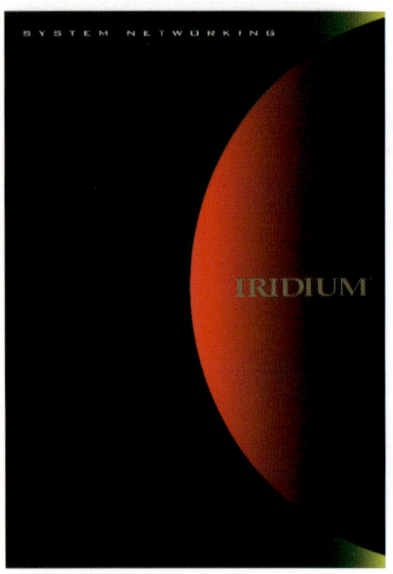

Client   2D
                INTERACTIVE,
                INC.
Design Firm   STORMSHIP
                STUDIOS
Designers/Illustrators
                ANNE
                DAMPHOUSSE,
                MIKE BRENNAN

Client   IRIDIUM
Design Firm   SUPON
                DESIGN GROUP.
Designer   JACQUES COUGHLIN

Client   HEARTLAND CAPABILITIES BROCHURE
Design Firm   LARSEN DESIGN + INTERACTIVE
Designers   TIM LARSEN, JERRY STENBACK

Client   QUILL CREATIVE, INC.
Design Firm   QUILL CREATIVE, INC.
Designer   STEVE M. UTLEY

Client   INVESTORS INDEPENDENT TRUST COMPANY
Design Firm   POLLMAN MARKETING ARTS, INC.
Designers   JENNIFER POLLMAN, SHEPHERD WILSON

INVESTORS INDEPENDENT TRUST COMPANY

Client   THE RICHARD E. JACOBS GROUP
Design Firm   HERIP DESIGN ASSOCIATES, INC.
Designers   WALTER M. HERIP, JOHN R. MENTER

Client   CONTINUUM HEALTHCARE
Design Firm   SAYLES GRAPHIC DESIGN
Designers   JOHN SAYLES, JENNIFER ELLIOTT

Client   RELIASTAR
Design Firm   LIZ J. DESIGN, INC.
Designer   NANCY JOHNSON

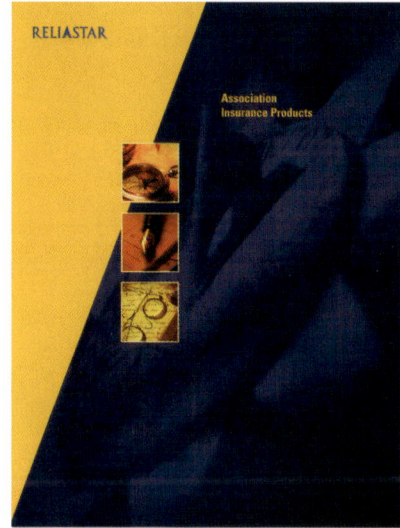

Design Firm   ROBINSON ADVERTISING + DESIGN
Designer   DANA ROBINSON

Client   CONTINGENCY PLANNING RESEARCH
Design Firm   ROSS & JACOBS, INC.
Designer   MARK ROSS

SOMETHING HAPPENS HERE

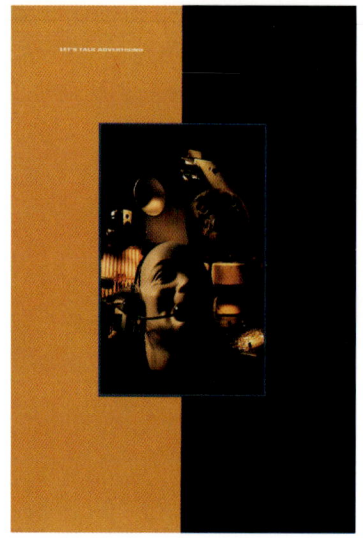

Client   QUILL CREATIVE, INC.
Design Firm QUILL CREATIVE, INC.
Designer   STEVE UTLEY

Client   SGI
Design Firm SGI
Designer   SCOTT GREENLEE

Client   THE GEORGE WASHINGTON UNIVERSITY
Design Firm SUPON DESIGN GROUP.
Designers JACQUES COUGHLIN, BRENT ALMOND

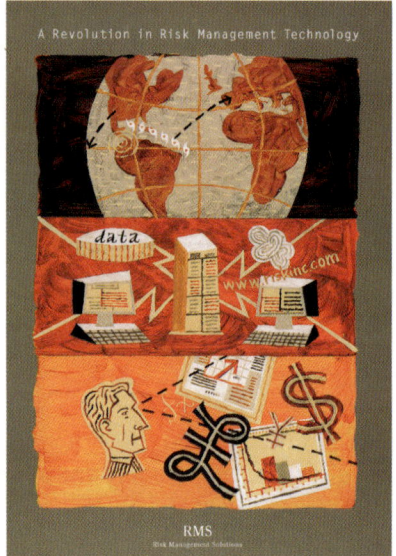

Client   MOLINA JEWELERS
Design Firm SULLIVAN MARKETING & COMMUNICATIONS
Designer   JACK SULLIVAN

Client   RISK MANAGEMENT
            SOLUTIONS
Design Firm LANDOR ASSOCIATES
Designers NANCY HOEFIG,
            JENNIFER BOSTIC

Client   DIVERSIFIED GRAPHICS
Design Firm SHANNON DESIGNS
Designer   ALYN SHANNON

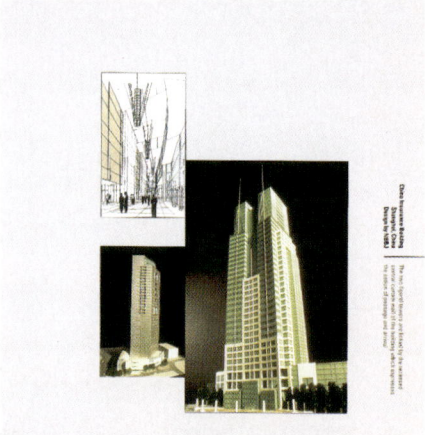

Client   NBBJ
Design Firm NBBJ GRAPHIC DESIGN
Designer   LEO RAYMUNDO

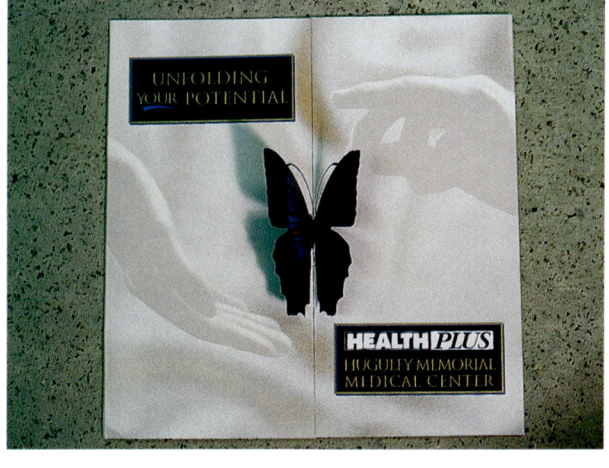

LOGOS

Client   YOUNG IMAGINATIONS
Design Firm   SACKETT DESIGN ASSOCIATES
Designer   MARK SACKETT

Client   3M
Design Firm   LIPPINCOTT & MARGULIES
Designer   RODNEY ABBOT

Client   VITAL RESEARCH
Design Firm   SMULLEN DESIGN
Designer   GRETCHEN VAN PELT

Client   LUCENT TECHNOLOGIES
Design Firm   LANDOR ASSOCIATES
Designers   MARGARET YOUNGBLOOD, WALLY KRANTZ, HENRICK OLSEN

Lucent Technologies
Bell Labs Innovations

Client   THE MANGO TREE OF NEW YORK
Design Firm   BURSTEIN/MAX ASSOCIATES, INC.
Designers   NAOMI BURSTEIN, HUGUETTE FRANCO

THE MANGO TREE
the ultimate in giftware

Client   TV ELECTRIC
Design Firm   GRIFFITH PHILLIPS CREATIVE
Designer   BRIAN NIEMANN

custom
SOLUTIONS

Client   APRIA HEALTHCARE
Design Firm   LANDOR ASSOCIATES
Creative Directors   MARGARET YOUNGBLOOD, COURTNEY REESER
Designer   DENISE GOLDMAN

APRIA HEALTHCARE

*A New Dimension
in Homecare*

Client   PARALLAX GRAPHICS
Design Firm   CALIFORNIA DESIGN INTERNATIONAL
Designers   SUZY LEUNG, CHRISTINE ARDITO

Client   BATAVIA NURSING & CONVALESCENT INN
Design Firm   PAVONE FITE FULWILER
Designer   JEFF FULWILER

Client   INDUSTRIAL METAL
Design Firm   MALCOLM GREAR DESIGNERS

PARALLAX GRAPHICS

BATAVIA
Nursing & Convalescent Inn

industrial metal

Client   DESIGN EDGE
Design Firm   KILMER & KILMER

Client   TANDEM (APPLICATION DEVELOPMENT)
Design Firm   JOE MILLER'S COMPANY
Designers   JOE MILLER, MICHAEL LAURETANO

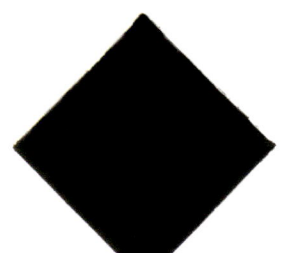

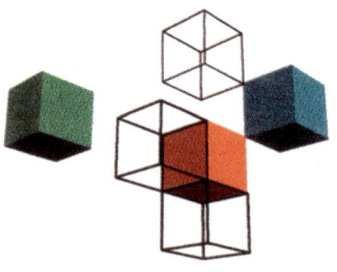

Client   FISHER DESIGN, INC.
Design Firm   FISHER DESIGN, INC.
Designer   RICHARD W. DEARDORFF

Client   MARJORIE GROSS & CO., INC.
            —CHARLES SCHWAB
Design Firm   TOM DOLLE DESIGN
Designer   TOM DOLLE

Client   THOMSON SOFTWARE, (NOW) AONIX
Design Firm   ADDISON WHITNEY
Designer   LORI EARNHARDT

Medcor

Aonix

Client   COSTELLO COMMUNICATIONS
Design Firm   COSTELLO COMMUNICATIONS
Designer   JAMES COSTELLO

Client   CARTA INTERACTIVE
Design Firm   TRACE
Designer   ALDIS STRAZDINS

COSTELLO COMMUNICATIONS

CARTA
INTERACTIVE

257

Client   GENERAL COATINGS (PAINTS)
Design Firm   DON BLAUWEISS ADVERTISING & DESIGN
Designer   DON BLAUWEISS

Client   ADX CREATIVE SERVICES
Design Firm   ADX CREATIVE SERVICES
Designer   KYLE KUMMER

Client   CAIRE, INC.
Design Firm   POLIVKA LOGAN DESIGN, INC.
Designer   CHRIS ADAMS

Client   TRW
Design Firm   JAMES ROBIE DESIGN ASSOCIATES
Designer   WAYNE FUJITA

Client   RHEMA
Design Firm   COLEMAN DESIGN GROUP, INC.
Designer   AMANDA GRUPE

Client   SCOTT FORESMAN ADDISON WESLEY
Design Firm   LIPPINCOTT & MARGULIES
Designers   KEN LOVE, MICHELLE CASSUTO

Client   GSP AIRPORT INTERNATIONAL
Design Firm   WESTHOUSE DESIGN
Designers   JACK DEL GADO, DANIEL JONES

Client   EVENTX IMAGEMAKERS
Design Firm   IDENTITY CENTER
Designers   WAYNE KOSTERMAN, DARIN HASLEY

Client   U.S. WEB
Design Firm   SARGENT & BERMAN
Designer   CHERYL GILLIS

Client   CLOSER LOOK CREATIVE
Design Firm   CLOSER LOOK CREATIVE
Designer   KATHLENE KIERNAN

Client   TELUS COMMUNICATIONS
Design Firm   LIPPINCOTT & MARGULIES
Designers   KEN LOVE, RYAN PAUL

Client   DOOSAN INDUSTRIES
Design Firm   LIPPINCOTT & MARGULIES
Designers   KEN LOVE, ALEX DE JÁNOSI

Client   THE CHILD CARE COMPANY
Design Firm   PAGANUCCI DESIGN, INC.
Designers   BOB PAGANUCCI, FRANK PAGANUCCI

Client   ANTARES LEVERAGED CAPITAL
Design Firm   THE MONOGRAM GROUP
Designer   MATTHEW BRETT

Client   COLLABORATIVE SOLUTIONS, INC.
Design Firm   3 MARKETEERS ADVERTISING
Designers   IN-HOUSE DESIGN TEAM

Client   PACIFIC TELESIS
Design Firm   AKAGI REMINGTON
Designers   DOROTHY REMINGTON, REGAN GRADET

Client   TARJAC, INC.
Design Firm   IN HOUSE GRAPHIC DESIGN, INC.
Designer   DENNIS ANGELO

Client   PAGE ONE BUSINESS PRODUCTIONS, L.L.C.
Design Firm   30SIXTY DESIGN, INC.
Designer   PÄR LARSSON

Client   AUTHORS BOOKSTORE AND CAFÉ
Design Firm   MADISON DESIGN
Designer   KIRSTEN BECK

Client   PKT TECHNOLOGIES
Design Firm   A TO Z COMMUNICATIONS, INC.
Designer   BOB DOWNING

Client HADASSAH
Design Firm CREATIVE SERVICES DEPARTMENT
Designer MICHAEL COHEN

Client NATIONAL HISPANIC HEALTH COALITION
Design Firm ALPHAWAVE DESIGNS
Designer DOUGLAS DUNBEBIN

Client HELENA LIONS SWIM TEAM
Design Firm CROWLEY WEBB & ASSOCIATES
Designer DION PENDER

Client MORTON PLAZA
Design Firm TRACY SABIN GRAPHIC DESIGN
Designer TRACY SABIN

Client THE GETTY TRUST
Design Firm JAMES ROBIE DESIGN ASSOCIATES
Designer ALEX CHAO

Client BROKERS NATIONAL LIFE ASSURANCE COMPANY
Design Firm GRAPHIC EDGE, INC.
Designer STEPHANIE PHAN ROECKER

Client ROGERS GLASSWORKS
Design Firm MINX DESIGN
Designer CECILIA M. SVEDA

Client ASIAN AMERICAN AIDS FOUNDATION
Design Firm DESIGNS IN THE WINDY CITY
Designer TUAN DO

Client JONAH LLC
Design Firm COMMUNICATION DESIGN, INC.
Designer ROBERT MEGANCK

Client   CARMEL VALLEY INN—SUNSET TENNIS CLASSIC
Design Firm THE WECKER GROUP
Designer   ROBERT J. WECKER

Client   DUTCHMILL DESIGN
Design Firm DUTCHMILL DESIGN
Designer   PATTI J. LACHANCE

Client   HYDRATECH, INC.
Design Firm DESIGN FOR INDUSTRY
Designer   KEVIN OPP

Client   CLOTHES THE DEAL (NOT FOR PROFIT ORGANIZATION)
Design Firm SHIMOKOCHI/REEVES
Designers   MAMORU SHIMOKOCHI, ANNE REEVES

Client   POTOMAC POLYMER CLAY GUILD
Design Firm DEVER DESIGNS
Designer   JEFFREY L. DEVER

Client   HAAGEN DAZS
Design Firm GILL FISHMAN ASSOCIATES
Designer   MICHAEL PERSONS

Client   INTERCOLLEGIATE ROWING ASSOC.
Design Firm JASPER & BRIDGE ASSOCIATES
Designer   KEN HALLEE

Client   SUMMIT VIEW SCHOOL
Design Firm JULIA TAM DESIGN
Designer   JULIA CHONG TAM

Client   PLANET COMMUNICATIONS
Design Firm SURFPUPPY MULTIMEDIA GROUP
Designer   KAREN MCKEE

Client ALLEN CENTER (HOUSTON)
Design Firm METZDORF, INC.
Designer LYLE METZDORF

Allen Center

Client ACTIVE ORTHOPAEDICS
Design Firm SCHNIDER & YOSHINA, LTD.
Art Director OSCAR SCHNIDER
Designer MARION DE BACKER

Client ATHERTON GROUP
Design Firm RKD, INC.
Designer RICHARD KLEIN

ATHERTON

Client ABGENIX
Design Firm MICHAEL PATRICK PARTNERS
Designers KARL KROMER, ROY TAZUMA

Client BRENHAM CLINIC
Design Firm METZDORF, INC.
Designers LYLE METZDORF, ROBERT VAN LENTEN

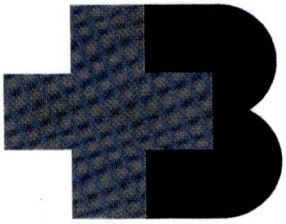

Brenham Clinic

Client BONIN AND ASSOCIATES FINE HOME BUILDERS
Design Firm ALPHAWAVE DESIGNS
Designer DOUGLAS DUNBEBIN

Client BILL BALLENBERG
Design Firm SKEGGS DESIGN
Designer GARY SKEGGS

Client CENTURY MIRROR & GLASS
Design Firm DON BLAUWEISS ADVERTISING & DESIGN
Designer DON BLAUWEISS

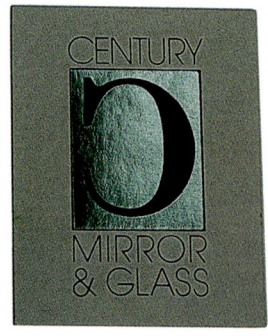

Client **COVALENT CORPORATION**
Design Firm **RKD, INC.**
Designer **JAMES CURL**

Client **DELAWARE VALLEY PHILHARMONIC**
Design Firm **COOK AND SHANOSKY ASSOCIATES, INC.**
Designers **ROGER COOK, MICHAEL MILLIGAN**

Client **COMMERCIAL PRESS**
Design Firm **CROUCH & NAEGELI/DESIGN GROUP WEST**
Designer **JIM NAEGELI**

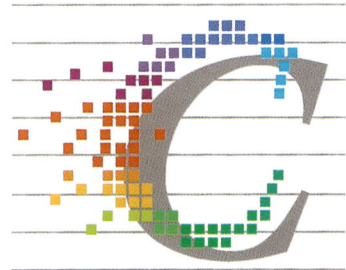

Client **DISNEY ONLINE**
Design Firm **DAVID VOGLER/DISNEY ONLINE**
Designers **DAVID VOGLER, BEN LUCE**

Client **EVANTAGE**
Design Firm **DESIGN MANIFESTO**
Designers **LISA CUMBEY, PAM WITBECK**

Client **ELOGEN, INC.**
Design Firm **LOVE PACKAGING GROUP**
Designer **BRIAN MILLER**

Client **FINATECH**
Design Firm **IMS**
Designer **JAMIE ANDERSON**

Client **FUCH'S**
Design Firm **MULLER + COMPANY**
Designer **TYLER SINGER**

Client   GO MART, INC.
Design Firm   RETAIL PLANNING ASSOCIATES, INC.
Designers   ANDY KRANEK, TIM SMITH

Client   HARTMAN'S LANDSCAPE
Design Firm   HERMSEN DESIGN ASSOCIATES, INC.
Designer   JACK HERMSEN

Client   INTERRA WEB SERVICES
Design Firm   AKAGI REMINGTON
Designers   DOUG AKAGI, DOROTHY REMINGTON

Client   J. GILBERT
Design Firm   MULLER + COMPANY
Designer   JON SIMONSEN

Client   ATMOSPHERICS
Design Firm   CLIFFORD SELBERT DESIGN COLLABORATIVE
Designers   ROBIN PERKINS, HEATHER WATSON

Client   HASTINGS FILTERS, INC.
Design Firm   LOVE PACKAGING GROUP
Designer   TRACY HOLDEMAN

Client   INPOWER, INC.
Design Firm   THE STEPHENZ GROUP
Designer   PHILLIP KIM

Client   THE MARTWICK GROUP
Design Firm   PARRIS ADVERTISING/DESIGN
Designer   PARRIS CHARGOIS

Client   MID-MICHIGAN MASONRY
Design Firm   HEART GRAPHIC DESIGN
Designer   CLARK MOST

Client   MITOKOR, INC.
Design Firm   GOSS KELLER MARTINEZ, INC.
Designers   FERNANDO M. MARTINEZ, JERRY GOEN

Client   MONTALBANO DEVELOPMENT, INC.
Design Firm   MONTALBANO DEVELOPMENT, INC.
Designers   TED BRASS, KENNIN SATO, GREG MONTALBANO, CHRIS MONTALBANO

Client   NEWS INTERNET SERVICES
Design Firm   ADV MARKETING GROUP, INC.
Designers   STEPHEN SOHL, JEAN-CHRISTIAN PHILIPPI

Client   INGEAR CORP.
Design Firm   VISUAL MARKETING ASSOCIATES, INC.
Designer   JASON SELKE

Client   FOTH & VAN DYKE—STRATEGIC ENVIRONMENTAL MANAGEMENT
Design Firm   FOTH & VAN DYKE
Designer   DANIEL GREEN

Client   OSCAR MAYER FOODS CORPORATION
Design Firm   PIRMAN COMMUNICATIONS
Designer   BRIAN PIRMAN

Client   WHEREHOUSE ENTERTAINMENT
Design Firm   RETAIL PLANNING ASSOCIATES, INC.
Designer   TIM A. FRAME

Client **SHADYSIDE PRESBYTERIAN CHURCH**
Design Firm **ADAM, FILIPPO & ASSOCIATES, INC.**
Designers **DAVID CHRISTIAN ZIMMERLY,**
ROBERT A. ADAM, AIMEE P. SANFORD

Client **GREEN DREAMS**
Designer **TODD DAVID NICKEL**

Client **NORTHFIELD SCHOOL**
Design Firm **LOVE PACKAGING GROUP**
Designer **BRIAN MILLER**

Client **CHRYSLER CORPORATION—COMMUNICATIONS GROUP**
Design Firm **ICONIX INC.**
Designer **SHERRI LAWTON**

Client **AMERICAN INSTITUTE OF GRAPHIC ARTS, NEW YORK**
Design Firm **J. GRAHAM HANSON DESIGN**
Designers **J. GRAHAM HANSON, IRIS TEO**

A Night at the Movies

Client **LEVERAGED LEARNING**
Design Firm **Z•D STUDIOS INC**
Designer **MARK SCHMITZ**

Client **GST INTERNET**
Design Firm **GST INTERNET**
Designer **KEITH SASAKI**

Client **SHOKT INTERNET PRODUCTIONS**
Design Firm **30SIXTY DESIGN, INC.**
Designer **RICKARD OLSSON**

Client **GORMAN'S**
Design Firm **THE HOPKINS GROUP**
Designers **ED DONALD, LYNETTE BOHN**

Client   JEEPERS!
Design Firm FRCH DESIGN WORLDWIDE
Designer   TIM FRAME

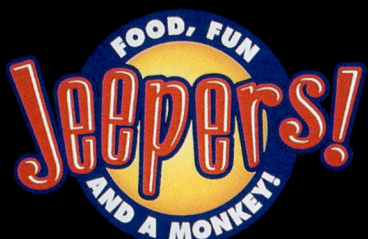

Client   BLAND GARVEY EADS MEDLOCK + DEPPE,
             ACCOUNTANTS & CONSULTANTS
Design Firm LAMBERT DESIGN
Designer   JOY CATHEY PRICE

Client   MICROSOFT
Design Firm LANDOR ASSOCIATES
Designers   BILL CHIARAVALLE, SCOTT CURTIS

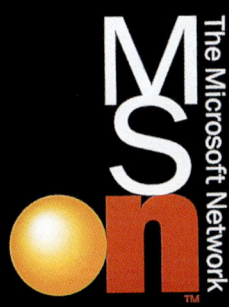

Client   SHANGHAI J.C. ORIENTAL HIGHTECH ENTERTAINMENT CO. LTD., P.R.C.
Design Firm GENSLER
Designers   TOM HORTON, CATHY NOE, LISA VAN ZANDT

Client   CAMERAD INC.
Design Firm SHIELDS DESIGN
Designer   CHARLES SHIELDS

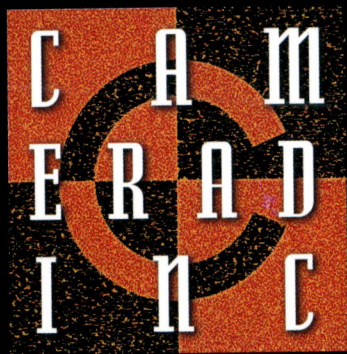

Client   TIMES SQUARE
Design Firm FRCH DESIGN WORLDWIDE
Designers   SHAWN DAVIES, TESSA WESTERMEYER

Client   CSE
Design Firm CSE
Art Director ROGER KENERLY II
Designer   LEO KOPELOW

Client   ACTIVE IMAGES
Design Firm COMICRAFT
Designers   JOHN MARASIGAN, RICHARD STARKINGS

Client   VARNAU CREATIVE GROUP
Design Firm VARNAU CREATIVE GROUP
Designer   TIM VARNAU

Client   NATIONAL CENTER FOR SUPERCOMPUTING
           APPLICATIONS OF THE UNIVERSITY OF ILLINOIS
Design Firm JACK DAVIS GRAPHICS
Designer   JACK W. DAVIS

Client   APPLIED PROFESSIONAL SYSTEMS
Design Firm DONALDSON MAKOSKI INC.
Designer   VIRGINIA BILODEAU

Client   BEANCOUNTERS BOOKKEEPING SERVICES
Design Firm TODD MALHOIT
Designer   TODD MALHOIT

Client   NOVELLUS SYSTEMS—ANGSTROMANIA 2
Design Firm LARSEN DESIGN OFFICE, INC.
Designer   SASCHA BOECKER

Client   DILLINGHAM CONSULTING
Design Firm FROGDESIGN TEAM
Designers FROGDESIGN TEAM

Design Firm GRAPHIC RESOURCES
Designers HARRY KNOX

Client   ELLEN BOGEN RUBENSTEIN
           EISDORFER & CO., LLP
Design Firm THE APPELBAUM COMPANY
Designers HARVEY APPELBAUM, NICK GUARRACINO

Client   MUSEUM OF FINE ARTS, BOSTON
Design Firm WONDRISKA RUSSO ASSOCIATES
Designer   ANNE ALLEN

Client FASHION INSTITUTE OF TECHNOLOGY
Design Firm RICHARD DANNE & ASSOCIATES
Designer RICHARD DANNE

Client HTI ASSOCIATES LLC
Design Firm SKEGGS DESIGN
Designer GARY SKEGGS

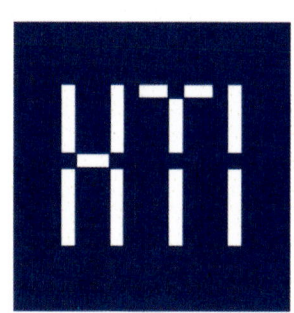

Client IDA—INTER DATA ACCESS
Design Firm DAVIES PACHECO & MURPHY ADVERTISING
Creative Director WALDO PACHECO
Designer MICHAEL WALSH

Client R + B SERVICES, INC.
Design Firm FLEURY DESIGN
Designer ELLEN FLEURY

Client JERRY WILLIAMS
Design Firm DESIGN MANIFESTO
Designers LISA CUMBEY, PAM WITBECK

Client NIEHAUS RYAN GROUP
Design Firm CALIFORNIA DESIGN INTERNATIONAL
Designers SUZY LEUNG, CHRISTINE ARDITO

Client GRAPHIC ARTISTS GUILD
Design Firm MICHAEL DORET GRAPHIC DESIGN
Designer MICHAEL DORET

Client ALEX CHRISTOPHER
Design Firm COMMUNICATION ARTS, INC.
Designer PATRICIA VAN HOOK

Client BRADLEY ACADEMY FOR THE VISUAL ARTS
Design Firm BRADLEY ACADEMY
Designer EDWARD KAHLER

Client PHIL RUDY PHOTOGRAPHY
Design Firm SHIELDS DESIGN
Designer CHARLES SHIELDS

269

Client UNIVERSAL INTERNET
Design Firm THE WECKER GROUP
Designer ROBERT J. WECKER

Client GATEWAY TRAVEL MANAGEMENT, INC.
Design Firm SEMAN DESIGN GROUP
Designer RICHARD M. SEMAN

Client APPLIED MATERIALS
Design Firm HOWRY DESIGN ASSOCIATES
Art Director JILL HOWRY
Designer TODD RICHARDS

Client NEW ENGLAND/ISRAEL MARKET GATEWAY
Design Firm GILL FISHMAN ASSOCIATES
Designer GILL FISHMAN

Client ANERGEN, INC. (BIOTECH COMPANY)
Design Firm HOWRY DESIGN ASSOCIATES
Designers GAYLE STEINBEIGLE, CLAY WILLIAMS

Client PURECHOICE
Design Firm HEDSTROM/BLESSING
Designer PAM GOEBEL

Client INOVA
Design Firm THE DUPUIS GROUP
Designer TIM SCHMIDT

Client WORLD ELECTRONIC COMMUNITY
Design Firm GILL FISHMAN ASSOCIATES
Designer MICHAEL PERSONS, ALICA OZYJOWSKI

Client THE SEVENTH-DAY
ADVENTIST CHURCH
INTERNATIONAL RELIGIOUS
LIBERTY ASSOCIATION
Design Firm DEVER DESIGNS
Designer JEFFREY L. DEVER

Client   SEATTLE SYMPHONY—SCHUBERTFEST
Design Firm   ART O MAT DESIGN
Designers   MARK KAUFMAN, JACQUELINE MCCARTHY

Client   OIL CHANGERS
Design Firm   ADDIS GROUP
Designers   RICK ATWOOD, JAMES ELI, JOHN MATTOS

Client   SCHWAN'S SALES ENTERPRISES
Design Firm   PEDERSEN GESK
Designers   KRIS MORGAN, MITCH LINDGREN

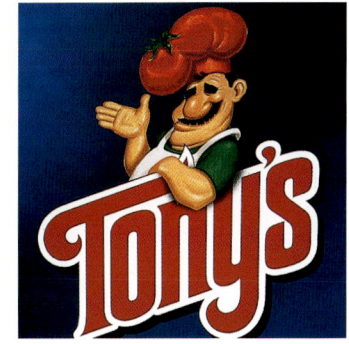

Client   STARBUCKS COFFEE COMPANY
Design Firm   HORNALL ANDERSON DESIGN WORKS, INC.
Designers   JACK ANDERSON, JULIE LOCK, JANA NISHI,
     JULIE KEENAN, JULIA LAPINE,
     MARY CHIN HUTCHISON

Client   EINSTEINS-NOAH BAGEL
Design Firm   WILLOUGHBY DESIGN GROUP
Designers   ANN WILLOUGHBY, DEB FRIDAY,
     MICHELLE SONDEREGGER, INGRED SIDIE

Client   CARL'S CAFÉ
Design Firm   RPA
Designer   TIM SMITH

Client   VIRTUAL VINEYARDS
Design Firm   GEE + CHUNG DESIGN
Designers   EARL GEE, FANI CHUNG

Client   PRAIRIE PRINT
Design Firm   INSIGHT DESIGN COMMUNICATIONS
Designers   SHERRIE HOLDEMAN, TRACY HOLDEMAN

Client   BOUDREUX'S
Design Firm   DESIGN SERVICES, INC.
Designers   ROD PARKER, NICOLE DUET

Client   ANITA PAULUS, DDS (FAMILY & COSMETIC DENTISTRY)
Design Firm   LAMBERT DESIGN
Designer   CHRISTIE LAMBERT

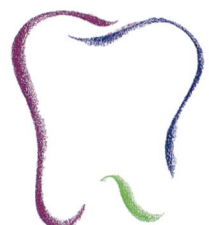

Client   AMERICAN FILM FESTIVAL
Design Firm   SCHNIDER & YOSHINA, LTD.
Art Director   OSCAR SCHNIDER
Designer   KARA HANNON

A CZECH
CINEMA
FESTIVAL

Client   INTERNATIONAL SPACE THEATER CONSORTIUM
Design Firm   METZDORF, INC.
Designer   ROBERT VAN LENTEN

INTERNATIONAL SPACE THEATER CONSORTIUM

Client   BRUTON/STROUBE STUDIOS
Design Firm   PHOENIX CREATIVE
Designer   ERIC THOELKE

BRUTON|STROUBE

Client   SIGHTS EPOSTCARD
Design Firm   FIFTH STREET DESIGN
Designers   J. CLIFTON MEEK, BRENTON D. BECK

Client   TOOLBOX PRODUCTIONS, INC.
Design Firm   SARGENT & BERMAN
Designer   PETER SARGENT

Client   ENVENTIVE MARKETING
Design Firm   STEEL WOOL DESIGN
Designer   KRISTY LEWIS

Client   AUTODESK—DESIGN-X
Design Firm   BRUCE YELASKA DESIGN
Designers   BRUCE YELASKA, JOHN SEMINERIO

Client   OUTBOARD MARINE CORP.—FICHT
Design Firm   DESIGN NORTH, INC.
Designer   PAT COWAN

Client   ALLEN AND SONS
Design Firm   ZGRAPHICS, LTD.
Designer   GREGG ROJEWSKI

FICHT
FUEL INJECTION

ALLEN
AND SONS

Client VIKING STAR ENTERPRISES
Design Firm STINSON DESIGN
Designers JEFF HEESCLI, MICHAEL STINSON

Client NORTHERN LIGHT
Design Firm GILL FISHMAN ASSOCIATES
Designers GILL FISHMAN, MICHAEL PERSONS, ALICIA OZYJOWSKI

Client BREAKING AWAY
Design Firm SARGENT & BERMAN
Designer PETER SARGENT

Client BUFFALO BILLS
Design Firm CROWLEY WEBB & ASSOCIATES
Designer DION PENDER

Client TODDLER TAXI
Design Firm DUTCHMILL DESIGN
Designer PATTI J. LACHANCE

Client WOOD TRUCKING
Design Firm FLUIDESIGN
Designers BLAKE DEJONGE, RANDI TRYQSTAD

Client HOT ROD HELL
Design Firm MIRES DESIGN
Art/Creative Director JOSÉ A. SERRANO
Designer JOSÉ A. SERRANO
Illustrator TRACY SABIN

Client TWA/DMB&B—ST. LOUIS
Design Firm PHOENIX CREATIVE
Creative Director GREG SULLENTRUP
Designer ED MANTELS-SEEKER

Client OCOTILLO ROCKET CLUB
Design Firm MIRES DESIGN
Art/Creative Director JOSÉ A. SERRANO
Designer JOSÉ A. SERRANO
Illustrator MARK MATTINGLY

Client   DR. POE
Design Firm   GILL FISHMAN ASSOCIATES
Designer   ALICIA OZYJOWSKI

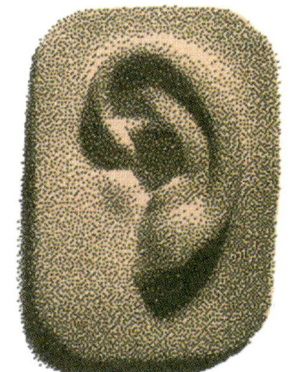

Client   FREESTYLE FAST FOOD FRANCHISE
Design Firm   AKAGI REMINGTON
Designer   LORSEN KOO

Client   AUTOGRAPH AUTHORITY
Design Firm   MULLER + COMPANY
Designer   JON SIMONSEN

Client   IMATION
Design Firm   INTERBRAND SCHECHTER
Designers   GERALD BERLINER, GARY STILOVICH

Client   GERBER OPTICAL
Design Firm   LERNER + COMPANY
Designer   BILL BOULEY

Client   HUGH BROWNE (PHOTORAPHER)
Design Firm   EDWARD WALTER DESIGN, INC.
Designer   MARTIN BRYNGIL

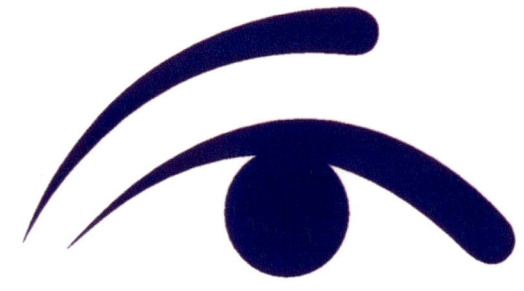

Client   NET IMPACT SYSTEMS, INC.
Design Firm   ELLIOTT VAN DEUTSCH
Designers   RACHEL DEUTSCH, ERIKA MAXWELL

Client   COLORADO YOUTH ARTS COUNCIL
Design Firm   COONTS DESIGN GROUP
Designer   MONTE MEAD

Client   ONLIVE!
Design Firm   MICHAEL PATRICK PARTNERS
Designers   KARL KROMER, ROBERT WONG, STACY HYUN

Client   GEORGE GOLDSMITH—THE TOMORROW LAB
Design Firm   DESIGN TRUST
Designer   DAVID CUNDY

Client   THE CLEVELAND CLINIC FOUNDATION
Design Firm   KAREN SKUNTA & COMPANY
Designers   KAREN L. HAUSER, KAREN A. SKUNTA

Client   ROCKWELL INTERNATIONAL
Design Firm   BASLER DESIGN GROUP
Designers   BILL BASLER, DREW DAVIES

Client   BUDDY BERKE'S STATHOUSE—POWERHOUSE
Design Firm   MIKE SALISBURY COMMUNICATIONS INC.
Designers   MARY EVELYN MCGOUGH, MIKE SALISBURY

Client   INTEL
Design Firm   MIRES DESIGN
Art/Creative Director SCOTT MIRES
Designer   SCOTT MIRES

Client   JACK DAVIS GRAPHICS
Design Firm   JACK DAVIS GRAPHICS
Designer   JACK W. DAVIS

Client   BRIGADOON.COM
Design Firm   GRAPHIC ASSOCIATES
Designers   WALLY LLOYD, HOUIE HAWK

Client   EAT DESIGN (HOLIDAY ICON)
Design Firm   EAT DESIGN
Designer   PATRICE EILTS-JOBE

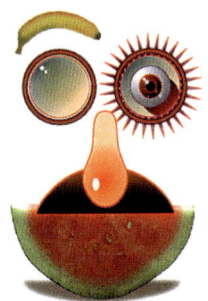

Client   NATURAL SELECTION FOODS
Design Firm JERRY TAKIGAWA DESIGN
Designer   GLENN JOHNSON

NATURAL
SELECTION
F O O D S

Client   REVELL & ASSOCIATES—OAKHURST MEDICAL GROUP
Design Firm SHIELDS DESIGN
Designer   CHARLES SHIELDS

OAKHURST
MEDICAL
GROUP

Client   OCEAN SPAR TECHNOLOGIES, L.L.C.
Design Firm DAIGLE DESIGN
Designer   CANDACE DAIGLE

Client   CHAOS LURES
Design Firm MIRES DESIGN
Art/Creative Director JÓSE A. SERRANO
Designer   JÓSE A. SERRANO
Illustrator   TRACY SABIN

Client   CHAOS LURES
Design Firm MIRES DESIGN
Art/Creative Director JÓSE A. SERRANO
Designer   JÓSE A. SERRANO
Illustrator   TRACY SABIN

Client   HARCOURT BRACE & CO.
Design Firm MIRES DESIGN
Art/Creative Director SCOTT MIRES
Designers   SCOTT MIRES, DEBORAH HORN
Illustrator   TRACY SABIN

Client   THE NBA
Design Firm THINK NEW IDEAS, LOS ANGELES
Creative Directors SCOTT MEDNICK, KEN ESKENAZI
Designers   PETER THORNBURGH, TOM THORNTON

Client   PLANET EXPEDITIONS
Design Firm UPPERCASE DESIGN
Designer   JUSTIN DEISTER

Client LAVERDONK DRESSAGE
Design Firm WORKHORSE DESIGN INC.
Designers CONSTANCE KOVAR, ANTHONY TAIBI

Client DEL MAR THOROUGHBRED CLUB
Design Firm CROUCH & NAEGELI/DESIGN GROUP WEST
Designer JIM NAEGELI

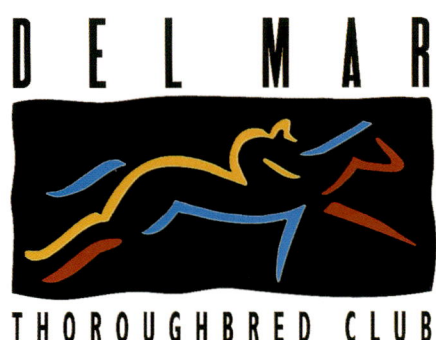

Client STARDUST TECHNOLOGIES, INC.
Design Firm JULIE MOORE CREATIVE
Designer JULIE MOORE

Client BROOKS BROTHERS
Design Firm DESGRIPPES GOBÉ & ASSOCIATES
Design Director CHRISTOPHER VICE

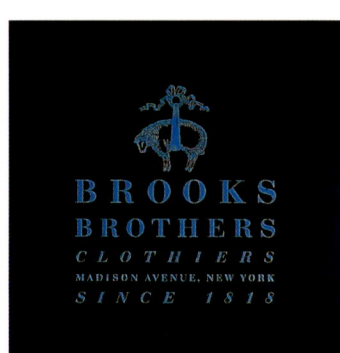

Client KAT-BOX KING, INC.
Design Firm NEWIDEAS, INC.
Designers CELESTE BRIGNAC, MARK PERRY, PATTY O. SEGER, DANA PETERS

Client MERCK—HEARTGARD
Design Firm ROBIN SHEPHERD STUDIOS
Designers MIKE BARNHART, LESLEY FOSTER

Client CHAPTER ONE PRODUCTIONS—DOG EARED AUDIO
Design Firm THE DELOR GROUP
Designers KEVIN WYATT, RUTH WYATT

Client MONGREL
Design Firm DESIGN MANIFESTO
Designers LISA CUMBEY, SUSAN SAWYER, PAM WITBECK

Client   HOLLAND BROTHERS
Design Firm   ADDIS GROUP
Designers   DEBBIE SMITH, DAVID LEONG

Client   HARVEST GROUNDS CAFE
Design Firm   KG ILLUSTRATION
Designer   CURT GEIDEMAN

Client   MADISON COUNTY, IL
Design Firm   BOB GAUEN GRAPHIC DESIGN
Designer   BOB GAUEN

Client   TSUNAMI DIVE GEAR
Design Firm   MIRES DESIGN
Art/Creative Director   JOHN BALL
Designers   JOHN BALL, DEBORAH HORN

Client   LIVE PICTURE
Design Firm   1185 DESIGN
Designers   PEGGY BURKE, JULIA FOUG

Client   AMERICAN EXPRESS
Design Firm   LUKE DAIGLE DESIGN
Designer   LUKE DAIGLE

Client   INTEGRAMED AMERICA
Design Firm   HANDLER DESIGN GROUP, INC.
Designer   BRUCE HANDLER

Client   TAYLOR GUITARS
Design Firm   MIRES DESIGN
Art/Creative Director   SCOTT MIRES
Designers   MIGUEL PEREZ, SCOTT MIRES

Client   RC CUSTOM CLEAN
Design Firm   WILLOUGHBY DESIGN GROUP
Designer   DEB FRIDAY

Client   ONE WORLD BREWING
Design Firm   HAYES GROUP
Creative Director MATT HAYES
Art Director/Designer MARK J. SUPLICKI

Client   CHINSKY'S KITCHEN
Design Firm   KIKU OBATA & COMPANY
Designer   JOE FLORESCA

Client   SWELL FASHION
Design Firm   66 COMMUNICATION INC.
Designer   CHIN-CHIH YANG

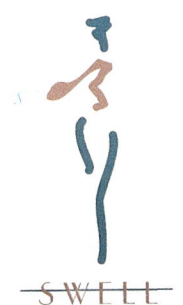

Client   BOYERSPORTS
Design Firm   SARGENT & BERMAN
Designer   PETER SARGENT

Client   BREW WORKS AT THE PARTY SOURCE
Design Firm   FRCH DESIGN WORLDWIDE
Designer   GARY CIERADKOWSKI

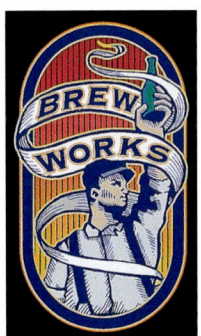

Client   RUSH PRESS (COMPANY SUMMER PICNIC)
Design Firm   CROUCH & NAEGELI/DESIGN GROUP WEST
Designer   JIM NAEGELI

Client   THE CLEVELAND INDIANS
Design Firm   HERIP DESIGN ASSOCIATES, INC.
Designers   JOHN R. MENTER, WALTER M. HERIP

Client   IMAGICOMM—INSPIRATIONAL NETWORK
Design Firm   LARRY SMITH & ASSOCIATES
Designer   MICHAEL BAILEY

279

Client   MARJORIE GROSS & CO., INC.
             CHARLES SCHWAB
Design Firm TOM DOLLE DESIGN
Designer   TOM DOLLE

Client   ALEX SHESHUNOFF
             NEW YORK NOW
Design Firm DESIGN TRUST
Designer   DAVID HO

Client   NORTHERN ILLINOIS UNIVERSITY
             FOUNDATION
Design Firm NORTHERN ILLINOIS UNIVERSITY
             OFFICE OF PUBLICATIONS
Designer   CAROL M. BENTHAL-BINGLEY

Client   CENTURIONS—KC CHAMBER OF COMMERCE
Design Firm EAT DESIGN
Designers   PATRICE EILTS-JOBE, KEVIN TRACY

Client   HANLEY-WOOD, INC.—"THE HOME OF THE FUTURE"
Design Firm WILLIAM J. KIRCHER & ASSOCIATES, INC.
Designer   BRUCE E. MORGAN

Client   KENT DELORD HOUSE MUSEUM
Design Firm RE: SALZMAN DESIGNS
Designer   RICK SALZMAN

Client   CENTRAL MARKET INCORPORATED
Design Firm DESIGNWISE GRAPHICS
Designer   JENNIFER SHOFFEY CARR

Client   J.T. DEVELOPMENT
Design Firm RIECHES BAIRD
Designer   CARRIE SANDOVAL

Client   MAIN STREET TRADING COMPANY
Design Firm SHIELDS DESIGN
Designer   CHARLES SHIELDS

Client   B&G FOODS, INC.
Design Firm APPLE DESIGNSOURCE INC.
Creative Director BARRY SEELIG
Designers   NANCY BROGDEN, JOHN RUTIG

Client   COMPUTER SMART CORP.
Design Firm   HANDLER DESIGN GROUP, INC.
Designer   BRUCE HANDLER

Client   EQUAL DIAGNOSTICS
Design Firm   BARTH AND CO.
Designers   ROB BARTH, MARCIE BARTH

Client   EQUITY TOYS
Design Firm   ALEXANDER ISLEY DESIGN
Designers   ALEXANDER ISLEY, CHARLES ROBERTSON

Client   ZENITH ELECTRONICS CORPORATION
Design Firm   BAGBY AND COMPANY
Designer   STEVEN BAGBY

Client   MONKEY STUDIOS
Design Firm   TRACY SABIN GRAPHIC DESIGN
Designer   TRACY SABIN

Client   LITHIA AUTOMOTIVE GROUP
Design Firm   LAURA KAY DESIGN
Designers   LAURA KAY, DONALD KAY

Client   SHIRRID, INC.
Design Firm   LIPPINCOTT & MARGULIES
Designers   KEN LOVE, RYAN PAUL

Client   GARY'S HOT RODS
Design Firm   MIRES DESIGN
Art/Creative Director JOSÉ A. SERRANO
Designers   JOSÉ A. SERRANO, MIGUEL PEREZ

Client   LOS ANGELES CONVENTION CENTER
Design Firm   JAMES ROBIE DESIGN ASSOCIATES
Designer   RICK YURK

Client   BLUE CROSS & BLUE SHIELD OF WESTERN PENNSYLVANIA—HIGHMARK
Design Firm   ADAM, FILIPPO & ASSOCIATES, INC.
Designers   DAVID CHRISTIAN ZIMMERLY, ROBERT A. ADAM

Client   FRASER PAPERS
Design Firm   LIPPINCOTT & MARGULIES
Designer   JERRY KUYPER

Client   LUCENT TECHNOLOGIES
Design Firm   LANDOR ASSOCIATES
Creative Director MARGARET YOUNGBLOOD
Designers   HENRIK OLSEN, WALLY KRANTZ

Client   INTERNATIONAL RESEARCH FOUNDATION FOR CHILDREN'S EYE CARE
Design Firm   SCHNIDER & YOSHINA, LTD.
Art Director   OSCAR SCHNIDER
Designer   LAURA EITZEN

Client   CMP MEDIA INC.
Design Firm   INTERBRAND SCHECHTER
Designers   GERALD BERLINER, JANINE BRUTTIN

Client   THE LOOP CORPORATION
Design Firm   HANSEN DESIGN COMPANY
Designer   PAT HANSEN

Client   RARITAN COMPUTER INC.
Design Firm   HENRY DREYFUSS ASSOCIATES
Project Manager JOHN BETTS
Designer   FRANCISCA SHERIF

Client   BETZ DEARBORN
Design Firm   INTERBRAND SCHECHTER
Designers   GERALD BERLINER, ANDREW BOGUCKI

Client   GTE
Design Firm   GRIFFITH PHILLIPS CREATIVE
Designer   TONY STUBBS

Client   ALLIN COMMUNICATIONS
Design Firm   JOHN BRADY DESIGN CONSULTANTS
Designers   JOHN BRADY, RICK MADISON

Client   SMITH STEELITE
Design Firm   LIPPINCOTT & MARGULIES
Designers   JERRY KUYPER, BARBARA SHENEFIELD

MICHAEL G. KESSLER & ASSOCIATES, LTD.

Corporate Investigative Strategies

HERRESHOFF MARINE MUSEUM

experian

Client TELECELLULAR, INC.
Design Firm CATHEY ASSOCIATES, INC.
Designer MATT WESTAPHER

Client RENT-A-WRITER
Design Firm IMS
Designer JAMIE ANDERSON

Client WHO WHAT WEAR
Design Firm RELIABLE DESIGN STUDIOS, INC.
Designer BILL KOBASZ

Client SOLUTIONS IQ
Design Firm LANDOR ASSOCIATES
Designers BILL CHIARAVALLE, SCOTT CURTIS

Client SCANSOURCE—QUICKSHIP
Design Firm MCELVENEY & PALOZZI
Designers JON WESTFALL, WILLIAM MCELVENEY

Client CHRYSLER CORPORATION
Design Firm RPA
Designer TIM SMITH

Client MICROSOFT—MSN, THE MICROSOFT NETWORK
Design Firm LANDOR ASSOCIATES
Designer BILL CHIARAVALLE

Client KING CASEY INC.
Design Firm KING CASEY INC.
Designer JOHN CHRZANOWSKI

Client NOVADYNE COMPUTER SYSTEMS, INC.
Design Firm THE INVISIONS GROUP LTD.
Designers JOHN CABOT LODGE, JONATHAN AMEN

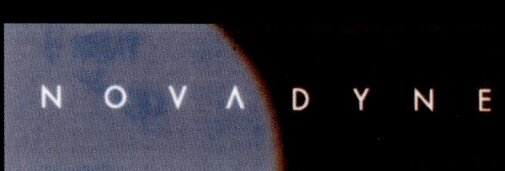

Client BRILL METALWORKS
Design Firm LAURA KAY DESIGN
Designers LAURA KAY, DONALD KAY

Client   AMERICAN SOCIETY OF HEALTH-SYSTEM PHARMACISTS
Design Firm   HC DESIGN
Designers   HOWARD CLARE, MARIA SESE PAUL

Client   XTENSION.COM
Design Firm   BRUCE YELASKA DESIGN
Designer   BRUCE YELASKA

Client   INTEGRAL PERIPHERALS
Design Firm   VOLAN DESIGN LLC
Creative Director MICHELE BRAVERMAN
Designer   MICHELLE VAN SANTEN

Client   DIFFUSION
Design Firm   1185 DESIGN
Designers   PEGGY BURKE, JULIA FOUG

Client   LEARNINGSMITH
Design Firm   COREY MCPHERSON NASH
Art Director KRISTEN REID
Designer   PADDY MCCOBB

Client   DIGITAL ARCHAEOLOGY
Design Firm   MULLER + COMPANY
Designer   JON SIMONSEN

Client   WTCA SERVICES CORP.
Design Firm   THE ARONSON GROUP
Designers   ADAM GREISS, NANA KOBAYASHI

Client   NATIONAL RECORD MART
Design Firm   LOUIS & PARTNERS

Client   CINCINNATI MILACRON
Design Firm   PAVONE FITE FULWILER
Designer   JEFF FULWILER

Client   NORNET
Design Firm   RILEY DESIGN ASSOCIATES
Designers   DANIEL RILEY, VONDRA DOHERTY

Client   COLOVISTA COUNTRY CLUB
Design Firm TOCQUIGNY ADVERTISING & DESIGN
Designer   LORI WALLS

Client   THE MOUNTAIN (WEB ICONS)
Design Firm ART O MAT DESIGN
Designers   MARK KAUFMAN, JACKI McCARTHY

Client   STEPHEN F. KRAVITZ
Design Firm SFK ADVERTISING & MARKETING
Designer   JODI SPECTER

Client   COLDWELL BANKERS GRAND TRADITIONS
Design Firm DESIGN ENTERPRISE
Designer   SCOTT CRIDER

Client   FLUIDESIGN
Design Firm FLUIDESIGN
Designers   RANDI TRYGSTAD, BLAKE DEJONGE

Client   HADLEY FRUIT ORCHARDS
Design Firm DENNIS S. JUETT & ASSOCIATES INC.
Designers   DENNIS S. JUETT, DENNIS SCOTT JUETT

Client   POKKA BEVERAGES, INC.
Design Firm PROFILE DESIGN
Designers   KENICHI NISHIWAKI, BRIAN JACOBSON, JEANNE NAMKUNG

Client   THE SEMINOLE TRIBE OF FLORIDA
              DEPT. OF ANTHROPOLOGY & GENEALOGY
Design Firm SYNERGY DESIGN GROUP
Designers   JOHN LoCASTRO, DAVID McGOWAN

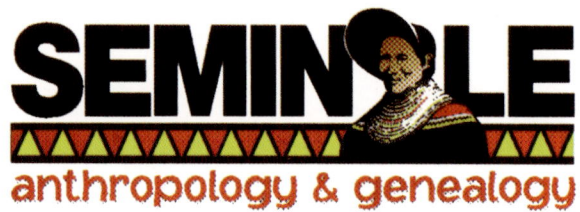

Client   ILLUMINET
Design Firm PHINNEY/BISCHOFF DESIGN HOUSE
Art Director LESLIE PHINNEY
Designer   JULI SAEGER

Client   NEW JERSEY CONSERVATION FOUNDATION
Design Firm JANET PAYNE
Designer   JANET PAYNE

Client — BELL-CARTER FOODS
Design Firm — ADDIS GROUP
Designers — RICK ATWOOD, ROBIN MACLEAN

Client — THE CYBERCOMM CORPORATION
Design Firm — BERKANO PRODUCTIONS, INC.
Designer — CATHERINE WILBERT

Client — THE MOUNTAIN MALL (WEB ICONS)
Design Firm — ART O MAT DESIGN
Designers — MARK KAUFMAN, JACKI MCCARTHY

Client — JIMMIE'S FOODS, INC.
Design Firm — PROFILE DESIGN
Designers — KENICHI NISHIWAKI, BRIAN JACOBSON, ANTHONY LUK

Client — LIGHTING STUDIO
Design Firm — DESIGN RANCH
Designers — GARY GNADE, DANETTE ANGERER, KIMBERLY COOKE

Client — THE HAHN COMPANY
Design Firm — COMMUNICATION ARTS, INC.
Designers — DAVID SHELTON, HENRY BEER

Client — THE BREADWORKS
Design Firm — A TO Z COMMUNICATIONS, INC.
Designer — EVAN WIMER

Client — SPORTSWAVE
Design Firm — JOHN BRADY DESIGN CONSULTANTS
Designers — JOHN BRADY, RICK MADISON

Client — BLUE FIN BILLIARDS
Design Firm — THE WECKER GROUP
Designer — ROBERT J. WECKER

Client — USA IN POLAND: AN INVITATIONAL EXHIBITION OF
U.S. POSTERS IN RZESZOW, POLAND
Design Firm — BOELTS BROS. ASSOCIATES
Designers — ERIC BOELTS, JACKSON BOELTS

Client QUALITY INN
Design Firm BABCOCK & SCHMID ASSOCIATES, INC.

Client ELECTRONIC BOOK TECHNOLOGIES, INC.
Design Firm STEWART MONDERER DESIGN, INC.
Designers STEWART MONDERER, AIME LECUSAY

Client 360° COMMUNICATIONS
Design Firm SIEGEL & GALE

Client GTE MAINSTREET INTERACTIVE TV
Design Firm TAYLOR DESIGN
Designers DANIEL TAYLOR, PETER MULLANEY

Client ASTROPOP COLLECTIBLES STORE
Design Firm MARTINI STUDIO
Designer SHELLEY DANYSH

Client CADMUS O'KEEFE
Design Firm CADMUS O'KEEFE
Designer BRIAN THOMSON

Client COMINCO FERTILIZERS—AGRIUM
Design Firm ADDISON WHITNEY
Designer LORI EARNHARDT

Client ELECTRONIC GRAPHIC ARTISTS OF DALLAS
Design Firm CATHEY ASSOCIATES, INC.
Designer GORDON CATHEY

Client INTERSPHERE
Design Firm RIECHES BAIRD
Designer CARRIE SANDOVAL

Client ASPCA
Design Firm PLATINUM DESIGN INC.
Creative Director KATHLEEN PHELPS
Designer KELLY HOGG

Client NORTH AMERICAN WATCH
Design Firm DESGRIPPES GOBÉ & ASSOCIATES
Design Director CHRISTOPHER VICE

Client BLITZ RESEARCH, INC.
Design Firm IMAGE ASSOCIATES, INC.
Designer LEIGH-ERIN MOORE SALMON

Client TIM SMITH DESIGN/COMMUNICATION
Design Firm TIM SMITH DESIGN/COMMUNICATION
Designer TIM SMITH

SMITH

Client MANPOLO INTERNATIONAL TRADING CORP.
Design Firm 66 COMMUNICATION INC.
Designer CHIN-CHIH YANG

Client DICKINSON-DOYLE, INC.
Design Firm DESIGN FOR INDUSTRY
Designers KEVIN OPP, DAVID KILBORN

DICKINSONDOYLE

Client MILL POND DEVELOPMENT CORPORATION
Design Firm CALDEWEY DESIGN
Designers JEFFREY CALDEWEY, HOLLY SCHEUMANN

MILL POND

Client DIMENSION ONE SPAS
Design Firm CROUCH & NAEGELI/DESIGN GROUP WEST
Designer JIM NAEGELI

DIMENSION ONE SPAS™

Client NEW YORK STATE ELECTRIC + GAS CORPORATION
Design Firm MICHAEL ORR + ASSOCIATES, INC.
Designer MICHAEL R. ORR

NysAir

Client INTERVAL
Design Firm SBG PARTNERS
Designers MARK BERGMAN, JESSIE MCANULTY

Client AMERICAN RECORDS MANAGEMENT ASSOC.
Design Firm GREGG & ASSOCIATES
Designer MICHELLE HICKS

Client   ROMORA BAY CLUB
Design Firm TOM FOWLER, INC.
Designers   THOMAS G. FOWLER, KARL S. MARUYAMA

Client   THE PHOENIX ZOO
Design Firm PAPAGALOS AND ASSOCIATES
Designers   NICHOLAS G. PAPAGALOS, DEREK BECKER

Client   AMERICAN NATIONAL BANK
Design Firm DOTZLER CREATIVE ARTS
Designer   DOTZLER CREATIVE ARTS

Client   PEREGRINE INCORPORATED
Design Firm THE COMARK GROUP
Designer   ERIC LIVINGSTON

Client   DOVETAIL LEARNING SYSTEMS
Design Firm STRONG PRODUCTIONS
Designers   TODD SCHATZBERG, MATT DOTY

Client   DEPARTMENT OF RELIGIOUS MINISTRIES
             THE MEDICAL CENTER AT PRINCETON
Design Firm PAMELA TANNURA GRAPHIC DESIGN
Designer   PAMELA TANNURA

Client   USPS—POSTMARK AMERICA
Design Firm KING CASEY
Designers   JOHN CHRZANOWSKI, STEVE BRENT

Client   H.C. BERGER BREWING COMPANY
Design Firm COONTS DESIGN GROUP
Designers   DAVID BACH, KIRK FLORY

Client   TODO WRAPS
Design Firm NBBJ GRAPHIC DESIGN
Designers   DOUG KEYES, LEO RAYMUNDO,
              DIANE ANDERSON

Client   MASTERCARD INTERNATIONAL
Design Firm INTERBRAND SCHECHTER
Designers   GERALD BERLINER,
              ANDREW BOGUCKI

Client   SCHWAN'S SALES ENTERPRISES
Design Firm PEDERSEN GESK
Designers   RONY ZIBARA, KRIS MORGAN

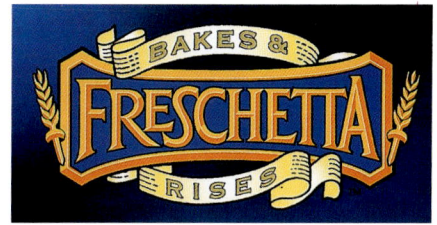

Client   QUILT ANTICS
Design Firm PAGANUCCI DESIGN INC.
Designers   BOB PAGANUCCI, FRANK PAGANUCCI

Client   SYMANTEC NORTON SECRET STUFF
Design Firm GEE + CHUNG DESIGN
Designer   EARL GEE

Client   TANNENBAUM'S OLD MARKET FLORIST
Design Firm DOTZLER CREATIVE ARTS
Designer   DOTZLER CREATIVE ARTS

Client   MILLER BREWING COMPANY
Design Firm LISTER BUTLER
Designer   JOHN LISTER

Client   PEPSI-COLA COMPANY
Design Firm PEDERSEN GESK
              IN COOPERATION WITH PEPSI-COLA
Designers   RONY ZIBARA, MITCH LINDGREN

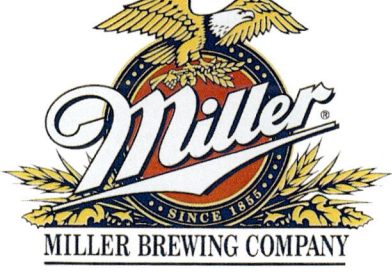

Client   TRANSIT VALLEY FAMILY DENTISTRY
Design Firm DESIGN FOR INDUSTRY
Designer   KEVIN OPP

Client   EDDIE BAUER—SAC JAC
Design Firm DAVID LEMLEY DESIGN
Designer   DAVID LEMLEY

Client   US NATIONAL SENIOR SPORTS CLASSIC
Design Firm   BOELTS BROS. ASSOCIATES
Designers   ERIC BOELTS, KERRY STRATFORD, JACKSON BOELTS

Client   UNIVERSAL SUPERSTARS
Design Firm   ANTISTA FAIRCLOUGH DESIGN
Designer   TOM ANTISTA

Client   MCI
Design Firm   INTERBRAND SCHECHTER
Executive Creative Director GERALD BERLINER

Client   MARKET STREET COMMUNICATIONS
Design Firm   ADX CREATIVE SERVICES
Designers   ERIC CLAPPIER, MICHAEL OBERHEU, KYLE RUMMER

Client   U.S. WEST FOUNDATION
Design Firm   COONTS DESIGN GROUP
Designer   MONTE MEAD

Client   MILLENNIUM MARKETING
Design Firm   SULLIVAN MARKETING & COMMUNICATIONS
Designer   JACK SULLIVAN

Client   POWERTEL
Design Firm   COPELAND HIRTHLER DESIGN + COMMUNICATIONS
Creative Directors BRAD COPELAND, GEORGE HIRTHLER
Designer   MICHELLE STIRNA
Producers   LAURA PERLEE, DONNA HARRIS, TOR GUNDERSON
Account Executives LESLIE MATTSON, LESLIE RAINER

Client   THE CORPORATE WORD
Design Firm   JOHN BRADY DESIGN CONSULTANTS
Designers   KATHY GRUBB, RICK MADISON

Client   DICK CORPORATION
Design Firm   ADAM, FILIPPO & ASSOCIATES, INC.
Designers   BLAIR GOOD, ROBERT A. ADAM

Client   WARNER BROS.
Design Firm   EVENSON DESIGN GROUP
Designers   STAN EVENSON, KAREN BARRANCO

Client   PORTER NOVELLI
Design Firm   PORTER NOVELLI CREATIVE
Designers   DONALD BURG, MICHAEL LEONE

Client   ART OF DESIGN
             —JACKI KAPPERS, GEMOLOGIST
Design Firm   SIGN HERE, INC.
Designer   LORI REYNOLDS

Client   MAKE-A-WISH FOUNDATION OF AMERICA
             —KIDS FOR WISH KIDS
Design Firm   TIEKEN DESIGN & CREATIVE SERVICES
Designers   FRED E. TIEKEN, LISA ROECA

Client   OGDEN ENTERTAINMENT INC.
Design Firm   COMMUNICATION ARTS, INC.
Designers   KELAN SMITH, HENRY BEER

Client   MARKETEAM INC.
Design Firm   H.O.T. DESIGN
Designer   T.L. ARY

Client   GEOSPHERE
Design Firm   RKD, INC.
Designer   CHRISTOPHER BUEHLER

Client   MUJU RESORT—SBW
Design Firm   THE GNU GROUP
Designers   JENI OLSEN, KWICHA PARK, NANCY DANIELS

Client · BARRY FISHLER DIRECT RESPONSE COPYWRITING
Design Firm · DAVID LEMLEY DESIGN
Designer · DAVID LEMLEY

Client · PET FAIR PRODUCTIONS
Design Firm · SHEEHAN DESIGN
Designer · JAMIE SHEEHAN

Client · ROLLERBLADE, INC.
Design Firm · ROLLERBLADE, INC.
Designer · MATTHEW HUBERTY

Client · LOMBARDI ELECTRIC
Design Firm · GRAPHICS NETWORK
Designer · M. SCANLAN

Client · SOUTH COAST CONSULTING, INC.
Design Firm · GRAPHICS NETWORK
Designers · T. CUTTER, M. SCANLAN

Client · FUTURES FOR CHILDREN
Design Firm · KILMER & KILMER, INC. DESIGN & ADVERTISING
Designers · RANDALL MARSHALL, RICHARD KILMER

Client · BUSINESS TECHNOLOGY SOLUTIONS
Design Firm · DAM CREATIVE
Designer · MARK K. PLATT

Client · DIX PRODUCTIONS
Design Firm · MULLER + COMPANY
Designer · DAVE SWEARINGEN

Client ATLAS SOFTWARE TECHNOLOGIES, INC.
Design Firm ATLAS ONLINE
Designer HEATHER MOORE

Client INTERNATIONAL SOCIETY FOR PERFORMANCE IMPROVEMENT
Design Firm FULLER DESIGNS, INC.
Designers AARON TAYLOR, DOUG FULLER

Client ROTISSERIA RESTAURANT
Design Firm BUSINESS GRAPHICS GROUP
Art Director CAM ROBERSON
Designer ERNEST SID

Client MOTION GRAPHICS COMMUNICATION
Design Firm LINCOLN DESIGN
Designer TOM LINCOLN

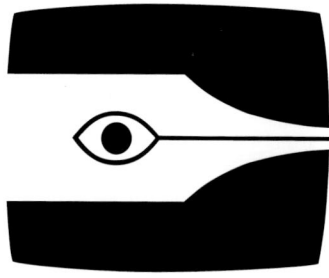

Client NATIONAL ASSOCIATION OF SERVICE MANAGERS NETWORK EXCHANGE
Design Firm ROBERT BARNES DESIGN
Designer ROBERT BARNES

Client QUANTUM SAIL DESIGN GROUP
Design Firm SUPON DESIGN GROUP.
Designer ANDREW BERMAN

Client SCUBALOGY, INC.
Design Firm CHRISTOPHER GORZ DESIGN
Designer CHRIS GORZ

Client CENTRAC LASERS
Design Firm HERIP DESIGN ASSOCIATES, INC.
Designer WALTER M. HERIP

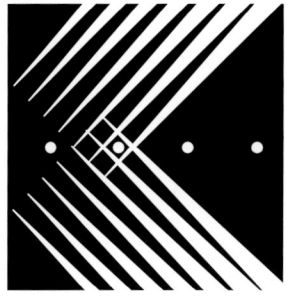

295

Client POTTS DESIGN
Design Firm KOR GROUP
Designers KAREN DENDY, AMY POTTS

Client McCAW
Design Firm HORNALL ANDERSON DESIGN WORKS, INC.
Designers JACK ANDERSON, SUZANNE HADDON, MICHAEL BRUGMAN,
ALAN FLORSHEIM, JULIE LOCK, JULIE KEENAN

Client DALLAS PUBLIC LIBRARY
Design Firm SULLIVAN PERKINS
Designer BRETT BARIDON

Client SPIRIT SPORTS, INC.
Design Firm McDERMOTT DESIGN
Designer BILL McDERMOTT

Client COMMISSION FOR THE 2004 OLYMPIAD
Design Firm GRAF, INC.
Designer LYDIMARIE APONTE

Client SLOWBURN CLOTHING CO.
Design Firm STREAMLINE DESIGN STUDIO
Designer KOUROSH GORJI

Client INNOVEX TECHNOLOGIES
Design Firm FAYE KLEIN DESIGN
Designer FAYE KLEIN

Client WEBER STATE UNIVERSITY
Design Firm BOB WINWARD & MARK BIDDLE
Designers BOB & MARK

Client   TUTTA LUNA
Design Firm   LOUEY/RUBINO DESIGN GROUP INC.
Designer   TAMMY KIM

Client   EVENT DESIGN
Design Firm   THE WELLER INSTITUTE
Designer   DON WELLER

EVENT DESIGN

Client   ALTA BEVERAGE COMPANY
Design Firm   HORNALL ANDERSON DESIGN WORKS, INC.
Designers   JACK ANDERSON, LARRY ANDERSON, JULIE KEENAN

Client   ZOË RESTAURANT
Design Firm   JOHN KNEAPLER DESIGN
Designers   JOHN KNEAPLER, MATT WALDMAN

Client   DESEO DEL CORAZON—COFFEE HOUSE
Design Firm   WALSH ASSOCIATES
Designer   TODD PYLAND

Café Deseo

Client   DIVI RESTAURANT
Design Firm   CUBE ADVERTISING & DESIGN
Designer   DAVID CHIOW

DIVI RESTAURANT

Client   DIVAN
Design Firm   MIRIELLO GRAFICO, INC.
Designers   COURTNEY MAYER, RON MIRIELLO

D I V A N

Client   METRO CORPORATION (SCALES MANUFACTURER)
Design Firm   PRODUCT COUNCIL LTD.
Designers   GREG FOSTER, ROBERT W. SHELDON

Client VILLAGE REALTY OF CENTRAL FLORIDA, INC.
Design Firm CORPORATE DESIGN ASSOCIATES
Designer JOE KRAWCZYK

Client THE WILLIE LANIER SCHOLARSHIP FUND
Design Firm DOYLE ROBINSON ADVERTISING/DESIGN
Designer DOYLE ROBINSON

The Willie Lanier
Scholarship Fund

Client REED SMITH SHAW & McCLAY
Design Firm ELIAS/SAVION ADVERTISING
Designer RONNIE SAVION

REED SMITH SHAW & McCLAY®

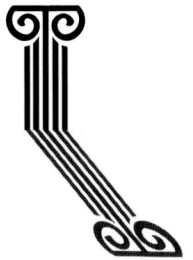

Client ALEXANDER TINTI
       ONE NIGHT STAND
Design Firm SAGMEISTER INC.
Designers STEFAN SAGMEISTER, HJALTI KARLSON

ONE NIGHT STAND THEATRE

Client MORSE DIESEL
Design Firm TONI SCHOWALTER DESIGN
Designer TONI SCHOWALTER

MorseDiesel
Construction/Consulting

Client LASALLE PARTNERS
       BANK ONE CENTER
Design Firm COMCORP, INC.
Designer DEBORAH WERNER, DAVE LAWRENCE

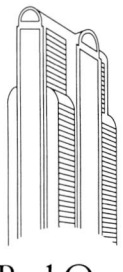

BankOne
CENTER

Client KANSAS CITY AD CLUB
Design Firm EAT DESIGN
Designers PATRICE EILTS-JOBE, PAUL PRATO

Client FRAMEWORK INC.
Design Firm SATELLITE DESIGN TECHNOLOGY INC.
Designers WALTER CLARKE, CARY MURNION

FRAMEWORK

Client SKIPPER'S RESTAURANT
Designer TODD DAVID NICKEL

Client HARCOURT BRACE
Design Firm MIRIELLO GRAFICO, INC.
Designers RON MIRIELLO, TRACY SABIN

Client JAMESTOWN COMMUNITY CENTER
Design Firm PUSH
Designers STEVE BARRETTO, TODD FOREMAN

Client QUARTER MOON ASSOCIATES
Design Firm VARNAU CREATIVE GROUP
Designer TIM VARNAU

Client J M EMBROIDERY
Design Firm WELLER INSTITUTE
Designer DON WELLER

Client GAMEKEEPERS' GRILL
Design Firm WELLER INSTITUTE
Designer DON WELLER

Client MAKE ★ A ★ CIRCUS
Design Firm LEE + YIN
Designer CHRIS YIN

Client PACIFIC PLACE
Design Firm HORNALL ANDERSON DESIGN WORKS, INC.
Designers JACK ANDERSON, HEIDI FAVOUR, DAVID BATES

Client   TAZEWELL COMMUNITY HOSPITAL
Design Firm MULLER + COMPANY
Designer   DAVE SWEARINGEN

Client   REDHAWK RANCH
Design Firm WELLER INSTITUTE
Designer   DON WELLER

Client   THUNDER BIRD GRILL
Design Firm WEBSTER DESIGN ASSOCIATES
Designer   PHIL THOMPSON

Client   TWO EAGLES PHOTO
Design Firm GARDINER DESIGN
Designer   DEBI GARDINER

Client   JUNEBUG PRODUCTIONS
Design Firm SCOTT BROWN DESIGN
Designer   SCOTT BROWN

Client   DREAM CATCHER INN
Design Firm WELLER INSTITUTE
Designer   DON WELLER

Client   JOHN C. BURNEY + COMPANY
Design Firm TRUDY COLE-ZIELANSKI DESIGN
Designer   TRUDY COLE-ZIELANSKI

Client   AIGA/ORANGE COUNTY
Design Firm DFACTO
Designer   MIKE OUSLEY

Client JACKRABBIT
Design Firm DOUBLE ENTENDRE
Designers RICHARD SMITH, DANIEL SMITH

Client ACCURATE LOCATING, INC.
Design Firm DOYLE ROBINSON ADVERTISING/DESIGN
Designer DOYLE ROBINSON

Client MARC SUITES
Design Firm KATIE WALLACE DESIGN
Designers KATIE WALLACE WEATHERINGTON, JEFF KENNARD

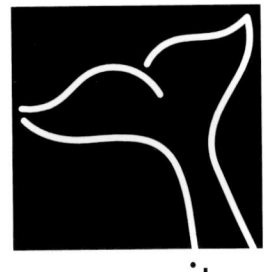

Client MUSEO DEL JAMÓN
Design Firm POD
Designer JOSÉ BILA RODRÍGUEZ

Client WHALE'S TALE SEAFOOD RESTAURANT
Design Firm MALOWANY.CHIOCCHI.INC.
Designer GENE MALOWANY

Client STARBUCKS COFFEE—YUKON BLEND
Design Firm DAVID LEMLEY DESIGN
Designer DAVID LEMLEY

Client PORCUPINE STUDIOS
Designer JEFF SHUBZDA

Client REPTILE
Design Firm LISKA AND ASSOCIATES
Designer HOLLE BODE

Client GUARDIAN POOL & FENCE SYSTEMS
Design Firm POONJA DESIGN
Designer SULEMAN POONJA

Client IEO
Design Firm X DESIGN COMPANY
Designer ALEX VALDERRAMA

Client GIANT STEPS
Design Firm KOR GROUP
Designers MB SAWYER, SAM ANTHONY, ANNE CALLAHAN

Client BIRMINGHAM CHAMBER MUSIC SOCIETY
Design Firm HOLLAND & HOLLAND ADVERTISING
Creative Director STEPHANIE HOLLAND
Art Director ELLEN HUTCHINS
Illustrator DWAYNE COLEMAN

Client CHILDREN'S MIRACLE NETWORK OF GREATER PHILADELPHIA
KIDS ON PARADE
Design Firm RANDI MARGRABIA DESIGN
Designer RANDI SHALIT MARGRABIA

Client PRETTY GOOD PRIVACY
Design Firm HORNALL ANDERSON DESIGN WORKS, INC.
Designers JACK ANDERSON, DEBRA HAMPTON, MICHAEL BRUGMAN,
HEIDI FAVOUR, JANA WILSON, KATHA DALTON

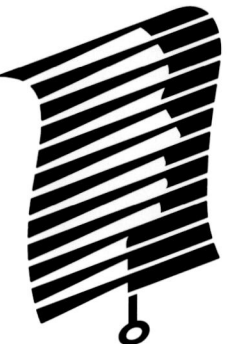

Client INDUSTRY PICTURES
Design Firm MIRES DESIGN
Art/Creative Director JOSÉ A. SERRANO
Designers DEBORAH HORN, JOSÉ A. SERRANO
Illustrator TRACY SABIN

Client PACT, INC.
Design Firm FRANEK DESIGN ASSOCIATES, INC.
Designer DAVID FRANEK

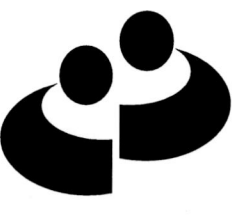

Client   CIRCADIA (FLAT BREAD BAKERY AND RESTAURANT)
Design Firm   DAVID LEMLEY DESIGN
Designer   DAVID LEMLEY

Client   DSI
Design Firm   TONI SCHOWALTER DESIGN
Designer   TONI SCHOWALTER

Client   SAWD 8 RECORDS
Design Firm   STREAMLINE DESIGN STUDIO
Designer   KOUROSH GORJI

Client   STARBUCKS COFFEE—ARABIAN MOCHA SANANI
Design Firm   DAVID LEMLEY DESIGN
Designer   DAVID LEMLEY

Client   STARBUCKS COFFEE
Design Firm   DAVID LEMLEY DESIGN
Designers   DAVID LEMLEY, ANDY ROHRMANN

Client   THE RESOURCE AREA FOR TEACHERS, INC.
Design Firm   POINT DESIGN
Designer   WILLIAM R. LOMAX

Client   THE CENTER FOR BETTER HEARING
Design Firm   BRAINSTORM!
Designer   BOB DOWNS

Client   ROADRUNNER SPORTS
Design Firm   LAURA COE DESIGN ASSOC.
Art Director   LAURA COE WRIGHT
Designer/Illustrator   RYOICHI YOTSUMOTO

Client GES EXPOSITION SERVICES PREFERRED CARRIER PROGRAM
Design Firm TIEKEN DESIGN & CREATIVE SERVICES
Designer FRED E. TIEKEN

Client MOTOROLA (RACING TEAM)
Design Firm KARNES PRICKETT DESIGN
Designer DAVE PRICKETT

Client PATHLORE SOFTWARE CORPORATION
Design Firm GRAPHICA, INC.
Designers DREW CRONENWETT, GEOFF RIECHEL

Client GRAHAM SCOTT DESIGNS
Design Firm GRAHAM SCOTT + CO.
Designer MIKE WHITNEY

Client DALLAS MUSEUM OF ART
Design Firm DITTMAR CREATIVE
Designer GREG DITTMAR

Client STARBUCKS COFFEE
Design Firm DAVID LEMLEY DESIGN
Designer DAVID LEMLEY

Client CYKO
Design Firm X DESIGN COMPANY
Designer ALEX VALDERRAMA

Client TRAVELIN' TOTS
Design Firm BIANCO MARCHILONIS DESIGN
Designers PETER BIANCO, ELLEN MACQUEEN

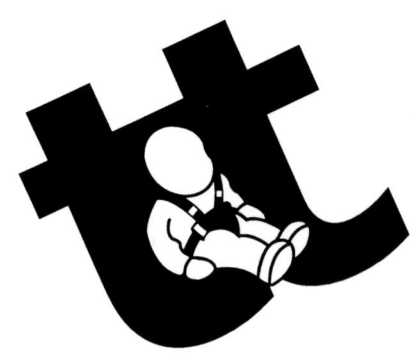

Preparing

for a healthy

baby

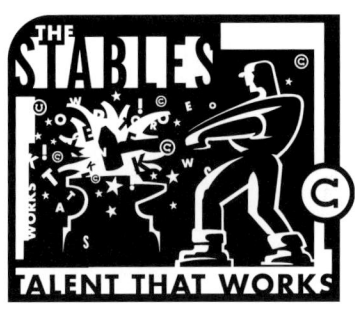

ALL POINTS
DISPATCH

DRAKE

Client   ELIAS STUDIOS
Design Firm   ELIAS/SAVION ADVERTISING
Designer   RONNIE SAVION

E L I A S
S T U D I O S

Client   EVOTECH, INC.
Design Firm   THE VISUAL GROUP
Designers   ARK STEIN, BILL MIFSUD

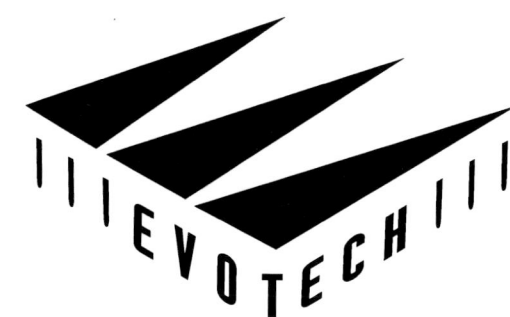

Client   EUGENE AREA CHAMBER OF COMMERCE
Design Firm   FUNK & ASSOCIATES
Designers   DAVID FUNK, TIM JORDAN

Client   HYBRID RECORDS
Design Firm   RON KELLUM
Designer   RON KELLUM

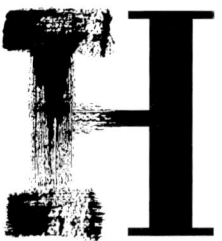

Client   HARRISON COUNTY DEVELOPMENT COMMISSION
Design Firm   THE PRIME TIME GROUP
Designer   BEN PRISK

HARRISON COUNTY
DEVELOPMENT COMMISSION

Client   HORTON ELECTRICAL CONSTRUCTION
Design Firm   HIRAM ASH DESIGN
Designer   HIRAM ASH

Client   INKLINGS DESIGN
Design Firm   INKLINGS DESIGN
Designer   JOHN GRUBER

INKLINGS
DESIGN SM

Client   THE IMPACT GROUP
Design Firm   SPANGLER ASSOCIATES
Designers   ALLEN WOODARD, MICHAEL CONNORS

Client   LUMINOUS CORP.
Design Firm   DIETZ DESIGN CO.
Designer   ROBERT DIETZ

Client   MIZAR
Design Firm   QUILL CREATIVE, INC.
Designer   STEVE M. UTLEY

Client   MOSPEED
Design Firm   MULLER + COMPANY
Designer   JOHN MULLER

Client   MATTY B ENTERTAINMENT (MUSICIAN)
Design Firm   MASTROGIANNIS DESIGN, INC.
Designer   PETER MASTROGIANNIS

Client   MOTHERS VOICES
Design Firm   THE SLOAN GROUP
Designer   LANA LE

Client   MAROON • INCORPORATED
Design Firm   VANTAGE ONE COMMUNICATIONS GROUP
Designer   MARIO RINI

Client   MEDICAL MISSION
Design Firm   MULLER + COMPANY
Designer   SUSAN WILSON

Client   ORLANDO SCIENCE CENTER
Design Firm   MAGIC PENCIL STUDIOS
Designer   SCOTT FELDMANN

Client   POINT-2-POINT TRANSPORTATION
Designer   EDWARD M. KENSICKI, JR.

Client   LIONEL PARIS, BUILDER
Design Firm   LISA HAWKESWORTH GRAPHIC DESIGN
Designer   LISA HAWKESWORTH

Client   PEACOCK PRODUCTS
Design Firm   DOERR ASSOCIATES
Designer   PRISCILLA WHITE STURGES

Client   PANDA GROUP INTERNATIONAL
Design Firm   MALOWANY.CHIOCCHI.INC.
Designers   TIM FISHER, GENE MALOWANY

Client   R. RETALLICK AND SONS, INC.
Design Firm   PINSONNAULT GRAPHICS
Designer   CYNTHIA PINSONNAULT

Client   VETRA
Design Firm   FULLER DESIGNS, INC.
Designers   DOUG FULLER, AARON TAYLOR

v e t r a

Client   WIENSTROER PAINTING CO.
Design Firm   ERVIN MARKETING CREATIVE COMMUNICATIONS
Designer   MIKE WHITNEY

Wienstroer Painting

Client   WRIGHTWOOD INDUSTRIES
Design Firm   IDENTITY CENTER
Designers   WAYNE KOSTERMAN, JASON BLASKOVITCH, DARIN HASLEY

Client   HIRO REAL ESTATE CO.
Design Firm E. CHRISTOPHER KLUMB ASSOCIATES, INC.
Designer   CHRISTOPHER KLUMB

Client   NEW MEXICO LOTTERY
Design Firm KILMER & KILMER, INC. DESIGN & ADVERTISING
Designers   BRENDA KILMER, RANDALL MARSHALL, RICHARD KILMER

Client   COMPOUNDING TECHNOLOGY, INC.
Design Firm DE GOEDE + OTHERS INC.
Designer   JAN DE GOEDE

Client   OJO MAGIC CORPORATION
Design Firm GIANOPOULOS DESIGN
Designer   DEAN GIANOPOULOS

Client   IAI CORPORATION
Design Firm BARRETT COMMUNICATIONS
Designer   NADINE FLOWERS

Client   THE RINK AT FOUNDERS CENTER
Design Firm RASSMAN DESIGN
Designers   JOHN RASSMAN, AMY RASSMAN, LYN D'AMATO

Client   THE LITCHFIELD INSURANCE COMPANY
Design Firm O'BRIEN DESIGN
Designer   ANN O'BRIEN

Client   ARTICLES
Design Firm DAM CREATIVE
Designer   MARK K. PLATT

Client   PENNSYLVANIA GENERAL ASSEMBLY
Design Firm   H2 DESIGN GROUP INC.
Art Director TIMOTHY HUSNI
Designer   GINO TAVOLETTI

Client   FOARD COLLINS DOERRE
Design Firm   TURNER DESIGN
Designer   BERT TURNER

Client   DOLLS SALON
Design Firm   KWGC ADVERTISING & DESIGN
Designer   JOHN KRAUS

Client   RED HAT SOFTWARE
Design Firm   BLANK
Designers   ADAM COHN, SUZANNE ULTMAN, ROBERT KENT WILSON

Client   MOAB.COM
Design Firm   SOLRANCH
Designers   MATT FINNIGAN, CARTER J. HOSTELLEY

Client   MERCRUISER
Design Firm   SHR PERCEPTUAL MANAGEMENT
Designer   MIKE BARTON

Client   GREYFOX
Design Firm   ST. JOHN DESIGN
Designer   STEPHEN ST. JOHN

Client   CONCORD SAVINGS BANK
Design Firm   WONDRISKA RUSSO ASSOCIATES
Designer   WILLIAM WONDRISKA

Client   WILDFLOWER BREAD COMPANY
Design Firm   ESTUDIO RAY
Designers   JOE RAY, CHRISTINE RAY, LESLIE LINK

Client   SHADE
Design Firm   JOE MILLER'S COMPANY
Designer   JOE MILLER

Client   BUSINESS RESOURCE AND INFORMATION NETWORK
Design Firm   SCHLATTER DESIGN
Designer   MICHAEL SCHLATTER

BRAIN

Client   MIAMI UNIVERSITY
Design Firm   PEG FAIMON DESIGN
Designer   PEG FAIMON

Client   TeleworX INC.
Design Firm   SUPON DESIGN GROUP.
Designer   SEAN ZINDREN

Client   THE GRAPELINE
Design Firm   JO DESIGN
Designer   JENI OLSEN

Client   SPROTTE & WATSON ARCHITECTURE AND PLANNING
Design Firm   POLLMAN MARKETING ARTS, INC.
Designer   JENNIFER POLLMAN

Client   AIM EXECUTIVE—STRATFORD GROUP
Design Firm   EDWARD HOWARD & CO.
Designer   BOB KELEMEN

STRATFORD GROUP

Client   ROMANEK PROPERTIES
Design Firm   MCKNIGHT KURLAND

Client   AGFA—EPHOTO
Design Firm   THE HUGHES COMMUNICATIONS GROUP, INC.
Art Director ROY HUGHES
Designer   ROBERT CROWLEY

Client   AUTOMALL ONLINE
Design Firm   FULLER DESIGNS, INC.
Designer   DOUG FULLER

Client   WRIGHT INVESTORS' SERVICE
Design Firm   CORPORATE BRANDING PARTNERSHIP
Designers   MICHAEL S. GLASS, JAMES R. GREGORY

WRIGHT

Client WARNER HOME VIDEO
Design Firm MICHAEL BROCK DESIGN
Designer MICHAEL BROCK

Client AMERICAN PHYSICAL THERAPY ASSOCIATION
Design Firm NEXT YEAR'S NEWS, INC.
Art Director PAULA ASHLEY
Designer ANDREA COLÓN

COMMUNITY HOME HEALTH SECTION
AMERICAN PHYSICAL THERAPY ASSOCIATION

Client SEATTLE DIRECT MARKETING ASSOCIATION
Design Firm GUTTMAN DESIGN
Designer SUZANNE GUTTMAN

SEATTLE **DIRECT MARKETING** ASSOCIATION

Client CENTER FOR REGIONAL ECONOMIC ISSUES
Design Firm FELDMAN DESIGN
Designer JAMIE FELDMAN

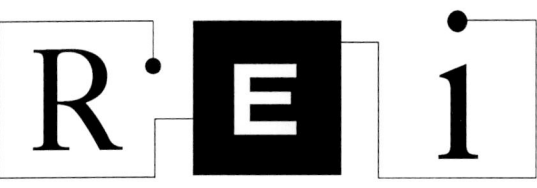

Client 1492 TECHNOLOGIES
Design Firm WEBSTER DESIGN ASSOCIATES
Designers DAVE WEBSTER, PHIL THOMPSON

1 4 9 2 TECHNOLOGIES

Client KIDSFIRST HEALTHGROUP, LTD.
Design Firm RICHARD ZEID, DESIGN
Designer RICHARD ZEID

KidsFirst HealthGroup, Ltd.

Client DATACARD
Design Firm LARSEN DESIGN + INTERACTIVE
Designers NANCY WHITTLESEY, DAVID SHULTZ

Client PLANRIGHT (FINANCIAL PLANNING SERVICES)
Design Firm ZUST & COMPANY
Designer MARK ZUST

Planright

Client MR. RAGS (CLOTHING STORE)
Design Firm NBBJ GRAPHIC DESIGN
Designer AMY LAM

Client JUDITH PHILLIPS PHOTOGRAPHY
Design Firm CHAMELEON CREATIVE, INC.
Designer MONA CORNWELL

MOTHERHOOD
A Photographic Celebration

Client BRIDGEPOINT TECHNOLOGY
Design Firm SHAWVAR ASSOCIATES
Designers PERCY M. AROW, MARK SHAWVAR

Client ZANTAZ
Design Firm KO DESIGN
Designer KYLE OGDEN

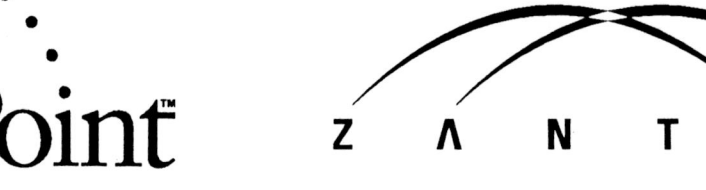

Client CLINIMETRICS
Design Firm ARTEMIS
Designer WES AOKI

Client PITTSBURGH NATIONAL BANK
Design Firm BRANDEGEE, INC.
Designer BRIAN LEE CAMPBELL

Client MAINSTAR
Design Firm SPANGLER ASSOCIATES
Designers MICHAEL CONNORS, ALLEN WOODARD

Client THE GLOBALSERVE CORPORATION
Design Firm NESNADNY + SCHWARTZ
Designer GREGORY OZNOWICH

Client WAVELENGTH TECHNOLOGIES
Design Firm IMAGE SOLUTIONS
Designer ANDREW PETITTI

Client GLOBALNET
Design Firm OBJECT DESIGN AND COMMUNICATIONS INC.
Designers NAWAF SOLIMAN, JENNIFER SCHOLTEN

Client DECISION INSIGHT
Design Firm MULLER + COMPANY
Designer TYLER SINGER

Client MARICULTURE
Design Firm HANSEN DESIGN COMPANY
Designers PAT HANSEN, KATE DODD

Client   DOW JONES & COMPANY
Design Firm   BELK MIGNOGNA ASSOCIATES
Designers   BRENNA GARRATT, HANS NEUBERT

Client   KIVA SOFTWARE
Design Firm   HALLECK DESIGN GROUP
Designer   WAYNE WRIGHT

Client   KATUN CORPORATION
Design Firm   KATUN CORPORATION
Designers   GREGORY J. MEYER, JOHN C. JENSEN

Client   QUANTUM-FIREBALL
Design Firm   JOE MILLER'S COMPANY
Designers   JOE MILLER, MAI NGUYEN

Client   STATE STREET BANK & TRUST, GLOBAL HUMAN RESOURCES
Design Firm   KOR GROUP
Designers   KAREN DENDY, ANNE CALLAHAN, MB SAWYER

Client   WEST END MOTOR CO.
Design Firm   MCDERMOTT DESIGN
Designer   BILL MCDERMOTT

Client   BRUCE CLARK PRODUCTIONS
Design Firm   HORNALL ANDERSON DESIGN WORKS, INC.
Designer   JACK ANDERSON

Client   THE DALAD GROUP
Design Firm   HERIP DESIGN ASSOCIATES, INC.
Designers   JOHN R. MENTER, WALTER M. HERIP

Client   IMAGIO
Design Firm   DIETZ DESIGN CO.
Designer   ROBERT DIETZ

Client   UNIVERSITY OF TEXAS PRESS
Design Firm   GEORGE LENOX DESIGN
Designer   GEORGE LENOX

315

Client   TCS CORPORATE SERVICES
Design Firm   DITTMAR CREATIVE
Designer   GREG DITTMAR

Client   AMERICAN ASSOCIATION OF BOTANICAL GARDENS & ARBORETA
Design Firm   LINDA GEORGE DESIGN
Designer   LINDA GEORGE

Client   SOUTH UMPQUA BANK
Design Firm   MORTENSEN DESIGN
Designer   GORDON MORTENSEN

Client   SEVEN PINES CONSULTING GROUP, INC.
Design Firm   JOWAISAS DESIGN
Designer   ELIZABETH JOWAISAS

Client   ROYAL AMERICAN LIFE INSURANCE CO.
Design Firm   LINCOLN DESIGN
Designer   TOM LINCOLN

Client   HORTICA, URBAN GARDENS
Design Firm   BARRY POWER GRAPHIC DESIGN
Designers   BARRY POWER, JUDITH MUSICK

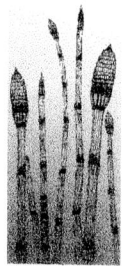

Client   UNITED STATES DEPARTMENT OF AGRICULTURE
Design Firm   SUPON DESIGN GROUP.
               U.S.D.A., OFFICE OF COMMUNICATION DESIGN CENTER
Designers   ANDY DOLAN, DAVID SUTTON

Client   OPUS CORPORATION—ELM CREEK
Design Firm   LARSEN DESIGN OFFICE, INC.
Designer   TODD MANNES

Index

Clients